D0197827

# the fearless gourmet

## decoding menus from around the world

NORMAN KOLPAS

MQP

**Special thanks to my wife Katie and our son Jake, Michael Friedman, Ljiljana Baird, Zaro Weil, Céline Hughes, Neil Gower, Julia Lloyd, and Jim Cornfield.**

Published by MQ Publications Ltd
12 The Ivories
6–8 Northampton Street
London N1 2HY
Tel: 020 7359 2244
Fax: 020 7359 1616
Email: mail@mqpublications.com

North American office
49 West 24th Street
New York, NY 10010
Email: information@mqpublicationsus.com

Website: www.mqpublications.com



ISBN: 1-84072-965-1

9 8 7 6 5 4 3 2 1



Printed in China

# Contents

# A word from the author

I wasn't always a Fearless Gourmet. But that all changed one rainy winter weekend when I was 15 years old.

You need a little background first. I'm a first-generation American of Eastern European Jewish heritage. That meant my mom served generous portions of overcooked meat, chicken, fish, and vegetables. Though my parents didn't keep a kosher home, pork (though curiously, not bacon) and all kinds of shellfish and crustaceans (though not shrimp) were considered unspeakably inedible in our household.

Of course, being good-hearted people who were eager to have their two sons assimilate into the American dream, my parents also always taught my brother and me that we should be good guests when invited to someone's home. "Always eat what's put in front of you," Mom cautioned us. And therein lurked a dilemma that suddenly materialized that rainy winter weekend.

My best friend Chuck's family were avid campers. His parents bought a camper van that had a pop-up roof, a built-in kitchen, and plenty of sleeping space. And I was lucky enough to get invited along on their weekend jaunts.

That one winter weekend, we'd settled at a campground on the beach north of Santa Barbara, California. While Chuck's parents went for a walk, we two unsociable teens stayed in the van and played cards.

Chuck's parents returned from their walk, jubilant. "Boys," Margaret exclaimed, "we found a stand selling fresh lobsters! We're going to cook them for dinner along with what we've brought along. It'll be a real feast!"

My heart and stomach sank. Lobster! The very thought disgusted me. Well, I thought, I'll just politely push it around my plate while I eat the other main course...which, you might have guessed, turned out to be pork chops.

I still don't know how I got through that dinner. I remember fighting the gag reflex, smiling all the while, and telling Margaret how delicious everything was.

And I never let on—at least not for 14 years. Shortly after I turned 29, I returned to the U.S. after seven years in London, during which time I traveled all over Europe and fearlessly enjoyed countless meals of pork, shellfish, and many other forbidden foods. The same night I settled into an apartment in New York City, Chuck flew in from L.A. for our first visit since I'd left the country.

We sat up late that night, reminiscing. Eventually, we talked about those camping trips. I finally told him the truth about that lobster-and-pork dinner.

Chuck laughed, of course, but his reaction seemed disproportionate to the revelation. I asked why.

"You only know half the story," he explained. "To this day, whenever Mom, Dad, and I reminisce, a moment always comes when Mom says, 'And do you remember how much Norm loved that dinner of lobster and pork chops?'"

Therein lies a lesson for any would-be Fearless Gourmet. The best way to conquer your fears, at the table or in life, is to face your fears head-on. More often than not, you'll find they aren't as frightening as you imagined. Lack of knowledge was possibly the reason you feared them in the first place. May you'll even wind up devouring what scared you!

That's the reason behind *The Fearless Gourmet.* Think of this book as a means by which you face anything unknown in the world of food. If you're confronted by an unfamiliar menu item or recipe, chances are you'll find an explanation of it here. If some unknown dish or ingredient makes you feel as apprehensive as I once did years ago about lobster and pork chops, read up on it in advance and start conquering your fears.

The book is organized by continents, regions, and countries for easy reference. Look up an unknown term, or anything you want to know more about, under what appears to you to be the key word in its name. Some dishes are so singular that they appear under their full names. And I've tried to avoid defining words that are obviously straight translations of familiar English terms—the Italian *zuppa,* for example, which means "soup."

Of course, from time to time you won't find what you're looking for. Even a book ten times the size of this one couldn't cover the whole world of food, and my goal for this book was to be both broad and deep—to cover a lot of territory without skimming the surface.

Rather, this book aims to give you enough information to make you confident in any restaurant you might enter; to look a possibly snooty waiter or shopkeeper in the eye, show him or her you know what you're talking about, and then ask the questions you need to ask and get the answers you need to get so you can order your food and enjoy your meal.

Think of this book as a buffet, or a *smorgasbord,* or a tapas bar. Okay, enough with the metaphors! Think of it as a place where you can sample a cuisine in morsels of information before you embark on your own more in-depth, fearless explorations.

NORMAN KOLPAS

Dining in
Europe

# British Isles

Although you can still find sorry examples of British cooking if you really make an effort, gone are the days of overcooked meats and watery, flavorless vegetables that stigmatized these fair isles for far too long. As well as the outstanding Indian and Chinese restaurants that have long been standbys across the nation (give thanks for these to the days of Empire), you'll also find cooks celebrating the very best of some of Britain's traditional dishes.

## CULINARY SURVIVAL

*"If the English can survive their food, they can survive anything."*

GEORGE BERNARD SHAW (1856-1950)

Back in the days before the Italian cooks Caterina de Medici brought along with her to the French royal court transformed France's cooking, that nation looked to England as a model of fine cuisine. And with good reason. The British Isles abound with outstanding meats, poultry, seafood, and produce, and many of its cooks reach back to centuries-old traditions in the process of transforming them into robust roast beef accompanied by Yorkshire pudding, home-baked creations like stargazy pie, soothing soups like cock-a-leekie, satisfying snacks such as Welsh rabbit (fret not: no animal is harmed in its preparation) or Cornish pasties, and comforting desserts like fool and trifle.

Don't overlook the opportunities offered by more casual restaurants across the British Isles. Street-corner cafés, affectionately referred to as "caffs" with a friendly sneer at the word's French roots, offer opportunities to enjoy honest home cooking of the meat-and-two-veg variety, often featuring such honest-to-goodness main dishes as toad-in-the-hole or steak and kidney pie accompanied by vegetables (over)cooked with care, such as Cockney-style bubble and squeak or Irish champ. Fish and chips shops sell fried-to-order batter-coated seafood fillets and deep-fried potatoes. Teashops soothe the soul in midafternoon with cupfuls of bracing tea accompanied by dainty sandwiches, cookies (biscuits to the Brits), and pastries, and such delicious baked goods as crumpets and scones, along with jam and great lashings of clotted cream. And the pubs you'll find everywhere, often several to the block, provide not just pints of good beer and other potables but also grub designed to sustain both body and soul.

**Angels on horseback**

Squint your eyes and knock back several pints of beer and you might, just might, be able to imagine how this combination of freshly shucked oysters rolled up inside strips of bacon and then broiled got their name. Though more likely served nowadays as an hors d'oeuvre, the delicious duo was traditionally offered at the end of a meal as a "savoury" course that followed dessert.

**Arbroath smokies**

From the eastern Scottish coastal town of the same name, this type of smoked haddock is generally prepared for serving by baking or broiling with butter.

**Bangers and mash**

The term "banger," referring to a firecracker, colorfully describes a good sausage, served in this case with mashed potatoes—and usually great lashings of gravy.

**Black bun**

No, it isn't a disease tracing back to medieval England, despite the sniggers you may hear when its name is spoken. Swallow your pride and dare to order this delicious yeast-leavened teatime bread, which gets its name for the color imparted to it by a wealth of sweet spices, candied and dried fruits, and nuts. You'd never know it from the exterior, though, which is always a thin layer of pristine plain dough that conceals the wealth inside until the first wedge-shaped slice is cut.

**Black pudding**

*The English Housewife's Book,* published in 1600, describes this dish as "small otemeale mixed with blood, and the liver of either sheep, calf or swine"—in other words, a rich blood sausage. You'll find this rustic favorite throughout northern England, sometimes boiled whole but more often sliced and pan-fried.

**Boxty**

Part potato pancake, part dumpling, part griddle scone, boxty is one of the simplest and most satisfying of Irish treats. The mixture of grated raw and mashed boiled potatoes, flour, milk, and egg is dropped in spoonfuls onto a hot greased griddle and cooked until golden brown on both sides, then served as an accompaniment to roast meat. Making boxty is such a basic requirement of any good traditional Irish cook that an old folk rhyme immortalized its importance for young women of an era long ago:

*Boxty on the griddle,*
*Boxty on the pan,*
*If you can't make boxty,*
*You'll never get your man!*

**Bubble and squeak**

A Cockney favorite, this economical Monday-morning reuse of Sunday dinner's vegetables feature cooked chopped potatoes, cabbage, or Brussels sprouts, and maybe—just maybe—a scrap or two of beef, ham, or pork, all fried up in generous dollops of hot bacon fat or beef dripping until brown and crispy-edged. In the process, the contents of the skillet make the hissing and popping noises that inspired its name.

**Butty**

This charming, nursery-like term refers to a traditional British sandwich, the name deriving from the fact that the two thin slices of bread for the sandwich are spread with butter. Beyond that, the filling determines the butty's personality, from simple and sweet jam butties to self-indulgent chip butties (yes, a sandwich of deep-fried potatoes), health-conscious butties filled with sprouts to elegant modern butties that might combine such *haute* ingredients as a combination of ripe French brie cheese and seedless grapes.

## **Some cheeses** of the British Isles

**The rich dairy lands of the British Isles give rise to dozens of fine regional cheeses. Here's a select trayful to watch out for.**

**BLARNEY** A mild cow's-milk cheese riddled with Swiss-cheese-like holes.

**CAERPHILLY** A slightly tart, crumbly white Welsh-style cow's-milk cheese.

**CHEDDAR** A firm cow's-milk cheese ranging from mildly nutty to rich and sharply tangy and from pale yellow to deep gold, depending on its age.

**CHESHIRE** A crumbly cow's-milk cheese that's young and mild in its "White" (pale yellow colored) or "Red" (deeper yellow-orange, colored with annatto seeds) varieties, rich and creamy in its blue-veined form. The famed 17th-century pub Ye Olde Cheshire Cheese, still in business in London today, was frequented by writers including Samuel Johnson and Charles Dickens.

**DOUBLE GLOUCESTER** A rich, mellow yet sharp-edged, golden-colored cow's-milk cheese.

**STILTON** The great British blue-veined cheese, made from cow's milk, creamy, rich, and sharp, so complex and enthralling that writer Clifton Fadiman described it as "the world's most regal Blue, exerting, like any true aristocrat, authority without aggressiveness. A Stilton's self-confidence springs from its past (the richest cream and milk) and its future, which can only be one of glory."

**WENSLEYDALE** From Yorkshire, a cow's-milk cheese that is smooth and tangy when fresh, rich and ever-so-slightly sweet when aged, and milder but richer than Stilton when prepared as a blue cheese.

**Champp**

Bash your boiled spuds ("potatoes" to you and me) with onions, leeks or green onions, and milk and you'll have before you Ireland's contribution to the subject of mashed potatoes. Then dip each forkful into the melted butter that sits like a pool of lava in the center of your mountainous portion, and you'll understand why this ranks as a great homespun dish. Want to take it a step further? Then turn to **Colcannon**.

**Christmas pudding**

Immortalized by Dickens in *A Christmas Carol,* this great English holiday dessert combines flour, sugar, bread crumbs, eggs, butter, suet, raisins, prunes, currants, nuts, dark beer, and sweet spices. Packed into a ceramic basin, the pudding is steamed for several hours until dense, moist, fragrant, and flavorful. It arrives at table decorated with a holly sprig and aflame with brandy. Hard sauce—a mixture of butter, sugar, and brandy—is spooned atop each serving.

**Clotted cream**

Use this term for the thick, spreadable, slightly sweet cream that results from scalding the unpasteurized product, then cooling it, and you'll avoid the inevitable turf war between Cornwall and Devonshire, who both claim it as their own and call it Cornish cream or Devonshire cream. Wherever you're served it, enjoy clotted cream in heaped spoonfuls as a spread for teatime scones or a topping for fresh berries.

**Cock-a-leekie**

The name is this humble Scottish soup's recipe in a nutshell: chicken and leeks, simmered together and served as a first course or main dish. Posher versions might also include some oatmeal as a thickener, or the pleasantly tangy addition of prunes.

**Colcannon**

Like champ, this is home-style Irish mashed potatoes (known colloquially as "praties"). Only this version includes not just green onions but also chopped leaves of kale, the flavorful, slightly bitter greens giving the resulting vegetable side dish a beautiful color befitting the Emerald Isles—and inspiring a favorite folk verse:

*Did you ever eat Colcannon*
*When 'twas made from yellowed cream,*
*And the kale and praties blended*
*Like the picture in a dream?*
*Did you ever take a forkful*
*And dip it in the lake*
*Of the clover-flavoured butter*
*That your mother used to make?*

**Crumpet**

Combining the best qualities of both bread and pancakes, these tea breads are made from a batter leavened with both yeast and baking soda. Poured into ring-shaped molds on a hot griddle, they develop golden-brown bottoms and pale tops riddled with holes just waiting to soak up melted butter or jam after toasting.

**Dublin coddle**

Generous slices of ham or bacon, plump pork sausages, and sliced potatoes and onions are baked together with the cooking liquid in which the meats were boiled to produce this incredibly satisfying Irish favorite.

**Eccles cakes**

The Lancashire town of Eccles gave birth to this deceptively simple-looking yet rich and complex-tasting pastry. Dried currants are mixed with sugar and butter, then enfolded in strips of puff pastry and baked to make plump bite-size treats.

## Lillian Gish and jockey's whips = fish and chips

Okay, so nowadays, unless you're deep in the Cockney heartland of East London, you're unlikely to hear anyone use rhyming slang to refer to fish (Lillian Gish) and chips (jockey's whips). But it did grab hold of your attention, didn't it?

Fish and chips deserves attention, being a glory of British cooking that gets less than its due because it's humble street food. But the best fish and chips shops, which you'll spot by the long lines stretching out the door at meal times, offer a culinary experience rivaling anything else in the Isles, or elsewhere. You'll get freshly deep-fried fillets of batter-dipped fish—crisp on the outside, moist and tender within—accompanied by big batons of deep-fried fresh potato, called "chips" in the British Isles and Commonwealth, and "French fries" in other parts of the world. A good shop will offer a wide range of seafood choices, with safe bets being cod, haddock, and plaice.

The customary condiment for fish and chips is malt vinegar, sprinkled from a bottle you'll find on the counter or tables. Its sharp flavor takes the edge off the greasiness that comes with frying. Orders were traditionally wrapped up in yesterday's newspaper, though today greaseproof paper or white paper are used—sometimes specially printed to resemble newsprint.

**Faggots**

Present-day political correctness makes many people uneasy about using this word, which derives from an Old English term for a bundle of sticks and, culinarily, refers simply and usually in the plural to rustic meatballs popular in Scotland and Wales. Similar to haggis, faggots usually are based on minced liver and other "variety meats," mixed with bread crumbs or oatmeal, eggs, onion, and spices, then shaped into fist-size balls, baked and served with thick gravy.

**Finnan haddie**

Not just labeled to provide a convenient rhyme for the classic song "My Heart Belongs to Daddy," this mellow-tasting golden smoked fish actually gets its name from the Scottish pronunciation for "Findon," its fishing village of origin, and "haddock," the species of fish in question. Cooked either by poaching or by sautéing in butter, finnan haddie makes a lovely, satisfying breakfast dish alongside eggs.

**Flummery**

Almost like eating a cocktail for dessert, this molded gelatin pudding, rich with egg yolks and sweet with sugar, gets its distinctive, even sophisticated, flavor from a combination of wine, brandy, and lemon juice. The word, derived from the Welsh *llymru,* has also become a dismissive term for a hollow compliment or nonsensical talk.

**Fool**

No one in a bell-decked jester's hat will come capering out of the kitchen when you order this traditional old English dessert. The name suggests only the utter simplicity of its preparation, combining sweetened pureed gooseberries or some other fruit with whipped cream or custard, then spooning it into individual serving dishes and chilling it.

**Haggis**

Long ago in London one Burns Night, the January-25th celebration of the birth of Scottish poet Robert Burns (1759-1796), my friends Windsor and Alan, who'd both studied at the University of Aberdeen, served me my first haggis, the traditional main course of such celebrations. The pudding is based on sheep's liver, heart, and lungs, minced and mixed with oatmeal, onions, and spices and then stuffed into a sheep's stomach and steamed. On Burns Night, the haggis is traditional carried into the dining room hot and steaming on a platter, accompanied by bagpipe music. Then a knife is plunged into it and the contents dished out, evoking deep affection or deep disgust. For those who feel the latter, bashed neeps (mashed turnips) help mask the flavor, while glassfuls of single-malt Scotch anesthetize the taste buds. Burns's "Address to a Haggis" is also traditionally recited, including his noble summation of the dish as "Great chieftain o' the puddin'-race!"

**Irish stew**

Ireland's country lamb or mutton is the featured meat in this rustic yet refined stew, slowly simmered with potatoes and onions and sometimes enhanced with carrots—and even barley to thicken the juices.

**Jugged hare**

The jug in question is an earthenware crock, in which game such as hare, or some other kind of meat or poultry, is marinated with vinegar or red wine for a day or two before being simmered as a stew with such other ingredients as onion, mushrooms, bacon, herbs, lemon juice, brandy—and, sometimes, the animal's blood, which thickens the final sauce.

**Kedgeree**

English colonists in India broadly adapted a native lentil-and-rice dish called *kitchari* to make this weekend breakfast or brunch favorite, in which curry powder seasons a mixture of flaked finnan haddie or kipper, rice, and hard-cooked eggs.

**Kipper**

Clean and split a fresh herring, soak it briefly in brine, and smoke it, and you'll have a kipper. All this is done before most cooks get their hands on this popular breakfast fish, which may be heated by soaking in boiling water or by broiling or sautéing it with butter before it is served with eggs.

# **Pub** grub

**One of the most pleasurable meals to be had across Britain is lunch in a pub. Look for one that specializes in handcrafted local "draught" beers rather than characterless corporate bottled products. Then take your pick from among these traditional pub favorites:**

**CORNISH PASTY** Wives in Cornwall smartly packed their coalminer husbands' lunches in edible containers they could fit into their pockets, heaping chopped meat and potatoes on a circle of sturdy dough and then folding it over to form a half-moon-shaped turnover before baking it. When you order one of these filling favorites, try not to think of the old folk saying that the Devil would never come to Cornwall "for fear of being baked in a pasty."

**PLOUGHMAN'S LUNCH** You can just imagine a farm laborer taking a break to devour the simple but satisfying contents of this pub favorite: a wedge or hunk of robust cheese such as Cheddar or blue-veined Stilton; some chutney or pickled onions; and a generous heel of crusty bread with butter. You can also imagine him leaving behind the lettuce leaves or sliced tomato that now typically also garnish the plate.

**SCOTCH EGG** Hard-cooked eggs are peeled, covered in fresh sausage meat, coated with bread crumbs, and deep-fried to make this satisfying treat, usually served cold with mustard or fruit chutney.

**STEAK AND KIDNEY PIE** This classic dish is a rich mixture of beefsteak and beef or veal kidney, stewed together and then enclosed in flaky pie pastry—sometimes just a top crust baked atop an ovenproof dish with the filling. If you're not one for so-called "variety meats," don't be put off by the steak's companion in this dish. The best cooks mince up the kidney so finely that it's all but unnoticeable save for the extra robust flavor it imparts.

**STEAK AND KIDNEY PUDDING** Like steak and kidney pie, only steamed in pastry inside a ceramic bowl known as a pudding basin.

For more information, check out the respected Campaign for Real Ale at www.camra.org.uk

**Lancashire hotpot**

From northeastern England, this is a rich stew of beef loin and kidneys, combined with ham, onions, mushrooms, and potatoes.

**Laverbread**

*Porphyra umbilicalis,* a seaweed species found along the coasts of Wales, Scotland, and Ireland and more commonly called laver, is the main ingredient in this staple most closely associated with Wales. The dark-green seaweed, the same species used to make Japanese *nori,* is cooked slowly and gently to form a thick sludge that may be eaten hot, mixed with oatmeal and fried with cakes, spread on fried bread, or served along with bacon and cockles for a hearty breakfast.

**Mulligatawny soup**

The Tamil word *milakutanni,* "pepper water," was co-opted in imperial India to describe a soup of chicken (or lamb) broth and onions lightly seasoned with such spices as red pepper and coriander seed, often sweetened with pieces of fresh apple, and then enriched with cream, coconut milk, almond milk, or even peanut butter.

**Oatcakes**

Cakes in name alone, these specialties from Scotland are actually robust, crumbly thick crackers made from butter or other shortening, oats, flour, baking soda, salt, and water, pressed out to the thinness of thick cardboard and baked until golden brown. You can find commercial varieties in stores featuring British foods, but they're very easy to make for yourself. Enjoy them with cheeses after dinner or as an accompaniment to breakfast eggs.

**Plum duff**

Oddly enough, this steamed sweet pudding doesn't usually have dried plums (a.k.a. prunes) in it at all, but rather currants or raisins. In other words, it's another term for spotted dick.

**Potted shrimps** Tiny, sweet bay shrimps, cooked and peeled, are nestled into a small ramekin or crock and covered with seasoned melted butter, then chilled, to make this popular British cold appetizer. Removed from the fridge a short while before serving to let the butter soften a bit, potted shrimps are accompanied by small triangles of toast or soft brown bread on which the shrimps and butter are spread together at table.

**Sally Lunn** Like France's *brioche*, the bread known as Sally Lunn is packed with eggs and butter. For more than three centuries, it's been a specialty of the city of Bath in southeastern England, where the definitive version is produced in a bakeshop/restaurant of the same name, historically believed to have been started by a French immigrant of the same name. There's one slight problem with that story, however. Some food historians believe that the name is an Anglicization of the French words *sol et lune*, "sun and moon," a reference to the bread's golden color and, perhaps even its round shape. No matter. Whichever explanation you accept, you'll enjoy Sally Lunn for its beauty, rich color, and compatibility with virtually any meal.

**Scone** Take your pick of the sources of this name: Gaelic *sgonn*, meaning a shapeless lump; the Low German *schoonbrod*, "fine bread;" or the Scottish town of Scone. Whatever their etymology, these sweet soda-leavened breads are what make British teatime so special, whether they're baked in the oven or cooked on top of a hot griddle. In England, most scones are small and circular in shape; Scottish scones, by contrast, are wedges cut from large rounds of dough. Savor the authentic delicacies hot with butter or clotted cream and jam.

## **Cockney rhyming slang** for favorite British foods

The Cockneys of East London have developed a time-honored slang based on rhyming words. Many, not surprisingly, cover favorite foods, including the following examples.

| | |
|---|---|
| **Army and Navy** | Gravy |
| **Clothes peg** | Egg |
| **Dog's eye** | Meat pie |
| **Giorgio Armani** | Sarnie (sandwich) |
| **Jack the Ripper** | Kipper |
| **Kate and Sidney** | Steak and kidney (pie or pudding) |
| **Loop the loop** | Soup |
| **Stand at ease** | Cheese |
| **Stop thief** | Beef |
| **Twist and shouts** | Sprouts |

**Scotch woodcock**

There's no game bird in sight in this "savoury," traditionally served after dessert (but also great for brunch): just toast, spread with anchovy butter, then topped with creamy scrambled eggs and a few more decorative anchovy fillets.

**Spotted dick**

Don't get the wrong idea from the name, which raises a smirk among Britons from school age on to old age. This steamed pudding, also called spotted dog, gets its name from a popular slang term for a Dalmatian dog, the classic firehouse dog also immortalized in the film *One Hundred and One Dalmatians* (itself based on Dodie Smith's book). Be that as it may, the fanciful name refers simply to the fact that the sweet bread-crumb-based pudding is generously studded with dried currants or raisins.

**Stargazy pie** One look at this savory Cornish fish pie explains the name. The heads of the pilchards or fresh sardines that fill it poke through along the edges of the crust, staring upward toward the heavens.

**Stovie** You can sense the affection Scots feel for this dish in the name itself, describing a slowly stovetop-cooked dish of buttered potatoes with onions fried in bacon fat or beef dripping.

**Toad-in-the-hole** You can just imagine an English mother or nanny coaxing a finicky youngster to eat by presenting this fancifully named dish: sausage baked inside a Yorkshire pudding batter.

**Treacle tart** A great example of delicious British nursery food, this sweet treat bakes bread crumbs and the molasses-like golden syrup known as treacle together in a tart shell. As a traditional British children's rhyme goes:

*Strawberry shortcake, treacle tart,*
*Tell me the name of my sweetheart.*

**Trifle** The term has more commonly come to mean something insignificant or unimportant. But the English dessert known as trifle is anything but, layering pieces of brandy- or sherry-moistened sponge cake with rich egg custard, whipped cream, and candied or fresh fruit. Sherry is the most common spirit used in trifle nowadays, and you'll even see the pudding referred to on some menus as "sherry trifle."

Sherry Trifle

**Welsh rabbit**

Best known of those British dishes traditionally served after dessert as a "savoury" course, this, as many people know, contains no rabbit at all—and in fact, you'll more often find it nowadays spelled as the less alarming Welsh "rarebit." Either way, it consists of shredded or grated Cheddar or other sharp cheese, mixed with such lively seasonings as powdered mustard, paprika, and Worcestershire sauce, melted and served over slices of toasted bread. Top it with poached eggs and you have a "buck rarebit."

**Yorkshire pudding**

Beat up a light batter of flour, eggs, and milk, then bake it in the pan drippings from roast beef, and you have this puffy, golden-brown treat, a traditional accompaniment to the roast whose fat contributes so much to its flavor. The pudding is an essential element in toad-in-the-hole.

## **The great** British breakfast

Even Anglophobes who doubt that fine dining exists in Britain have to admit that breakfast there was and always will be a glorious experience. From big-city hotel dining rooms to humble transport "caffs" along the highways, you can rely on finding a bounty of delicious breakfast items.

The basics include fried eggs with thick strips of bacon and plump sausages—a classic "fry-up" that is often embellished with sliced bread fried in the bacon fat until golden brown, sautéed mushrooms, a broiled tomato half, and sometimes baked beans out of a can. Indeed, many "caffs" will offer just such platefuls to customers all day long. More casually still, you can order a bacon sandwich—hot strips of griddle-cooked bacon between slices of toasted and buttered white bread. Friends of mine in the U.K. can't eat one of these without slathering the bacon with H.P. Sauce, a fruity-tasting, sweet, sharp, savory condiment. Breakfast can also include other items mentioned in this chapter, such as Arbroath smokies, finnan haddie, kedgeree, kippers, marmalade, and oatcakes.

# France, Switzerland, and Belgium

French cuisine can evoke fear within the culinary novice, and understandably so. No people are more adept at effortlessly making the uninitiated feel unsophisticated; none are quicker sternly to correct a mispronounced word rather than warmly offering encouragement to someone struggling with their language. Add centuries of tradition, and a more varied selection of particularly named cheeses, sauces, garnishes, wines, and other dining folderol, and you have, quite literally, a recipe for confusion and trepidation.

But fear not!

Much of the confusion felt by the uninitiated when confronted with French foods comes from the language barrier. Still more comes from the fact that, historically, French cooks, particularly those who created the hallmarks of *haute cuisine,* literally the "high cooking" of the finest restaurants, have used their culinary creations to honor great events, statesmen, artists, or the social elite—from *Béarnaise* to *à la Impératrice,* Marengo to Rossini—leading to dishes with appellations that bear no relation to their defining ingredients. The definitions that follow will help guide you through the truly foreign land that a French menu can sometimes seem.

Know, too, that the non-*haute* cooking to be found in the more humble restaurants of provincial France have gained increasing prominence in French restaurants all around the world, offering enthusiastic guests tastes of what is traditionally referred to as "*la vraie cuisine de bonne femme*"—the true cuisine of a good woman. Look for foods from the German-bordering provinces of Alsace and Lorraine, including robust *choucroute garnie* and *potée*; the fish *quenelles* of nearby Burgundy and its dishes cooked with its red wines, earning the designation *Bourguignonne*; the humble but delicious foods of the northwestern provinces of Normandy and Brittany, including *crêpes* and *galettes* and *pré salé* lamb; the rich and elegant specialties of Bordeaux in the southwest, home to great red wines along with such ingredients as *foie gras* and truffles; the hearty fare of the Languedoc, bordering the Pyrenees, including *cassoulet, garbure,* and *pipérade*; and sunswept Provence, famed for such fragrant and generous-hearted dishes as *aïoli, bouillabaisse,* and *ratatouille.*

Know, too, that French cuisine, all too often mischaracterized as calorie-laden, also gave the world in the latter decades of the 20th century the lighter, fresher trends of *nouvelle cuisine* ("new cooking") and *cuisine minceur* ("slimmer's cooking"). Both approaches focus on highlighting and intensifying the natural tastes of high-quality ingredients, and have thus influenced creative chefs far beyond France's borders.

Switzerland to France's east and Belgium to its northwest often get lumped in together with French food during culinary conversations. Obviously, that's being done here as well. But each country's cuisine is worthy of singular accolades. Beyond *fondue,* Swiss cooking shows dynamic influences not just from the neighboring Burgundy region to its west but also Germany to the north, Italy to the south, and Austria to its east. Belgian cuisine, meanwhile, presents a satisfying amalgam of not just northeastern French but also German (to the east) and Dutch (north) cooking styles, visible and edible in such specialties as *waterzooi* and *carbonnade.*

## THE FRENCH CONSIDERATION OF THE TABLE

*"The French approach to food is characteristic; they bring to their consideration of the table the same appreciation, respect, intelligence and lively interest that they have for the other arts, for painting, for literature, and for the theatre. We foreigners living in France respect and appreciate this point of view but deplore their too strict observance of a tradition which will not admit the slightest deviation in a seasoning or the suppression of a single ingredient."*

ALICE B. TOKLAS, *The Alice B. Toklas Cookbook* (1954)

**Aïoli** — Most often this term refers to a Provençal version of mayonnaise, that thick emulsion of egg yolks and olive oil, abundantly scented with pureed garlic, which is used as a sauce, dip, or spread. (The name literally means "garlic-oil.") In Provence, however, it means even more: the *grand aïoli*, an entire casual feast of fish, meats, and vegetables, at which the sauce sits gloriously as the centerpiece.

**Aligot** — Mashed potatoes at their most sublime, this puree of spuds from Aubrac in south-central France combines them with garlic and fresh cheese to make a fragrant, thick, slightly stringy, intensely satisfying side dish.

**Amoricaine, à la** — Also *à la Américaine*, "American-style," referring to an *haute cuisine* lobster preparation in which pieces of the crustacean are sautéed in olive oil, simmered with tomatoes, white wine, garlic, and shallots, and served in a sauce based on the cooking liquid, butter, cayenne pepper, brandy, lemon juice, and the lobster's coral (another word for roe, or eggs) and liver. The term also applies to a similar sauce for eggs or other seafood.

**Amuse-gueules** — Literally "amuse the gullet," these unordered, complimentary little bites, sips, or slurps of savory food are sometimes offered by the chef to guests immediately after they are seated. All manner of ingredients or preparation styles may be used, but generally the results are a big impression of color, shape, texture, and flavor in a surprisingly small mouthful of food—an announcement, the chef hopes, that an extraordinary meal will follow. I've enjoyed *amuse-gueules* as diverse as a salty-sweet scooplet of fresh tomato sorbet in a miniature bite-size Parmesan cone; a miniature

Champagne flute fillet with hot fresh pea soup in its bottom, chilled pea soup on top; and a slice of house-smoked salmon on a miniature fresh sweet corn *blini*.

**Argenteuil**

See this designation coupled with a dish and you'll know it includes fresh white asparagus, a specialty of the region of the same name near Paris, or green asparagus.

**Baeckeoffe**

This family-style casserole from Alsace layers potatoes with pork, beef, and veal, sometimes enriched with pigs' feet and sometimes replaced with lamb, slowly oven-braising them in white wine. Traditionally prepared for lunch on Sunday, it is assembled before leaving for morning mass and eaten afterward. The name means "baker's oven," referring to the fact that families would drop off their casseroles to cook at the local bakery on their way to church.

**Ballotine**

Literally "little bundle," this describes a large fillet of poultry, meat, or fish rolled up around a fine-textured stuffing, tied securely, cooked in broth, and then sliced. It is often served hot in a sauce based on the cooking liquid.

**Bavarois**

A "Bavarian cream" dessert of custard, gelatin, and whipped cream, blended together and chilled in an elaborately shaped mold that yields an impressive presentation when unmolded. Different flavorings, from vanilla to chocolate or coffee to fruit purees, are typically added, often in combination to give the finished dessert an even more elaborate appearance.

**Béarnaise**

The early 19th-century restaurant Pavillon Henri IV, near Paris, paid tribute to Henri IV (1553–1610), a native of the southwestern province of Béarn, with the creation of this sauce. Traditionally served with steak, it is made by beating together egg yolks, melted butter, white wine, vinegar, shallots, and tarragon, proving that French chefs well understood the Atkins diet two centuries ago.

**Béchamel**

Louis de Béchamel, a 17th-century financier who served as royal steward to Louis XIV, invented this classic "white" sauce, made by preparing the cooked flour-and-butter paste known as *roux*, slowly whisking in hot milk, and then simmering until thick with a bay leaf, mace (the dried husk of a nutmeg), and a chunk of onion studded with a couple of cloves. Countless other French sauces have their start with *béchamel*, including *Mornay* and *Piemontaise*, and it is also used to bind together fillings for savory *crêpes* and to form the basis for the golden-brown upper crust of a savory *gratin*. Blame badly prepared *béchamel* sauces, not simmered long enough to eliminate the flour's taste, for anything with pretensions to French cuisine that more readily brings to mind eating library paste.

**Beurre blanc**

A "white butter" sauce made by simmering shallots in white wine and wine vinegar until the liquid reduces to an intense essence, then gradually whisking in cubes of butter to form a thick, creamy, warm sauce for seafood or poultry.

**Beurre noir**

Literally "black butter," this sauce for seafood, vegetables, eggs, brains, or sweetbreads is based on butter cooked until it turns nut-brown, then enhanced with a splash of vinegar, chopped parsley, and pungent, salty little caper berries.

**Bisque**

A cream- or egg yolk-enriched soup of pureed crab, crayfish, or lobster. The crushed shells are also used to give the soup its intense flavor. Since *bisquer* is also old-fashioned slang for "to be vexed," a French wit once remarked on the thought of being too ill to eat such a rich soup, *"Je bisque en songeant"*—"I am vexed even to dream of such a thing."

**Blanquette**

"Little white" describes a stew of white meat (such as veal in *blanquette de veau*, or lamb in *blanquette d'agneau*) that is gently braised in white wine with mushrooms and small onions and then served in a sauce made from its cooking liquid enriched and thickened with cream, egg yolks, and butter.

**Boeuf à la ficelle**

"Beef on a string" aptly describes this simple, delicious way to cook a prime piece of fillet. It's tied up with string, then lowered into a pot of gently simmering, rich broth to cook before being sliced and served in the broth with a selection of vegetables that have cooked along with it. Think of this as the upscale version of *pot-au-feu*.

**Bombe**

Don't even think of dropping this weapon-shaped dessert on an enemy! Various flavors and colors of softened ice cream or sorbet are typically packed in a bomb-shaped mold to form decorative layers, then frozen solid and unmolded to be cut into wedges for serving.

**Bonne femme, à la**
"In the style of a good woman," this describes any savory main course served with a humble, home-style garnish such as potatoes, onions, mushrooms, and bacon.

**Bordelaise, à la**
Meaning "in the style of Bordeaux," this refers to grilled meats served with a sauce of Bordeaux wine, the concentrated broth known as *demiglace*, shallots, and herbs, as well as a garnish of poached bone marrow.

**Boudin**
French for a particular type of plump, juicy sausage, the name bears a similarity to the English word "pudding" (hence that country's "blood pudding"). Two of the most familiar *boudins* are *boudin noir* (black pudding), a pork sausage whose color and flavor come from the pig's blood; and *boudin blanc*, a mild sausage usually made with veal and enriched with milk or cream. *Boudins* are typically cooked first by simmering in water and then by browning them off in a skillet or on a griddle.

**Bouillabaisse**
The phrase "a mixed catch" has never tasted so good as it does in this fisherman's stew from the port city of Marseilles. You'll find a dozen or more different kinds of seafood in the pot, including halibut, snapper, or cod; eel; shellfish such as clams, mussels, and scallops; sometimes lobster or shrimp; and always mild-tasting John Dory, known by the French *rascasse*. Any combination of the above are simmered with white wine, tomatoes, olive oil, garlic, leeks, onions, dried orange peel, and saffron. Seasoning each serving at table is a generous dollop of *rouille*, a thick mayonnaise-like sauce made by pounding together garlic, olive oil, egg yolks, water, bread crumbs, and fresh or dried hot red chilies.

**Bouquetière, à la**

"In a florist's style," meaning any savory main dish served with a virtual bouquet of fresh seasonal vegetables.

**Bourguignonne, à la**

Meaning "in the style of Burgundy," this sauce features that region's robust red wine as a braising liquid for beef, usually accompanied by onions, mushrooms, and bacon; or, without the bacon, for fish.

**Bourride**

A close cousin to *bouillabaisse,* this Mediterranean seafood soup is milder and simpler than that big, brash creation. Poached fish fillets are served in a soup made by stirring seafood broth into *aïoli,* then gently heating the mixture until thick. The soup is traditionally poured into a tureen or deep bowls in which crusts of rustic bread have been scattered.

**Brandade**

The salt cod, or *morue,* of which many cooks are fond throughout France reaches its epiphany in this preparation from the south, which gets its name from the local dialect for "stirred." The dried fish is first soaked in several changes of cold water, then boiled and drained; after the fish has been skinned and boned, its flakes are beaten with hot milk, olive oil, and sometimes garlic to make a voluptuous warm paste enjoyed as a spread with crisp croutons of sliced French bread.

**Carbonnade**

From the Flemish lands of northwestern France and Belgium, this country-style braise features chunks or slices of beef layered with caramelized onions and slowly cooked with dark beer until intensely rich-tasting and meltingly tender. In times past, salt-preserved beef was often used instead of fresh, further intensifying the final results.

**Cassoulet**

You might at first be astonished by the incredible mystique surrounding this ancient, humble peasant bean dish from the Languedoc region of southern France. One voluptuous, earthy taste, however, will likely make you a convert. Dried white beans are gently baked for hours in an earthenware casserole with such meats as preserved goose or duck, fresh lamb or pork, and Toulouse sausage, along with plenty of garlic and other aromatic vegetables, broth, and sometimes tomatoes. A brown crust forms on the top and is repeatedly broken with a spoon and folded down into the beans, further enriching them, and a final crust of browned bread crumbs is sometimes baked on top. The results define the notion of stick-to-your-ribs winter food. As the legendary cookbook author Julia Child observed, "*Cassoulet*, that best of bean feasts, is everyday fare for a peasant but ambrosia for a gastronome, though its ideal consumer is a 300-pound blocking back who has been splitting firewood nonstop for the last twelve hours on a subzero day in Manitoba."

**Chantilly**

See this name, a reference to Vatel, who was chef at the Château Chantilly in the early 18th century, and you know the dessert so designated will feature that chef's most enduring creation: sweetened whipped cream.

**Charcuterie**

The broad French category of preserved meats, from cured hams and sausages to all kinds of pâté and terrine. Often, a *charcuterie* assortment is enjoyed as an appetizer or for a light but satisfying lunch accompanied by bread.

**Charlotte**

I know a girl named Charlotte whose gastronome uncle always tries to make sure she has a *charlotte* as her birthday cake. She'll never get bored, because the term applies to two different kinds of widely varied desserts formed in and then unmolded from a round, deep, straight-sided tin called a *charlotte* mold. One category is known collectively as fruit *charlottes,* made by lining the mold with buttered bread, filling it with a fruit puree (apple is the classic choice), and baking it. The other is cream-filled *charlottes,* in which the mold is usually lined with cake, filled with some sort of cream mixture and then chilled; the most famous of these is a *charlotte russe,* in which a sponge-cake lining is filled with a rich Bavarian cream (*bavarois* in French) made by combining custard, whipped cream, and gelatin.

**Choucroute garnie**

Those with an ear finely attuned to foreign tongues might recognize that *choucroute* is just the French way of saying "sauerkraut." Ah, but then there's the *garnie* that transports the humbled salted and pickled cabbage to gastronomic glory in the northwestern provinces of Alsace or Strasbourg. No mere garnish, the sausages, bacon, ham, goose fat, onions, herbs, and spices with which the *sauerkraut* is gently simmered in broth and white wine or beer for several hours endows the humble cabbage with incredibly rich, complex flavor—and the meats with melting tenderness and a delightful tang. Enjoy the results with boiled potatoes or, in some restaurants, pureed yellow split peas, and quench your thirst with white wine or beer, whichever figured in the cooking.

## **French** cheeses

**"How," pondered the French World War II general and subsequent prime minister Charles de Gaulle, "can anyone be expected to govern a nation with 325 cheeses?"**

***Exactement!***

Every town and region of France does, indeed, seem to have one or more of its own special cheeses, part of the reason that dining in France can be an experience at once delightful and bewildering. With that in mind, keep an *oeuil* (eye, *en français*) open when dining for some of these well known and widely available varieties, and use them as your starting point for further explorations.

**BOURSAULT** A triple-cream cow's-milk cheese from the north, soft, rich, and slightly salty.

**BOURSIN** A triple-cream cow's-milk cheese from Normandy and the Île-de-France, rich and spreadable, often flavored with garlic and herbs.

**BRIE** From the Île-de-France, this acclaimed, creamy cow's-milk cheese is prepared in large, flat disks that ripen to a rich, tangy flavor and an oozing consistency within its white rind.

**BRILLAT-SAVARIN** A triple-cream cheese resembling a plump Brie or Camembert, named to honor Jean Anthelme Brillat-Savarin, the 18th- to 19th-century gastronome who wrote *The Physiology of Taste,* famed for his observation generally condensed and translated into English as "you are what you eat."

**CAMEMBERT** From Normandy, this is similar to brie but somewhat milder and formed into smaller, thicker disks.

**CANTAL** A rich, robust, sweet cow's-milk cheese from the Auvergne region in central France.

## **French** cheeses

**CHÈVRE** The general term for French goat's-milk cheeses, which can range from mild, soft, creamy, and slightly tangy when young and fresh to firm, crumbly, and pungent when aged.

**COMTÉ** A chewy aged cow's-milk cheese from the Franche-Comté region in northeastern France.

**EXPLORATEUR** A close cousin to brie produced with triple-rich cream and made in narrower, thicker disks.

**FROMAGE FRAIS** Literally "fresh cheese," this is a soft, mild curd cheese, similar to cream or mild yogurt, that may be enjoyed for breakfast or, lightly sweetened and garnished with fresh fruit, as a dessert.

**MUNSTER** A robust-tasting cow's-milk cheese, usually formed into flat cylinders.

**PONT L'EVÊQUE** A resilient-textured mild cow's-milk cheese with a distinctive yellow rind.

**PORT SALUT** A very milky, smooth-textured cow's-milk cheese, prepared in thick disks.

**REBLOCHON** A mild-tasting, rich and creamy, soft cow's-milk cheese.

**ROQUEFORT** France's superb blue cheese, made from sheep's milk formed into tall cylinders, with a creamy consistency and a distinctive rich, sharp, tangy flavor.

**TOMME** A low-fat pressed cheese made from sheep's, goat's, or cow's milk.

**Clafoutis**

Originally from the Limousin region, but now a countrywide favorite, this humble, warm dessert features fresh fruit baked in a sweet batter of eggs and egg yolks, flour, and milk. Cherries are the traditional choice, and the very first of the season get celebrated in a *clafoutis*.

**Coeur à la crème**

This "cream heart" is actually a lightly sweetened, creamy fresh white cheese prepared in a porcelain mold shaped like a heart (*coeur*), then unmolded and served for dessert with fresh fruit, often assorted berries.

**Coq au vin**

A tough old rooster, the *coq*, finds eternal tenderness in this classic farmhouse dish, in which the bird is cut up and slowly braised in red or white wine, traditionally cooked with and accompanied by cubes of bacon, baby onions, mushrooms, and a garnish of crisp bread croutons.

**Coquilles Saint-Jacques**

Fresh scallops rapidly cooked in a variety of simple ways depending on the region, sometimes given a *gratin* topping with *béchamel* sauce.

**Cornichons**

Small, bite-size baby cucumbers are pickled with vinegar and spices to make these sharp-tasting accompaniments for various kinds of pâté, *charcuterie*, and other dishes including *pot-au-feu*.

**Court bouillon**

A "short broth" usually made by simmering aromatic vegetables such as onions, carrots, and celery in water with a little white wine and/or vinegar with bay leaf, parsley, and other herbs, producing a mildly flavored cooking liquid most often used for seafood. The liquid is discarded after cooking.

**Crème brûlée**

"Burnt cream," as the name translates, has traveled far beyond the confines of France to become one of the most popular desserts in restaurants everywhere. Thick, rich egg custard is poured into shallow porcelain dishes and chilled. Then, a layer of granulated sugar is sprinkled evenly over the custard's surface before it is burnt—in fact, melted and caramelized, by intense heat. Traditionally this was done with a red-hot poker called a salamander, or by putting the dishes briefly beneath an intense heating element such as a broiler. Many chefs nowadays flavor the custard in a wide variety of ways—chocolate, ginger, coffee, berries, even floral essences—instead of the customary vanilla. They also prefer to melt the sugar with a small hand-held kitchen blowtorch.

**Crème fraîche**

A favorite enrichment for a wide variety of both savory and sweet French dishes, this cultured cream possesses a luxuriously thick consistency and pleasant hint of sour flavor that only underscores its richness.

**Crêpes**

These large, tissue-thin pancakes are loved throughout France. Made with white wheat flour, they are traditionally served rolled up or folded around a sweet filling, including *crêpes Suzettes*, which are flavored with orange liqueur; pleasantly sour buckwheat *crêpes* traditionally are the vehicle for savory fillings such as cheese and ham. For the best, most down-to-earth *crêpes* in any good-sized French settlement, look for a *crêperie*, a casual restaurant specializing in them.

**Croquembouche** The name, which translates as "crunch in the mouth," captures a particular pleasure of this dessert. Little hollow bite-size balls of *choux* pastry, the same mixture used to make cream puffs and *éclairs* and *gougère,* are filled with whipped cream or custard, dipped in molten caramelized sugar syrup, and then stacked to form a conical tree shape. Each guest is served several balls removed from the tree, which crunch when bitten into.

**Crudités** An assortment of fresh seasonal vegetables served in all their glorious rawness (to which the name refers), usually accompanied with a vinaigrette or other dressing for dipping, or just coarse salt.

**Daube** Coming from the same root word as the English "daub," the name for this Provençal country stew literally means "mess," a reference to the casual way in which it is composed of meat, broth, wine, root vegetables, herbs, and salt pork or pork rinds. The wide-bottomed, narrow-necked earthenware pot in which it cooks, called a *daubière,* guards against evaporation during the several hours of cooking, as does a flour-and-water paste usually employed to seal on its lid. The leftovers are often molded to make a cold luncheon dish called *daube en gelée,* which sets thanks to the sauce's rich gelatin content.

**Demi-deuil, en**

"Half-mourning" fancifully describes the appearance of this specialty from France's alpine region, where slices of black truffle are slipped between the skin and flesh of a sausage-stuffed chicken before it is poached.

**Dijonnaise**

When you see this adjectival reference to the city of Dijon in a recipe's name you will know that famed Dijon mustard is likely to play a distinctive role in its sauce.

**Duxelles**

Take lots of finely chopped mushrooms and a good dose of shallots. Sauté them in butter, oil, or a mixture of the two, and something intriguing gradually occurs. At first, the spongy mushrooms give up all their liquid, and the pan holds a watery, unappetizing mess. Gradually, however, the liquid evaporates, the mixture darkens in color, and it becomes a dark brown paste concentrating intense mushroom flavor. The 17th-century chef La Varenne created, or at least codified, the paste and named it in tribute to his employer, the Marquis d'Uxelles. The honor endures today in the kitchens not just of French chefs but any enterprising cooks who use *duxelles* to flavor stuffings for pasta, *crêpes*, seafood, poultry, or meat; or as the basis for a mushroom sauce or a creamy mushroom soup.

**Escargots**

You probably know that *escargots* is French for snails, and slam shut the trapdoor of your mind at that thought. Open the door and reconsider trying them, though. Try to think of snails as the mushrooms of the animal world, earthy-tasting, pleasantly chewy, and wondrously receptive to (and entirely disguised by) the garlic butter in which they're most often served. Then take note of the fact that, before being served, the snails are put on a week-long fast, and then cleansed in a mixture of water, salt, and vinegar before being poached in *court bouillon*. All this is done in preparation for whichever manner they're subsequently prepared for the table.

**Flamiche**

A rustic savory tart from Picardy of leeks, onions, or even pumpkin, enriched with egg and cream.

**Foie gras**

Ah! Those two little French words sound so much more appealing than their translation: "fat liver." The organ in question belongs to a goose, or sometimes a duck, that is force-fed a calorie-rich porridge of cornmeal and fat for six weeks in a process designed to cause its liver to swell to many times normal size, more than two pounds in weight, and turning it as rich and smooth as butter. Considered one of the pinnacles of French *haute cuisine*, this specialty of Strasbourg and Toulouse may be simply sliced and briefly sautéed, baked inside the buttery egg bread known as *brioche*, formed into a pâté or terrine, or used as the most luxurious of garnishes.

**Fondue**

"Melted" cheese is the briefest way to sum up this favorite casual main dish from France's alpine regions (and neighboring Switzerland, *mais oui!*). Good cheeses of the region such as *Beaufort*, *Emmental*, or *Gruyère* are melted with white wine, nutmeg, and a splash of cherry-scented kirsch in a garlic-rubbed earthenware pot. Then cubes of crusty bread are speared on long forks to dip in the luscious, thick mixture. One old custom holds that a woman who loses her bread cube in the pot owes a kiss to every man at the table, or at least the man seated to her right. What better reason could there be to enjoy *fondue* as a romantic dinner for two?

**Galette**

This term refers to any of several different preparations in the form of a round, flat cake. Some *galettes* are sweet, such as the classic *galette des rois,* "kings' cake," made with puffed pastry and the almond-flavored pastry cream known as *frangipane,* served traditionally at parties celebrating Twelfth Night. (A dried bean hidden inside before baking represents the baby Jesus, and whoever gets it in his or her slice becomes "king" or "queen" of the celebration.) More often still, a *galette* may simply be a shortbread cookie or a simple flat pastrylike cake, or it can also refer to a thick golden-brown cake of sliced or shredded potatoes baked in the oven to serve as a side dish.

**Galantine**

Imagine a pâté of veal and pork poached inside a whole boneless chicken (or pheasant or even fillet of veal), then served cold in slices as an elegant hors d'oeuvre and there you have this classic French dish, its name derived from the Old French word for chicken, *galine.*

**Garbure**

Rustic soup serves as main course in this traditional dish from Béarn in southwestern France. Into a pot of boiling water, in order of cooking time, go potatoes, beans, peas, sometimes roasted chestnuts, fresh herbs, garlic, then sausage, ham, and preserved goose with its rich, flavorful fat. The result should be so thick that a wooden spoon can stand up in it. Dry crusts of country bread go into the bowls, and the soup is ladled in. Drink red wine with *garbure,* and stir the dregs of your glass into the last few spoonfuls in your bowl to make a *goudale,* believed to sustain good health and ward off doctors.

**Gougère**

The cooked paste of flour, butter, and eggs known as *choux* pastry, also the basis for such sweet pastries as cream puffs, *éclairs,* and *croquembouche,* can be combined with grated cheese, piped into small ball shapes, and then baked to make immensely satisfying little appetizer puffs, popular at wine tastings in Burgundy. Try stopping at popping just one into your mouth.

**Gratin**

Meaning "crust," this describes the golden-brown surface that forms atop a savory or sweet recipe baked in a shallow dish of the same name and topped with a creamy, cheesy sauce such as *Mornay* or with bread crumbs and butter. A *gratinée à l'oignon* is classic French onion soup with a crust of melted cheese, a legendary form of early-morning sustenance for workers in the old Les Halles market (which 19th-century writer Emile Zola evocatively described as "The Belly of Paris" in the title of a novel largely set there). *Gratin dauphinois* describes a baked dish of thinly sliced potatoes slathered with cream and baked until tender and golden. Interestingly, the French slang for "the upper crust," society's snootiest level, is *le gratin.*

**Impératrice, à la Julienne**

Meaning "in the style of the Empress," specifically Napoleon III's wife Eugénie, these words appear most often on French menus nowadays after *riz,* describing a molded rice-and-custard pudding studded with candied fruit and scented with the kirsch, a spirit distilled from cherry pits.

**Julienne**

This French kitchen term may be found in recipes written in many other languages as well. It refers both to food cut into long, thin strips and to the act of cutting them.

## **A mussel-shell** utensil

Try this popular French bistro trick for eating *moules marinière*. After removing and enjoying the succulent meat from your first shell, wipe off the hinged shell, which should close easily when squeezed between thumb and fingertips and then spring back open when released. Holding and manipulating the shell in this way, use the narrow end of the shell to extract the meat from the remaining mussels, raising it to your lips and then releasing it from the shell.

**Lyonnaise, à la**

Meaning "in the style of Lyons" in east-central France, this usually means cooked with lots of onions, whether the main ingredient is potatoes, eggs, tripe, steak, or roasted meat.

**Madeleine**

Delicately scented with orange-flower water, these scallop-shell-shaped little sponge cakes were immortalized in *À La Recherche du Temps Perdu* (*Remembrance of Times Past*) by early-20th-century French writer Marcel Proust. A number of different cooks laid claim to inventing them, but the best are reputedly made in the northeastern town of Commercy in Lorraine.

**Marengo**

This dish of chicken (or sometimes veal) cooked with white wine, cognac, tomatoes, and garlic was first prepared by Napoleon's cook, Dunand, to celebrate victory over Austrian forces at Marengo on June 14, 1880.

**Marinière**

Meaning "sailor-style," this term usually applies to *moules*, mussels, steamed in their shells with olive oil, garlic, and white wine, then served heaped in bowls with the resulting briny broth.

**Mesclun**

First, and most importantly, don't mispronounce this "mescaline," a psychedelic extract of the peyote cactus. Properly pronounced "mez-clah," *mesclun* literally means mixture, referring to an assortment of little salad leaves prized in Provence, including arugula, purslane, chervil, dandelion leaves, and radicchio, and traditionally served as a simple salad with vinaigrette dressing.

**Meunière**

The "miller's wife" to whom this designation referred would typically cook sole or trout by dusting it lightly with some of the mill's flour before sautéing it in butter and finishing it with fresh lemon juice and parsley.

**Meurette**

A Burgundian term describing dishes prepared with red wine, particularly eggs poached in a buttery sauce featuring Burgundy, red wine vinegar, butter, and shallots.

**Mille-feuille**

This pastry of "a thousand leaves" is constructed from baked layers of flaky puff dough, interspersed with cream or thick custard. To temper its intensity, enjoy this with good strong coffee.

**Mornay**

A sauce made from *béchamel*, enriched with tangy grated Parmesan or *Gruyère* cheese, then spooned over or combined with vegetables, seafood, chicken, or eggs. It's amazing how a *Mornay* sauce can transform humble cauliflower when that vegetable is briefly cooked, spread in a baking dish, covered with the sauce, and baked until its surface develops a golden-brown *gratin*.

**Mousseline**

Meaning "little froth," this refers to a sauce (such as Hollandaise) or an ingredient (usually pureed seafood, to be shaped into dumplings and poached) lightened by whipped cream.

**Navarin**

Some claim the name comes from the Battle of Navarino in 1827, a joint French-British-Russian naval victory over Turkey and Egypt. More likely, however, it refers to the turnips (*navets*) that traditionally accompany the meat—along with carrots, onions, potatoes, and tomatoes—in this garlicky lamb stew.

**Niçoise**

Meaning generally "in the style of Nice," this term is more specifically paired most often with *salade* to designate a classic southern French salad of tomatoes, bell peppers, cucumbers, green onions, black olives, hard-cooked eggs, canned tuna, and anchovy fillets. Though less traditional, most versions nowadays also include cold boiled potatoes and green beans.

**Normande, à la**

The rich cream of Normandy is a tip-off of dishes prepared in this style, such as seafood. So, too, might the apples, cider, or Calvados, the local applejack.

**Paillard**

Pronounced "pie-yard," this term refers to a thin cutlet of chicken, veal, turkey, or other meat that has been pounded flat for cooking, usually by grilling or pan-frying.

**Pan bagnat**

From the area of Nice, this "bathed bread" consists of a loaf of French bread stuffed with a mixture of tomatoes, roasted bell peppers, olives, possibly tender young fava beans, some olive oil, and maybe a splash of vinegar. Canned tuna and anchovy fillets often join in the fun to make a sort of *salade Niçoise* sandwich, and the stuffed loaf is wrapped and weighted to let the flavors mingle for several hours before slicing and serving.

**Papillote, en**

"In paper" refers to any of a wide range of savory or sweet dishes, but most often tender, quick-cooking seafood, sealed inside a folded and pleated sheet of parchment paper and then baked. The paper, often replaced nowadays by aluminum foil, seals in the juices, yielding moist, flavorful results. The trapped steam puffs up the packet, making for an impressive presentation when the balloonlike object is carefully slit open at table, releasing a cloud of fragrant steam.

**Pâté**

This describes any of a wide range of finely ground mixtures of meat or poultry and seasonings, packed into a usually loaf-shaped mold, cooked, and served cold in slices as an appetizer. Literally "pastried," the name is a reference to the pastry casing that once enclosed it but now seldom does. Pâtés can range from rustic, such as a coarse country-style *pâté de campagne,* to rich and refined like a classic *pâté de foie gras.*

**Périgourdine**

Refers to a dish prepared in the style of Périgord, meaning generously flavored with truffles and sometimes also featuring the region's *foie gras.*

**Pets de nonne**

Truth be told, you won't find these deep-fried little Burgundian appetizer puffs of flour, water, butter, cheese, and eggs on the menus of that many restaurants. But, honestly, how could anyone resist including in this book a dish whose name translates as "nun's farts"?

**Pipérade**

A favorite Basque dish, this consists of bell peppers (hence the name) sautéed with onions and garlic, then mixed with beaten egg to form a soft, flavorful scramble. Enjoy it for breakfast, lunch, or dinner.

**Pissaladière**

Yes, the name of this tart from Nice sounds suspiciously like the pizza of nearby Italy, and with good reason. A large, thin sheet of rich dough is traditionally topped with onions sautéed in olive oil, chopped garlic, black olives, and a crisscross pattern of anchovy fillets (but no cheese), then baked to make a gloriously fragrant casual appetizer or luncheon treat. The name comes from the local dialect *pissalat,* the name for a pungent paste of anchovies and herbs sometimes used in place of the fillets.

**Pistou**

This extravagant but rustic Provençal summertime vegetable soup takes its name from the sauce of fresh basil, tomatoes, garlic, olive oil, and sometimes Parmesan cheese. Yes, that sauce sounds like a close cousin in both ingredients and name of the pesto of neighboring northwestern Italy. So elementally good is a well made *pistou* that, declares Richard Olney in *Simple French Food,* "The thing, in itself, is like some unleashed earth force, sowing exhilaration in its wake."

**Pithiviers**

The central French town where this sweet pastry dessert originated gives its name to the construction of two layers of buttery, flaky puff pastry. Between these layers is sandwiched a layer of *frangipane,* a thick mixture of buttercream and almond paste. Sometimes fruit such as pears are added, too.

**Pot-au-feu**

From the "pot on the fire" comes this simple country dish of beef poached with vegetables in broth, traditionally served accompanied by coarse salt and a jar of *cornichons.*

**Potée** As simple and obvious as the name appears, this term generally describes anything cooked in an earthenware pot. More specifically, it refers to a humble but delicious soup of cabbage, potatoes, and other vegetables, enriched and flavored with a big chunk of salt pork.

**Poule-au-pot** France's King Henri IV (1553-1610) promised his people an era so prosperous that there would be "a chicken in every pot." This traditional dish may well be what the good king was describing, a whole, plump chicken poached with vegetables in rich broth, then sliced and served with the vegetables and its cooking liquid.

**Pré salé** "Pre-salted" refers to lamb that has grazed on the salty coastal pastures of Normandy, literally pre-seasoning their meat.

**Printanier** Expect springtime (*le printemps*) vegetables as part of any dish that bears this designation, including *potage printanier,* a Provençal soup featuring baby artichokes, fava beans, new potatoes, and Swiss chard; *salade printanière,* a spring vegetable salad; and the classic *Navarin printanier,* a stew of lamb and vegetables.

**Quenelles** In Lyons, these fluffy dumplings of fresh pike are made by pureeing the raw fish with eggs, cream, and seasonings, then poaching them in large egglike shapes. The *quenelles* are usually served with Nantua sauce. Other seafood (as well as poultry, especially chicken) may also be used. Indeed, the dying words of the great French chef and author Marie-Antoine Carème (1784-1833), reputedly spoken to a favorite student, were, "My lad, the *quenelles* of sole were splendid, but the peas were poor. You should shake the pan gently, all the time, like this."

**Quiche**

A casual, country-style luncheon tart from northeastern France, this is a savory egg custard baked inside a pastry casing. The name *quiche* derives from *küche,* "cake" in nearby Germany. The dish comes in its most familiar form as *quiche Lorraine,* a popular version from the Lorraine region, with bits of bacon studding the smooth, rich filling. As well as in casual French restaurants, quiches are also sold in France from "*quiche* wagons," that set up shop in public marketplaces.

**Raclette**

Made with a Savoyard cheese of the same name, this alpine French and Swiss specialty is traditionally made by holding a block of the cheese close to an open fire. This melts a thin layer of its surface, which is then scraped onto a plate to be enjoyed with boiled potatoes and perhaps a bite of *cornichon.* Nowadays, ingenious electric tabletop grills for melting the cheese are the norm. Whenever possible (and safe), opt for the fire.

**Ratatouille**

The goodness of this vegetable stew from Provence is evident in its name, combining *rata,* military slang for food at its most humble, with a variation on a slang term meaning to stir things up. The things in this case are chunks or slices of eggplant, tomatoes, zucchini, onions, garlic, and bell peppers, which simmer slowly together until they achieve melting tenderness while their flavors blend into an intense essence of summertime. *Ratatouille* may be serve hot or cold, as an accompaniment, appetizer, or salad.

**Rillettes**

A rich, thick appetizer, this spread made of seasoned, shredded pork or goose meat is cooked and preserved in rendered pork or goose fat.

**Rösti**

Many consider this humble potato dish one of the pinnacles of the Swiss kitchen. Shredded potatoes are shaped into a thin cake and packed into a hot skillet. It is cooked in melted butter until golden brown and crisp on both sides, and tender within. Usually served as an accompaniment to meat or poultry dishes, *rösti,* sometimes prepared in smaller cakes, may also be used as a beautiful platform upon which main courses are placed, soaking up their juices in the process.

**Sauté**

From the verb *sauter,* meaning "to jump," this term refers to a broad class of French dishes cooked on the stovetop in a pan of the same name. Broad and shallow, the sloping sides of the pan allow a dexterous cook to cause small pieces of food to flip or jump with a twist of the wrist. Sautéing at its most simple involves cooking any small pieces of food quickly in a little hot oil or fat over high heat. But a dish termed *sauté* begins with that browning process—applied to pieces of poultry, meat, or seafood—and then continues with the introduction of flavorful liquids and garnishes, the lowering of the heat, and the final cooking until the main ingredients is done and its accompaniments form a casual sauce. Still other *sautés,* in which the main ingredients cook through quickly, may be finished with a flourish by removing the food from the pan and then deglazing the caramelized juices on the pan's bottom with some broth, wine, or other tasty liquid to make a quick sauce.

**Soufflé**

Shh! As clichéd as this dish may be among French restaurant classics, its name, appropriately derived from the word for "whisper," still has the power to evoke awe among diners. In classic savory or sweet hot *soufflés*, pureed or melted ingredients, such as seafood, asparagus, cheese, or chocolate are combined with beaten egg whites and baked in a circular dish until the mixture rises to glorious heights. Frozen *soufflés* combine sweet ingredients with whipped cream or egg whites and are then frozen in a dish surmounted by a paper collar that contains the "risen" part until its rock-solid. The term also refers to oval-shaped pieces of potato—*pommes soufflés*—that are fried twice to puff them up.

**Steak-frites**

Even the most Francophobic traveler will likely feel comfortable spotting this on the menu of virtually every French bistro in existence. It's a shorthand way of listing a pan-fried, grilled, or broiled steak accompanied by a mound of crisp French-fried potatoes.

**Tapenade**

A classic spread from Provence, made by coarsely pureeing black olives, anchovies, garlic, olive oil, capers (*tapeno* in the local dialect), and seasonings.

**Tarte Tatin**

The Tatin sisters, early-20th-century innkeepers in the town of Lamotte-Beuvron between Toulouse and Paris, reputedly invented this upside-down tart of caramelized apples. It has become so fashionable beyond France's borders that its name is now misapplied to pallid imitations. A true *tarte Tatin* begins by caramelizing sliced, carefully arranged apples with butter and sugar in an ovenproof pan; then, a round of pastry is placed on top and the tart finishes cooking in the oven. It is then unmolded and flipped over to serve.

**Tartiflette**

This specialty of eastern France's Alpine region could be the ultimate cholesterol-rich French comfort food. Sliced potatoes, crisp bacon, and mushrooms are layered and baked in a casserole dish together with *Reblochon* cheese and cream to make a rich, golden-brown, bubbling-hot self-indulgent dish.

**Terrine**

From *terre*, meaning "earth," this refers both to an earthenware dish and to a pâté prepared in it.

**Tournedos Rossini**

This luxurious dish was created in the 19th century at the Café Foy in Paris to honor its upstairs neighbor, Italian opera composer Gioacchino Rossini. Thick beef fillets are fried in butter, placed atop butter-fried slices of bread, topped with truffles and *foie gras*, and then napped in a sauce of Madeira wine and beef stock. Considering those ingredients, you could conceivably encounter a chef who isn't versed in either classic culinary nomenclature or opera naming this dish *tournedos Périgourdine*.

**Le Trou Normande**

In the northwestern French province of Normandy, and at Normandy-style restaurants anywhere, you might be fortunate enough to be offered *le trou Normande*, literally "the Normandy hole" (or "break" or "trough"). This *moment digestif* settles the appetites between courses of a robust meal by offering each guest a small glass of Calvados, the applejack brandy of the region. More refined restaurants might instead transform the Calvados into a sorbet whose iciness makes the alcohol slide down all the more smoothly. If the opportunity arises, do not pass up *le trou Normande*—but be prepared to feel the consequences the next morning!

**Truffé**

Literally meaning "truffled," the Black Diamonds of Périgord are one of the glories of French cuisine. This specialty of the Périgord region is a usually golfball-sized, firm black fungus that grows underground near the roots of oak trees. Truffles are so highly aromatic, with a heady scent that often gives rise to sexual allusions, that a little of it usually goes a long way, shaved or chopped to flavor eggs, pâtés, poultry or meats, and other dishes. Indeed, smart chefs usually store whole truffles alongside raw eggs in their shells, then cook the eggs, which absorb some of the intoxicating flavor without any sacrifice of the precious truffles. You'll likely pay a hefty price for any dish involving truffles; but, if you're inclined to enjoy life's more esoteric, exotic (or even erotic) pleasures, then the experience will likely be very much worth the expense.

**Vichyssoise**

Though the name and the style are distinctively French, and it stars on French menus, this soup shares dual citizenship with the United States. In the mid 20th century, chef Louis Diat at New York City's Ritz-Carlton Hotel took the rustic leek-and-potato soup that any country housewife might have made back in his hometown of Vichy, pureed it, enriched it with cream, and served it cold, garnished with chopped fresh chives.

## **The glories of** French bread

**BAGUETTE** Meaning "stick," this is the traditional long, slender, golden-brown loaf of French bread.

**BOULE** Meaning "ball," this is a round loaf of bread.

**BRIOCHE** Common lore has it that when Marie-Antoinette, King Louis XVI's queen, was informed that the peasants of France were hungry and didn't even have bread to eat, she replied, "Let them eat cake!" Actually, that was an antiroyal rumor started by the philosopher Jean-Jacques Rousseau, and what he actually attributed to a certain princess were the words, "*Qu'ils mangent de la brioche!*" Though not strictly a cake, *brioche* is about as close as bread can come to being cake, made as it is from a dough so packed with butter and eggs that the resulting loaf has a deep golden color, a rich flavor, and an almost cakelike texture. You'll usually find it as large or individual circular loaves baked in fluted molds, each bread surmounted by a ball-size topknot of dough referred to as its *tête*, or head. Enjoy *brioche* with coffee for breakfast, or sliced as the basis for deluxe sandwiches. *Brioche* dough also turns up as a luxuriant casing in which humble sausages may be baked, and small loaves may be hollowed out to form edible serving containers for scrambled eggs, thick creamy stews, or other savory mixtures.

**CROISSANT** A golden, crescent-shaped breakfast roll made from yeast-leavened dough that has been interleaved with butter to produce fine, flaky results.

**DEMI-BAGUETTE** This "half-baguette" is just a smaller, more slender version of its bigger cousin.

## **The glories of** French bread

**FICELLE** Literally "string," this is a thin mini loaf, as much crust as crumb, suitable for a single serving.

**FOUGASSE** Similar to Italian *focaccia,* this flat bread of southern France is sometimes baked in a ladder shape and strewn with herbs and olive oil.

**FLUTE** As the name describes, a thin, small baguette.

**MICHE** Another term for a country loaf, it is a round and large everyday bread.

**PAIN AU CHOCOLAT** Buttery, flaky croissant dough is rolled up around bittersweet chocolate before being baked until golden brown. It is often enjoyed with breakfast coffee.

**PAIN DE MIE** Literally "crumb bread," this is France's version of the standard loaf-shaped white bread that is sliced for use in sandwiches.

### Waterzooie

As the first two syllables imply, this Belgian main-course soup begins with water, in which chicken or a mixture of fresh fish (always including chunks of eel, as well as such local choices as carp, perch, tench, pike, and roach) are poached along with some fortifying broth, perhaps, aromatic vegetables, and white wine for the fish. Before serving, the broth of the poultry version will be enriched with a mixture of beaten egg yolks and cream, the seafood version with butter and bread crumbs.

# Holland and Scandinavia

The nations of northern Europe all share cuisines that have been shaped by their surrounding seas, harsh winters, and long nights. Expect generous, simple, but flavorful fare featuring lots of seafood, including herrings and such spectacular salmon treats as *gravlax*. Robust meat dishes include such treats as reindeer and preserved meats such as Iceland's distinctive *hangikjöt,* as well as fortifying stews like *hutspot.*

## ALL YOU NEED IS...BUTTER!

*"Food should be prepared with butter and love."*

SWEDISH PROVERB

I recall an entire afternoon I once spent early one spring back in 1980 in downtown Oslo searching for fresh eggplant, zucchini, and tomatoes so I could prepare a French *ratatouille* for my hosts. We miraculously turned up a few wrinkled specimens, and after I'd cut away the moldy spots I was able to prepare enough of the side dish to serve a couple of tablespoons to each person. While I'm sure there have been great advances in produce shipping since then, that typified for me the way that northern European cuisines rely heavily on vegetables that store well through the nongrowing seasons, especially the potatoes that accompany so many meals and star in such specialties as Jansson's *frestelse*; and the dried peas you'll find featured in soups such as Holland's *erwtensoep*.

Whenever possible, seek out some form of the buffet typified by Sweden's *smorgasbord* and given similar names in other northern European countries. Served in various versions for breakfast, lunch, or dinner, it expresses the warm hospitality and joyful eating that endures in a sometimes harsh climate.

And speaking of joyful eating, not enough can be said about the wondrous pastries and other baked confections found in Denmark and other countries of northern Europe. Danish pastry, known locally as *Wienerbrod*, is perhaps the best known of such creations. But all the nations of this region also glory in buttery cookies and other pastry treats. And don't miss Sweden's famed *ostkaka*, an unusual take on the concept of cheesecake that shows how ingenious that nation is in making wondrous treats from humble ingredients.

**Aebleskiver**

These rich, sweet, eggy Danish treats are made with a batter resembling that for pancakes, but they're cooked in an iron pan usually containing about seven hemispherical depressions, which gives the resulting golden-brown cakes a round shape resembling cream puffs or doughnut holes. *Aebleskiver* are served hot, generally with jam or dusted with powdered sugar. They're especially popular during the holiday season.

**Broodje**

Dutch "little rolls" are the popular form of sandwich in the Netherlands, with the fist-size breads split, buttered, and generally stuffed with such fillings as sliced cheese or meats, shrimp, or seafood salads to make a light-but-satisfying lunch. The humble everydayness of these treats is evident in the Dutch saying, *"Als de boter duur wordt, leert men het broodje droog eten"*—"When butter is expensive, one learns to eat *broodje* dry."

**Erwtensoep**

The Netherlands' definitive version of split pea soup starts with the dried legumes, cooked with aromatic vegetables, smoked ham hock and sausage to make a thick porridge. An old Dutch rhyme recounts the consequences of enjoying too much of this good thing:

*Aan de oever van de Nete*
*Heb ik erwtensoep gegeten.*
*Wat mij danig heeft gespeten*
*Want ik liet heel vieze windjes.*

*On the banks of the Nete river*
*I ate a bowl of split pea soup.*
*Which I have awfully regretted*
*Because I left lively winds.*

**Fårikål**

Considered by many to be Norway's national dish, this slowly simmered stew of lamb and cabbage (the two ingredients that make up the name), layered together in a casserole and generously seasoned with whole black peppercorns, is accompanied by boiled potatoes to soak up the juices.

**Frikadeller**

Finely ground veal and pork are combined with bread crumbs, grated onion, milk, and seasonings to make these smooth, satisfying little Danish patties, which are fried in butter and served with boiled potatoes.

**Gravlax**

The Swedish name is a contraction for *gravad lax*, "buried salmon," describing the original method by which this delicious appetizer was preserved centuries ago. Today, cooks instead sandwich two large salmon fillets with a mixture of sugar, salt, pepper, and lots of fresh dill, then press them down not with earth but with boards and weights and refrigerate them. The curing process yields firm yet tender flesh with a delightfully complex flavor, best enjoyed thinly sliced with some buttered brown bread. A sweetened sauce of mustard and dill is usually served alongside.

**Hangikjöt**

Literally "hung meat," Iceland's signature smoked meat, typically made with lamb, mutton, or horsemeat, is first cured for a couple of days in a brine of salt, sugar, and saltpeter, and then smoked for a couple of weeks with smoldering juniper, birch, or willow wood. Gourmets might then slice the preserved meat into thin strips and serve it with melon, much as the Italians might do with *prosciutto*. More traditionally, especially for Christmas, the meat will be simmered until tender and served with a creamy white sauce and tangy red cabbage.

**Hutspot**

This Dutch version of a hotpot is a stewed meat casserole generally featuring beef flank steak, slowly cooked together with assorted root vegetables that are often mashed together at serving time.

**Jansson's frestelse**

Different stories attempt to explain this dish's name, "Jansson's temptation." Some say the Swedish opera singer Pelle Janzon reputedly first devised it a century ago; others that the name comes from the 19th-century leader of a Swedish religious cult, who yielded to the dish's charms. Whatever the source, this comfort-food recipe features sliced potatoes layered with anchovy fillets and butter-sautéed onions. These are drizzled with cream, covered with bread crumbs, and then baked until crusty and tender. One can only imagine the reaction of the opera star's fellow singers, or the zealot's followers, when they got too close.

# **Northern Europe's** herrings

The people of Scandinavia and other northern European countries prize the abundant herrings of their surrounding seas. Rich and flavorful, the fish's flesh takes excellently to pickling and smoking, giving rise to a number of classic treatments you'll find in restaurants and delis everywhere. They may at first seem an acquired taste, but it takes little more than a few bites to acquire it!

**BORNHOLMER** Named for the Danish island of Bornholm in the Baltic Sea, these small herrings are hot-smoked over fragrant alderwood and served with buttered rye bread.

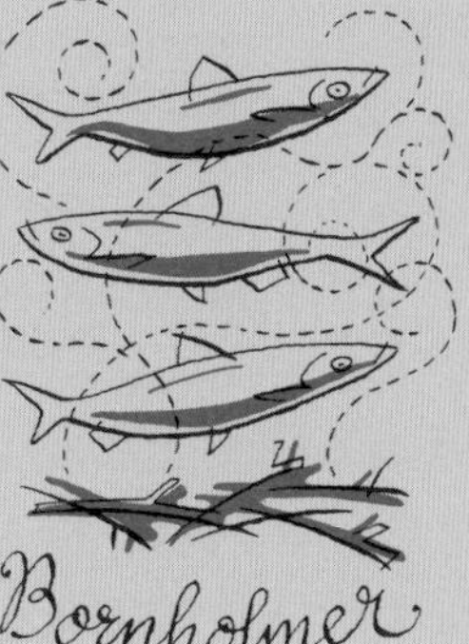


**BUCKLING** Popular in both Holland and Britain, these briefly salted whole herrings are hot-smoked and then served cold with lemon and horseradish cream.

**GLASSBLOWER'S** Sweden's signature herring style, made by layering salted herring fillets with onions, carrots, horseradish, and bay leaves in a glass jar filled with sweetened vinegar.

**MATJES** Fillets of these young springtime herrings, "little girls" in German, are lightly cured with a salt-and-sugar brine and then served with raw onion.

**Kalakukko**

Next time you're in Finland, make a pilgrimage to the eastern town of Kuopio for this local specialty (which you may also find in Finnish restaurants elsewhere). A mixture of chopped local fish fillets, pork, and salt is enclosed inside a bread dough of rye and oat flours, then slowly baked for as long as 20 hours to make a sort of large seafood pasty that is sliced and served with boiled potatoes.

**Karjalanpiirakat**

These low, cup-shaped Finnish pastries from Karelia, on the Russian borderlands, are typically filled with a custardy rice pudding, to enjoy as a sweet snack or dessert. They may also be prepared with a mixture of mashed potatoes and egg to make a savory snack or lunchtime treat.

**Kjøttkaker**

These Norwegian pork-meat burgers are often enjoyed as a casual meal accompanied by boiled potatoes, sautéed onions, and gravy.

**Knäckerbröd**

Spread with butter, these thin unleavened crackers of rye flour or oats are common accompaniments to breakfast meats and cheeses in Finland.

**Koldtbord**

Norway's answer to the *smorgasbord* is often enjoyed as the morning meal and usually includes boiled eggs, herring, and salmon along with meats and cheeses.

**Laufabraud**

Iceland's "leaf bread" is made from an unleavened wheat flour dough enriched with animal fat, rolled ultra-thin (folk wisdom says you should be able to read a newspaper through it), pressed with a decorative pattern, and then deep-fried. Serve it as an accompaniment to thinly sliced *hangikjöt.*

## **A Norwegian** shrimp feast

Norwegian shrimp fishermen generally make their catch at nighttime and boil the shrimp on board their boats. First thing in the morning, smart locals and tourists head for the harbor in Oslo and other coastal cities and towns to greet the fishermen, who sell the sweet, fresh, ready-to-peel-and-eat shrimp by the bagful right from their boats.

**Ostkaka**

From the dairylands of the southern Swedish province of Småand, this simple but delicious dessert is made by combining fresh curd cheese, cream, eggs, flour, sugar, and ground almonds, then baking them in a cake pan until set. *Ostkaka* is enjoyed warm from the oven or cold, usually topped with jam and whipped cream.

**Poffertjes**

Dutch dessert pancakes, these puffy little pancakes resemble Danish *aebleskiver*, and they're cooked in a similar fashion in a heavy pan containing about a dozen rounded depressions into which the batter is dropped. Yeast may be used to leaven the batter, and a handful of buckwheat flour may be included along with the wheat flour, giving the results an earthy, pleasantly sour tang. Enjoy them with melted butter and icing sugar, or berry jam.

**Rapu**

The word is Finnish for "crayfish," but two such short syllables can hardly begin to evoke the rapture this freshwater crustacean kindles in Finns during the precious weeks from late July to September when they're in season. The little creatures, looking like miniature lobsters, are gathered (more than 225,000 pounds annually during the brief season) and generally boiled in water seasoned with salt and fresh dill, then served by the pile. Diners twist off and savor the succulent tails, then suck every last drop of sweet juices from the shell.

**Rødgrød med fløde**

"Red gruel with cream" hardly captures the satisfying appeal of this thickened puree of raspberries and currants, served cold in soup bowls and drizzled with cream to make a dessert that sends grown Swedes right back to childhood.

**Smorgasbord**

Literally "bread and butter table" in Swedish, the term *smorgasbord* modestly describes a buffet of immodest proportions through which guests work plate after delicious plate. The meal proceeds from lighter cold dishes to more robust hot ones, with a change of plate for every trip to the buffet. A couple of rules: don't mix seafood dishes with other offerings; and always start with a fresh plate for each successive visit to the buffet. Begin with assorted herrings (see **Northern Europe's herrings**), then proceed to other kinds of pickled, smoked, or cooked fish. Next come cold cuts of meat and fresh and pickled vegetables and salads. Then, enjoy such hot dishes as meatballs and croquettes, roast or fried chicken, roast potatoes and cooked green vegetables. Finally, refresh yourself with cheeses, fruit, and light desserts. And, oh yes, there'll inevitably be good bread and butter to round out the table.

**Smørrebrød**

Danish for "buttered bread," this term describes Denmark's most glorious lunchtime tradition: a wide assortment of open-faced sandwiches consisting of thinly sliced and buttered white or brown bread toped with an imaginative array of toppings, from cheeses; to seafood such as pickled herring (see **Northern Europe's herrings**) or poached baby shrimp; to salami, ham, and other cured meats; to sliced cold cooked meats such as roast beef or pork. Wash it all down with a refreshing Danish beer.

**Voileipäpöytä**

Translating as "butter-bread-table," this is Finland's version of the *smorgasbord*. Expect the starring bread to be the local rye bread, known as *ruisleipä*, accompanied by generous doses of pickled herring, sausages, and smoked meats (including reindeer, deliciously lean and only slightly gamey).

**Vorschmack**

Say the Germanic name of this popular Finnish dish and you can't help but smack your lips! This odd-but-enticing hashlike mixture of ground herring, lamb, beef, onions, garlic, and spices was reputedly introduced to the country by the Finnish military hero C.G.E. Mannerheim (1867–1951). It is cooked slowly in butter, mixed with meat gravy, and served as an appetizer or main dish topped with sour cream.

**Wienerbrod**

That which most of the English-speaking world refers to as "Danish pastry," the Danes call "Vienna bread." Go figure! Typically based on a sweet yeast-leavened dough repeatedly folded and layered with butter, it bakes up light, rich, and flaky. Danish pastries come in a wide range of shapes and sizes, with fillings ranging from sweetened cheese to nuts to fruit.

# Germany, Austria, and Central Europe

I group these countries together not just because they comprised my itinerary for a memorable culinary automobile tour over the 1985–1986 holiday season. This part of middle Europe has seen so much political change over the past couple of centuries that its culinary landmarks seem to have swapped back and forth as often as its borders and regimes have changed.

## SWIMMING LESSONS

*"To taste good, fish must swim three times—in water, in butter, and in wine."*

POLISH PROVERB

What do all these cuisines have in common? They share a fondness for well seasoned soups and stews such as Poland's *bigos* and Hungarian goulash that have the power to ward off the chilliest of winters. Preserved meats, particularly in the form of sausage (see **Wurst for the better**) abound.

Central Europe's nations also feature a wealth of surprisingly subtle fish dishes, making the most of the creatures that live in the region's lakes and rivers and in the cold waters of the North Sea and the Baltic Sea. Witness, for excellent example, the many forms of herring to be found here, including Bismarck, rollmops, and *matjes.* Central Europeans also revel in the glories of the garden, transforming them into cold soups like *chlodnik,* the seemingly omnipresent side dish *rotkohl,* and countless dishes in which potatoes star, including *himmel und erde.*

Most memorable for many visitors and natives of the region alike are the creations of central European pastry chefs. Treats like *dobostorte, Sachertorte,* and *strudel* are highlights of the dining day, expressing the joy folks in this part of the world feel for the pleasures of the table.

**Baba**

Also called *babka,* this classic Polish coffee cake is based on a sweet yeast-leavened dough, baked in an often-fluted ring mold. The Czechs have a similar treat, known as a *babobka;* so do the Poles, *buka.*

**Biersuppe**

Leave it to the Germans to base a soup on beer thickened and enriched with egg yolks and sour cream. Two different versions of the dish diverge from that point. Savory *biersuppe* will be served with copious bread cubes and shredded Swiss cheese for a first course. But the mixture may also be sweetened with sugar and seasoned with lemon, cinnamon, and raisins to make a warming holiday drink enjoyed like eggnog.

**Bigos**

The national dish of Poland, resembling France's *choucroute garnie,* this huntsman's-style stew combines game, pork, beef, ham, and the garlicky fresh or smoked pork sausage known as *kielbasa,* with *sauerkraut* and/or fresh cabbage, onions, dried mushrooms, apples, tomatoes, meat broth, and possibly a splash of Madeira.

**Bismarck**

From Germany, these fresh herring fillets are briefly marinated in vinegar with onions, juniper berries, and chilies.

**Bündnerfleisch**

This German or Swiss-style salt-cured, dried beef is pressed during the preserving process into dense rectangular bricks. The meat is cut into ultra-thin slices, the better to enjoy its intense meaty flavor and surprisingly delicate texture.

**Chlodnik**

This cold summertime soup from Poland features cucumbers, beets, green onions, radishes, and other crisp vegetables in a bracing broth laced with lemon juice or vinegar, sour cream, and dill.

**Csípetke**

Similar to Austria's *spaetzle,* these Hungarian dumplings or tiny egg-and-flour noodles are pinched by hand from a lump of dough and dropped into water to boil as a companion to goulash and other saucy stews. In an old-fashioned quip, some folk say that they've a lifetime of eating *csípetke* enables them to tell, at a taste, whether the cook who made them was right-handed or left-handed.

**Eintopf**

This German term literally means "one-pot," referring to a sturdy casserole cooking dish and to the easy-to-make stew cooked within it. Meat, usually in the form of bacon or ham, is creatively and flavorfully stretched by more humble ingredients such as potatoes or rice. Traditionally, a German housewife would prepare an *eintopf* when her labor was required elsewhere, such as doing laundry or helping with the harvest.

**Goulash**

Alternately spelled *gulyas* or *gourlasch,* this Hungarian huntsman's stew or soup is enjoyed throughout central Europe. Cubes of beef, veal, or pork are simmered in broth with diced onion and potato, whole caraway seeds, and the hot paprika that gives the mixture its distinctive brick-red color and bracing but not usually overwhelming spiciness. Interestingly, the paprika, now such a definitive element of goulash, did not become common in Hungary until the 18th century. You might also find such ingredients as tomatoes, bell peppers, and garlic, but seldom if ever sour cream, in various versions.

**Hasenpfeffer**

Literally "black-pepper hare," this country-style German stew has rabbit, liberally flavored with the namesake pepper as well as onions, herbs, and sometimes touches of lemon and even bitter chocolate. Seek out the robust, flavorful dish if you can find it, thus rescuing it from its primary source of fame today as part of the Yiddish-based playground catchphrase uttered in the opening sequence of the 1970s sitcom *Laverne & Shirley*: "*Schlemiel, schlemazel, hasenpfeffer* incorporated."

**Himmel und erde**

The "heaven" part of this German dish's name (*himmel*) refers to the apples that make up half of its primary contents; the "earth" half (*erde*) refers to potatoes. Both ingredients are cut up, cooked, and mashed together along with butter and sautéed bacon and onions to make a surprisingly satisfying side dish.

**Kaiserschmarren**

Delightfully named, this traditional Austrian dessert means "the emperor's nonsense" or "the emperor's little bit of fluff." The Emperor Franz Joseph I reputedly referred to the soufflé-like sweet as *schmarren* in response to his wife Elisabeth's complaint over how rich it was. A flour-and-egg batter lightened with fluffy beaten egg whites and enhanced by rum and raisins is baked and then dished up with a warm sauce of berries or other fresh fruit.

**Leberknödel**

German "liver dumplings" made by simmering in broth, balls formed from a ground mixture of beef or veal liver, bread, onions, egg, and seasonings. Not the lightest or most elegant of culinary creations, these are nonetheless true middle-European comfort food.

**Matjes**

Fillets of these young springtime herrings, "little girls" in German, are lightly cured with a salt-and-sugar brine and then served with raw onion.

**Mazurek**

This traditional Polish pastry is based on a sweet dough rich with butter and eggs. It is baked in a thin layer and topped with jam, candied fruit, toasted almonds, or an icing-sugar glaze.

**Paczki**

Poland's popular dessert doughnuts are sometimes soaked with rum and almost always stuffed with jam, often a beautifully perfumed variety made from rose petals. Bittersweet plum paste is also a popular filling.

**Palatschinken**

The Austrian answer to French *crêpes*, these are traditionally enjoyed for dessert. The thin pancakes are folded twice into a wedge shape or rolled up around a filling of jam or other fruit preserves or sweetened curd cheese, then baked.

**Paprikás**

See this word on a Hungarian menu, or on the carte of any other kitchen specializing in central European cuisine, and you know for sure that the dish will be liberally seasoned with mild to hot paprika, the ground dried red chili pepper that is today a defining characteristic of the cuisine. Veal or chicken, the most common proteins cooked in this style, is generally simmered slowly with broth and the spice, and then enriched with cream or sour cream, stirred in just before serving. Interestingly, paprika only entered Hungarian kitchens in the mid 16th century, following the invasion of central Europe by Turks of the Ottoman Empire, who in turn first acquired the spice from Spanish or Portuguese traders who first brought chili to Europe from the New World: a perfect example of how convoluted food history can be!

**Placek swiateczny**

For Christmas Eve, Polish cooks traditionally make this tender, rich, sweet cake studded with nuts and dried fruit and enhanced with a splash of vodka or brandy. The cake is usually prepared a few days ahead of time and wrapped airtight to give its flavors extra time to mingle and mature.

**Pörkölt**

Use a higher concentration of onions and paprika in a chunky version of a goulashlike stew made with beef, pork, mutton, duck, goose, or game, and leave out the cream or sour cream, and you wind up with this stew.

**Rollmops**

Fillets are rolled up around sliced onions or gherkins and pickled for at least a week in spiced vinegar brine in this German-style favorite.

**Rotkohl**

Cooked red cabbage is a customary side dish in this part of Europe, usually simmered slowly with a nice balance of sour (vinegar or lemon juice) and sweet (sugar) ingredients.

**Rouladen**

These large German "rolls" of flattened steak or other meat enclose a stuffing of bacon, pickled vegetables, onions, and seasonings such as mustard. Tied and braised in broth, the finished roll is cut into thick slices and usually served with potatoes and *rotkohl*.

**Salzberger nockerl**

The hills of Salzburg have inspired the rolling heights of this traditional Austrian baked dessert based on whipped eggs. The egg mixtures is usually mounded in a baking dish, sometimes atop a layer of sautéed berries or other fruit.

# **A gallery** of schnitzels

**HOLSTEIN SCHNITZEL** Named to honor the German diplomat Friedrich von Holstein (1837–1909), this is basically a *Wiener schnitzel* topped with a fried egg, anchovy fillets, and capers.

**JÄGERSCHNITZEL** A "huntsman-style" schnitzel in which the sliced meat is lightly floured, browned in oil, and simmered until tender with stock and aromatic vegetables, and then garnished with bacon, mushrooms, and pearl onions.

**TIROLERSCHNITZEL** In the style of the Austrian Alpine range, this is usually a breaded pork schnitzel served with a cream sauce.

**WIENER SCHNITZEL** The famed "Viennese slice," as the name literally means, is veal, pork, beef, or chicken, coated with flour, egg, and bread crumbs and then fried until golden. A classic version should be so big and thin—pounded to those dimensions with a meat mallet—that its edges overlap the rim of a dinner plate. According to the folk wisdom of old Vienna, it should be so perfectly fried that a gentleman could sit down on it without staining the seat of his trousers.

**ZIGEUNERSCHNITZEL** This "gypsy-style" schnitzel is served with a spicy sauce made with tomatoes and paprika.

## **Wurst for** the better

Nowhere will you find a greater variety of sausages, or *wurst,* than in Germany and the neighboring countries of middle Europe. The best of the *wurst* listed here can be found on the menus of restaurants, casual cafés, and snack stands alike. As the American humorist Dave Barry observed in his 1991 book *Dave Barry's Only Travel Guide You'll Ever Need,* "Eating in Germany is easy, because there is basically only one kind of food, called the 'wurst.'"

**BERLINERWURST** A Berlin-style sausage made from coarsely ground cured pork and finely ground beef, smoked and precooked. Served cold, in slices.

**BIERWURST** Traditionally marinated in beer, the source of its name, this cold sliced precooked sausage is made of pork seasoned with juniper, garlic, and cardamom.

**BLUTWURST** A dark sausage made with pork meat, fat, and blood, seasoned with herbs. Precooked, it is served cold, sliced.

**BOCKWURST** A large, mild sausage mostly of ground veal, some pork, milk, egg, and herbs, it is boiled before serving whole.

**BRATWURST** A fine, light-colored frying sausage of pork or veal, it is sometimes lightly smoked.

**BRAUNSCHWEIGER** This is the most common form of *leberwurst.*

## **Wurst for** the better

**FRANKFURTERWURST** Familiar around the world as the "hot dog," this long, slender sausage from the city of Frankfurt is made of a finely ground mixture of beef and pork, combined with mild seasonings and a touch of saltpeter to maintain a rosy pink color, and then lightly smoked. Frankfurters are usually boiled or grilled.

**KIELBASA** The most typical versions of this Polish sausage combine ground pork, liberal amounts of pork fat, and a generous share of garlic. You'll find fresh, air-dried, and smoked versions.

**KNACKWURST** The German word for "snap" captures the pleasures of biting into these plump pork-and-beef sausages scented with garlic and cumin, cooked by either boiling or grilling.

**LEBERWURST** A precooked fine-textured "liver sausage" usually eaten as a spread.

**NÜRNBERGERWURST** From Nuremburg, Germany, this fresh sausage made of pork, bacon fat, herbs, seasonings, and usually a splash of cherry-scented kirsch, is typically pan-fried in butter.

**RINDFLEISCHKOCHWURST** A finely textured sausage combining lean beef with pork fat, it is seasoned with coriander seed and air-dried. It is usually boiled.

**WIENERWURST** A "Vienna sausage," this cured, smoked sausage is made from finely ground pork and beef or veal, and is usually boiled or grilled.

**Sauerbraten**

Germany's sweet-and-sour pot-roasted beef is one of that nation's definitive dishes. The meat is first marinated in a sharp, vinegary brine for several days, then cooked with onions, carrots, celery, and herbs. To give the finished meat and its sauce a sweet edge, caramelized sugar and often crumbled gingersnap cookies are added toward the end of cooking. Richer versions of the dish also include a final embellishment of sour cream. Potatoes, often in the form of dumplings, are served alongside to soak up the abundant juices; *rotkohl* makes another fitting accompaniment.

**Sauerkraut**

Germany's "sour cabbage" is made by layering copious amounts of shredded fresh cabbage with coarse salt in a barrel or tub and weighting it down to keep the vegetable submerged in the juices that the salt draws from it. Gradually, the cabbage ferments, giving *sauerkraut* its distinctive sour tang. Although *sauerkraut* may be served as a side dish on its own, straight from the barrel, it is often more creatively simmered with broth, beer, or wine, spices, and smoked or salt-cured pork in the form of ham or sausage to make a robust main dish.

**Schlagobers**

Admit it: whipped cream just sounds more gloriously indulgent when referred to as *schlagobers*. That's the Austrian term for the lightly sweetened beaten cream that is invariably heaped atop the great pastries and cakes of Vienna, the nation's capital, as well as its other cities and towns.

**Schnitzel**

The German word *schnitzel* literally means "slice," referring more specifically to thin cutlets—whether veal, pork, chicken, or some other protein—that are fried and finished in various imaginative ways. See **A gallery of schnitzels**.

**Spaetzle**

Austria's "little sparrows" are tiny dumplings formed either by pinching bits of eggy dough with the fingertips or forcing it through the holes of a colander or a special *spaetzle*-making tool, from which it drops into simmering water to cook for several minutes until the puffed-up, plump birdlike shapes rise to the surface of the pot. Skimmed and tossed with butter, the *spaetzle* may be served alongside a *schnitzel*, goulash, *paprikás* or any other main course.

**Wiener backhendl**

Austria's legendary Viennese-style fried chicken is made simply but superbly by dusting pieces of the poultry with seasoned flour and shallow-frying them in a skillet of hot oil until they're a deep golden brown. The traditional accompaniment to this dish is a warm, vinegary, bacon-laced potato salad.

**Zrazy**

This country-style Polish main course features thin pieces of pan-fried veal, beef, or lamb, simmered until tender with broth, onions, mushrooms, and herbs.

## **The pastry** shop

Middle European bakers have raised pastry to a high art. Be sure to sample one of these treats midmorning or midafternoon in the nearest *konditorei* (pastry shop). When offered one of the option of *mit schlag* (with whipped cream) with one of the following classic options, always say *"ja!"*

**DOBOSTORTE** This drum-shaped cake is made by alternating seven thin layers of a light vanilla or chocolate sponge cake with a rich chocolate buttercream filling, then coating the entire assembly with still more of the buttercream. As a finishing touch, the top is covered with a layer of hot caramel syrup, which is scored with a knife to mark the wedges into which the cake will be cut for serving.

**GUGELHUPF** This classic Viennese coffee cake of egg-enriched yeast dough is layered with poppy seeds or nuts and baked in a fluted, ring-shaped mold. Rumor has it that the actress Katharina Schatt, mistress of the Emperor Franz Josef I of Austria, tempted him with her home-baked *gugelhupf*. (No smutty jokes, please!)

**KIPFERL** The name for vanilla-flavored, crescent-shaped little Austrian cookies, these are usually made with finely ground nuts such as almonds or hazelnuts and buttery dough.

**LEBKUCHEN** These are German-style spice cookies made from a dough of flour, honey, molasses, cinnamon, allspice, nutmeg, cloves, ginger, and other sweet spices. They are traditionally shaped by pressing the dough into elaborate engraved molds. During the holiday season, these molds yield up the walls and roofs of elaborate *lebkuchen* houses decorated with icing and candies, and are popularly known as gingerbread houses.

**LINZERTORTE** From the Austrian town of Linz, this tart features a base of ground almond pastry topped with a layer of raspberry jam that peeks through a latticework of more almond pastry.

**SACHERTORTE** From Vienna's Hotel Sacher, this rich chocolate sponge layer cake is filled with apricot jam and covered with bittersweet chocolate icing.

**SCHWARZWÄLDER KIRSCHTORTE** Literally a "Black Forest cherry cake," this rich German chocolate layer cake has a tart-sweet cherry filling.

**STOLLEN** A traditional Christmas fruit bread popular throughout middle Europe, this freeform loaf is based on a sweet yeast dough enriched with eggs and butter, studded with almond slivers and rum-soaked candied fruit, then baked and covered with a snowy topping of powdered sugar. *Dresdener stollen,* those made in the style of the German city of Dresden, are most renowned.

**STRUDEL** Sheets of rich dough so ultra-thin they're almost translucent are rolled up around sweet and spicy fillings such as apples, poppy seeds, or nuts and then baked until golden brown to make this classic pastry, served in slices.

# Russia and Eastern Europe

The old Soviet Union and its Eastern Bloc may be long gone. But the same culinary traditions that preceded that catastrophic 20th-century flash-in-the-historical-pan endure after its passing, continuing to unite cultures in a far more profound way than politics ever did.

## THE TRUE PROVIDERS

*"The rich would have to eat money if poor people did not provide food."*

RUSSIAN PROVERB

Covering as it does a vast geographic expanse, from the Baltic Sea to the Black Sea, the Ural Mountains to the Kamchatka Peninsula, this region offers an incredibly varied buffet of tastes. Estonia, northernmost of the Baltic States, shows the influence of nearby Scandinavia, while Latvian and Lithuanian kitchens reflect more of the cooking styles of Germany and Poland. Southeastern European cuisine is more closely allied to that of Greece and Turkey, while in easternmost Siberia you'll find food more akin to Asian cuisine.

Russian and Ukrainian cooking, like that of its neighboring Eastern European countries, shows deep peasant roots, evident in soups like *borscht* and *shchi*, and in the dumplings so dear to everyone (see **A world of robust Eastern European dumplings**). No doubt, many such dishes also reflect the harsh winters so prevalent in this part of the European continent, featuring staples that store well such as potatoes and smoked meats, and preparations designed to warm and sustain body and soul alike. Yet, the cuisines of this region also bear the elaborate marks of the pre-Communist Imperial era, when chefs created grand dishes like beef Stroganoff and *kulebiaka*, and when *zakuski* tables overflowed with *blini* and caviar.

**Blini**

Russia's signature small, thin yeasted pancakes are usually made with earthy, tangy buckwheat flour, to serve as a platform for caviar, pickled herrings, smoked fish, sautéed mushrooms, or sweet jams. It's common practice to apply melted butter liberally to *blini* before topping them, and to add a dollop of sour cream before popping them in your mouth. Before Lent, Russians traditionally build entire lavish feasts around *blini* and assorted embellishments, along with great quantities of vodka.

**Borscht**

Also sometimes found spelled *borsch* or *bortsch*, or *barszcz* in Polish, this is Eastern Europe's signature vegetable soup, found on tables in Russia, Poland, and elsewhere. Beets are the defining factor here, giving the soup its distinctive deep red color and sweet flavor. You'll also generally find shredded or chopped cabbage as well as other vegetables such as carrots, onions, and potatoes, making the soup a close cousin to the more humble *shchi*. At its grandest, a good *borscht* also includes meat, and may even be served in two courses—first the rich vegetable soup, then the sliced meat—with accompanying *piroshki*. At its simplest, a vegetarian beet *borscht* can also be served cold as a refreshing first course, frequently garnished with a dollop of sour cream.

**Botvinya**

This elegant Russian cold brothy soup features shredded leaves of fresh spinach or its tart-tasting cousin, sorrel, combined with poached sturgeon or salmon fillets and a healthy splash of *kvass*, a bracingly sour grain spirit. At serving time, each portion may be further laced with sparkling wine or sherry and a dollop of sour cream.

**Chlodnik**

In Poland, summer vegetables are showcased in this cold soup of chopped cucumbers, beets, radishes, and green onions, seasoned with lemon juice or vinegar, sour cream, and chopped fresh dill, then garnished with chopped hard-cooked egg. In particularly upscale versions, you might also find a few chilled shrimp or crayfish.

**Golabki**

Stuffed cabbage, Polish-style, usually features a filling of ground pork stretched with rice and sometimes chopped *sauerkraut,* rolled up in individual cabbage leaves that are then simmered with a sauce of tomatoes and sometimes mushrooms.

**Kasha**

With their earthy, pleasantly sour flavor, buckwheat grouts—known in these parts as *kasha*—are a staple starchy side dish of Russian and Eastern European tables. Traditionally, the grains are combined with sautéed chopped onion before being steamed in water or broth.

**Kulebiaka**

In the most elegant version of this Russian main dish, a filling of flaked salmon, rice, and chopped hard-cooked egg is enclosed in flaky pastry, then baked, cut into slices, and garnished with an occasionally dill-laced sour cream sauce. More humble versions have cabbage instead of salmon, though still to considerably delicious effect.

**Leib**

Estonian rye-based black bread is truly considered the staff of life, so much so that meals traditionally begin with the words *Jätku leiba,* "May your bread last."

**Pashka**

The faithful among the Russian Orthodox church include this rich cheesecake as part of their Easter celebrations. A mixture of fine curd cheese, eggs, fresh cream or sour cream, candied fruit, and almonds is baked in a four-sided pyramid-shaped mold, then decorated with still more candied fruit, usually forming religious symbols.

**Pojarski**

The invention of a Polish innkeeper in czarist Russian, who immortalized himself in the dish's name, this may look at first glance like a breaded, butter-fried cutlet of veal or chicken. In fact, in this more economical but no less delicious dish, chopped meat or poultry is substituted for the more expensive cuts, which are shaped into cutlets before they're coated with bread crumbs.

**Shashlik**

These fire-licked lamb kebabs are a specialty of Russia's more southwesterly neighbors, betraying the influence of the nearby Middle East.

**Shchi**

A cousin of *borscht*, this humble, robust vegetable soup features cabbage, along with such other vegetables as carrots, onions, leeks, turnips, celery, and tomatoes. Beef, fresh or smoked pork, or sausage may be added to transform the soup into a main course. In winter, *sauerkraut* will often replace the fresh cabbage.

# **A world of** robust Eastern European dumplings

**PELMENI** Small Russian boiled dumplings filled with meat, sometimes referred to as Siberian dumplings.

**PIEROGI** Large, plump, Eastern European half-moon-shaped dumplings, usually filled with a mixture of potatoes and onions but also available with a wide variety of other savory and sweet fillings. *Pierogi* may be either boiled or sautéed in butter.

**PÎRÂGI** These Latvian baked dumplings are generally stuffed with a spiced mixture of bacon or ham.

**PIROSHKI** Also sometimes spelled *pirozhki,* these crescent-shaped, finger-sized baked dumplings may be filled with seasoned mixtures of chopped meat, fish, eggs, mushrooms, cabbage, or onion. You'll often find them accompanying *borscht* or *shchi.*

**SALTANOSIAI** Literally "cold noses" in Lithuanian, these are sweet little egg-dough dumplings stuffed with fresh blueberries or blueberry preserves, briefly boiled and then served hot or cold with a topping of sour cream and sugar.

**VARENNIKI** Traditional Ukrainian dumplings with savory or sweet fillings ranging from potatoes to cheese to chopped meat to fresh or preserved fruit. They are usually boiled, their name deriving from the Ukrainian word for that cooking method.

**Maybe it's the cold weather or harsh lives that so many people in this part of the world led in past times. Probably, the cause is a combination of both factors. Whatever the explanation, you'll find all kinds of dumplings featured on menus throughout Eastern Europe and Russia. Herewith, a tasting sampler.**

## **Zakuski:** feasting on morsels, Russian-style

The term *zakuski* comes from a Russian word for "morsels," a precious and appealing way to describe a generous array of tempting morsels offered as a welcome at Russian country homes to revive houseguests after their long trek. Now traditionally offered at the beginning of a meal, they include everything from smoked and pickled fish to caviar, sliced vegetables to marinated mushrooms and other pickles, cold cuts to sliced cheeses to assorted dumplings (see **A world of robust Eastern European dumplings**). Ready to wash it all down, of course, will be bottles of vodka, a powerful but clean-tasting spirit that has the ability both to whet the appetite and to cleanse the palate.

**Stroganoff**

Count Paul Stroganoff, a famed gourmet in 19th-century Russia, was immortalized when his personal chef bestowed his name upon this elegant, rich dish, one of Russian cuisine's most widely known. Thin slices of beefsteak are sautéed in butter and oil along with onions and mushrooms, then finished in a sauce of beef broth, wine, tomato, sour cream, mustard, and lemon juice. Rice or noodles form a bed for the finished dish, soaking up every last drop of luscious sauce. Nowadays, you'll also find turkey, pork, or veal versions as well.

**Ukha**

Don't let the name, which sounds like an expression of disgust, keep you from sampling this surprisingly fine Russian peasant dish. Mild white fish fillets are simmered and then served in a simple seasoned broth, garnished with fresh dill and lime.

# **Caviar:** a glorious treat

The salt-cured roe, or tiny fish eggs, of several species of sturgeon, caviar is indeed a glorious treat. Don't be put off by the thought of its being fish eggs (you eat chicken eggs, don't you?); or of it tasting fishy (the best caviar in peak quality will carry only delicate, pleasant hints of the sea). Caviar is traditionally served with small slices of toast trimmed of their crusts, or with Russian blini, and chopped egg, onion or chives, and sour cream may join it as garnishes. Caviar itself may become an extravagant garnish, usually for seafood or egg dishes. Today, the world's best caviar comes from the Baltic and Caspian seas, and the names applied to it refer to either the species of sturgeon it came from or a particular way in which the eggs were processed. Caviar is so highly priced nowadays that it's a popular product for smugglers. So, yes, you shouldn't "spread it about like marmalade."

**BELUGA** Generally the highest-priced caviar from the species of the same name, with large eggs colored black or pearly gray.

**MALOSSOL** Meaning "lightly salted" in Russian, this refers to the highest grade of caviar from any species.

**OSETROVA OR OSETRA** From a smaller species of sturgeon known by that name, yielding smaller, dark eggs.

**PAYASNAYA** Pressed caviar, made by taking broken or immature eggs from *sevruga* or *osetrova*, salting them more heavily, and pressing them into brick-shaped blocks.

**SEVRUGA** From a small sturgeon species, small dark-gray eggs with excellent flavor.

**"Wit," wrote the great English playwright, songwriter, and actor Noel Coward, "ought to be a glorious treat like caviar; never spread it about like marmalade."**

# Spain and Portugal

Occupying as they do the Iberian Peninsula, that big block-shaped landmass dipping toward Africa from Europe's southwestern corner, Spain and Portugal share geography, history, and culinary influences.

## PRIORITIES IN ORDER

*"Sopa y amor, lo primero lo mejor."*

*"Of soup and love, the first is best."*

SPANISH PROVERB

Both countries pay homage to the olive tree, which provides not only its fruit as a ubiquitous hors d'oeuvre but also wondrously fruity olive oil, the preferred cooking medium. Both enjoy the rich seafood that comes with a lengthy coastline, Portugal hugging the rugged Atlantic, Spain—though it, too, has Atlantic shoreline—more closely attuned to the Mediterranean. Both also show the influence of Europe's historical tides, from the Greeks who brought the cultivation not only of olives but also wheat; to Celts, who fostered pork as a preferred meat; to Moors and Berbers, who introduced such staples as rice, almonds, citrus fruit, and artichokes, as well as exotic spices from the Middle and Far East, most notably saffron. Add to that the New World produce Columbus brought back from his journeys in the late 15th century—chief among them tomatoes and bell peppers—and you have one of Europe's most enthrallingly diverse pantries.

Portuguese cooking puts particular emphasis on seafood, from its relatively narrow western edge of the peninsula. You'll find wonderful dishes featuring not just fresh fish and shellfish but also *bacalhau*, the ubiquitous salt cod. Cooking tends to be simple and straightforward, with tomatoes, bell peppers, and onions as well as garlic, vinegar, and lemon adding particular character.

Seafood figures prominently in Spanish cooking, too, showcased in signature dishes such as *paella* and *zarzuela*. Meat, poultry, and game from the interior also get their due, most notably *cocido* and its most glorious incarnation, *olla podrida*. Tomatoes, garlic, bell peppers, and olive oil—all memorably joined in the cold soup called *gazpacho*—lend character to many dishes, not least the bite-size offerings to be found in Spain's omnipresent tapas bars.

**Açorda**

Portugal's most basic form of soup starts with rich broth that is then thickened with peasant bread and beaten egg and made fragrant with chopped garlic. In coastal areas, shrimp or other seafood may also be added.

**Alioli**

Whether spelled in this Spanish form or with an extra "l" in the Catalan *allioli*, this sauce is a close cousin to France's *aïoli*. The suave emulsion of garlic, olive oil, bread crumbs, and sometimes egg yolks to bind and enrich the mixture, may accompany all manner of savory appetizers, entrées, and sides.

**Bacalao**

Salt cod, known as *bacalao* in Spain and *bacalhau* in Portugal, became institutionalized in the Iberian Peninsula through a combination of economics and faith. Because liberal catches of Atlantic codfish were so easily and reliably preserved by gutting and salting the fish, it became a widely accessible form of protein for rich and poor alike. Meanwhile, the longstanding Roman Catholic practice of shunning all animal proteins but fish on Fridays made salt cod a mainstay for folks living inland, far from the sea. To make the cardboardlike, very briny dried fish edible again, it is soaked in several changes of cold water for 12 hours to a day and a half, depending on how long it was originally salted. The soaking not only softens it but also removes some of the considerable salt. Then it may be cooked in a variety of ways, including simmering with tomatoes, onions, bell peppers, olive oil, and garlic; or mashing with bread crumbs, potatoes, and eggs, to be fried in ball or disc shapes. In one popular Spanish appetizer or *tapa*, *pimientos rellenos al bacalao*, mild yet flavorful roasted red *piquillo* peppers are stuffed with a flour-and-milk-thickened puree of salt cod, then dipped in flour and egg and fried in oil.

**Bacalhau**

See **Bacalao**.

**Chorizo**

Although it is now a staple of virtually all Spanish-speaking countries, as well as Portugal where it is known as *chouriço*, this garlicky, paprika-spiced pork sausage probably traces its roots back to Estremadura in west-central Spain. There, before it is stuffed into sausage casings, some of the homemade, freshly ground and seasoned chorizo is traditionally cooked in a pot and eaten communally as a dish called *la prueba*, the "proof" or "test" of its goodness. Chorizo is enjoyed not only on its own sliced as one of many tapas offerings but also as a robust complement to vegetables, beans, or eggs, and in such signature main courses as *cocido* and *paella*.

**Chouriço**

See **Chorizo**.

**Cocido**

Iberia's one-dish meal, known as *cocido* in Spain and the similar *cozido* in Portugal, combines all manner of meats, poultry, or seafood slowly simmered together with vegetables and broth in a large earthenware casserole, or *olla*. The most famous version of *cocido* is the *olla podrida*.

**Crema Catalana**

"Catalan cream" is Spain's answer to French *crème brûlée*, a rich egg custard that is chilled and then topped with a brittle layer of caramelized sugar. (Indeed, outside of Catalonia, it may also be referred to as *crema quemada*, a direct equivalent of the French name.) A traditional dessert for St. Joseph's Day, it is sometimes referred to as *crema San José*.

**Empanada**

Literally "breaded," this term refers to a popular savory pie of well seasoned meat or seafood with vegetables, baked in a large circular pan and served in wedges as an appetizer, *tapa*, or luncheon dish. It is thought to be the ancestor of the half-moon-shaped, individual-portion *empanadas* of Latin America.

**Escalivada**

Its name meaning "grilled," this is to Catalan Spain what *ratatouille* is to Provence in France. Eggplant, bell peppers, and onions are rubbed with olive oil, grilled, chopped, and tossed together with more olive oil, some garlic, and a little salt and pepper to make a popular side dish usually enjoyed at room temperature.

**Gazpacho**

A specialty of Andalusia in southern Spain, this cold soup traditionally is made by pureeing together fresh tomatoes, bell peppers, garlic, olive oil, vinegar, salt, and pepper. Sometimes, bread crumbs serve as a thickening agent, explaining the name's origin, which is Arabic for "soaked bread." Indeed, original *gazpachos* were nothing more than mixtures of bread, olive oil, and water, awaiting the tomatoes and bell peppers Spanish explorers brought back from the New World. At its best, *gazpacho* is served with a lavish array of garnishes, including more tomatoes, onions, and bell peppers, plus chopped cucumber, hard-cooked eggs, and crisp garlic-and-oil croutons. In Malaga, you'll also find a white *gazpacho* featuring almonds and grapes, while Cadiz is known for a hot *gazpacho* made with beans.

**Ibérico**

Black Ibérico pigs of southwestern Spain, a breed descended from wild boars, are the source of what many connoisseurs consider Spain's finest cured ham, *jamón Ibérico*—also referred to sometimes as *jamón pata negra* for the distinctive pigs' black feet. In addition to the animals' wild ancestry, much of the flavor comes from the fact that the best of these hams—those designated *jamón Ibérico de bellota*—come from animals that fatten exclusively on acorns (*bellotas*) in their final months. The hams are packed with sea salt for nine days and then cured for nine months and aged in drying rooms for a year and a half or more, depending on size. The resulting meat, eaten on its own in tissue-thin slices, is rich and complex in flavor, but surprisingly light and clean-tasting at the same time.

**Leche frita**

If you know even the most basic Spanish, the name alone will be enough to intrigue you: "fried milk." In fact, this dessert is a milk-and-egg custard, left to chill until firm, then cut into square or diamond shapes, coated with egg and breadcrumbs, and fried in oil or clarified butter until the crust is crisp and golden.

**Linguiça**

This Portuguese cured dried sausage is made from ground pork, with liberal doses of garlic and paprika. Though it takes its name from the word for "tongue," it includes none of that meat. The name refers to its long, slightly flattened shape.

**Manchego**

This firm, tangy cheese from the plains of La Mancha, source of its Spanish name, was originally made from sheep's milk, though nowadays you're just as likely to find cow's-milk versions. Enjoyed both fresh and aged, it makes frequent appearances among tapas offerings, though it is also used in cooking and makes a popular dessert accompanied by quince paste or fresh fruit.

**Membrillo**

Take quinces, those bitter-tasting cousins of the apple, and cook them down to a puree with sugar and cinnamon, and you get this beguiling jam, which sets to a paste thick enough to slice. *membrillo* makes a popular dessert when combined with slices of manchego cheese.

**Olla podrida**

The "putrid pot" of the Spanish table is anything but the mess implied by its name, a throwback to olden days when it evolved from a big, ever-simmering, ever-replenished earthenware pot (*olla*) into which thrifty cooks would continuously toss scraps of meat and vegetables. Today, this glorious version of *cocido* might include such widely assorted ingredients as fresh and cured pork and beef, sausages, pigs' ears and tails, chickens, game birds, and all kinds of vegetables. No wonder Don Quixote, the hero of the great Spanish novel by Miguel de Cervantes Saavedra, describes *olla podrida* as "a grand dish, eaten only by canons and bishops."

**Pa amb tomàquet**

From Spain's Catalan region comes this comforting *tapa* of "bread with tomato." The bread in question will be a rustic country loaf, cut into slices, slicked with olive oil, and grilled until crusty and brown. Garlic cloves and fresh tomatoes are then rubbed across the toasted surface, transferring their fragrant flavors to the bread, which receives another anointing with fruity olive oil and a light sprinkling of salt and pepper before being served, still warm.

**Paella**

The definitive dish of Spain's Mediterranean coast is a moist pilaf of rice turned golden and fragrant with saffron and studded with seafood such as shrimp, crab, lobster, clams, squid, and mussels; poultry and game, including chicken and rabbit;

## **The edible lids** of Spain

Long ago in the sherry bars of Spain, barkeepers would thoughtfully place little edible lids (*tapas*) of sliced bread atop their patrons' glasses to keep the sherry clean in the dusty surroundings. Soon, the bartenders began to crown those lids with tasty bits of food such as chorizo, Serrano ham, or manchego cheese.

Down through the centuries, tapas became more and more elaborate, eventually migrating off the tops of sherry glasses onto small plates that guests in the bar would order to complement their meal. Today, an assortment of tapas would certainly begin with simple, time-honored bites of cheese and cured pork, as well as olives, fried almonds, and other nibbles; but they'd then likely move onto cooked treats as wide ranging as Catalan *pa amb tomàquet*; small fried fritters of *bacalao*, ham, or poultry; chunks or wedges of *tortilla*; marinated anchovies and other bites of cooked seafood; artichoke hearts sautéed in olive oil with garlic and bits of ham; *empanadas*; the meatballs known as *albóndigas* (see **Mexico** chapter); fried or roasted potatoes doused with spices or accompanied by *romesco* sauce for dipping; and on and on.

Different tapas bars, of course, feature different specialties. For that reason, folk will often make an evening of wandering from bar to bar—a journey known as a *tapeo*—to sample their favorite dishes, with a glass of sherry at each stop, of course.

cured meats such as ham and chorizo sausage; and vegetables including not only garlic and onions but also tomato, peas, bell peppers, and sometimes green beans. Some *paellas* may also feature snails. *Paella*'s name comes from its cooking vessel, the *paellera*, a wide, shallow iron pan that provides the perfect heat distribution to render the rice tender but chewy, with just the right level of moisture to achieve an almost but not quite soupy consistency.

**Plancha, a la**

Don't take your Spanish-English dictionary too literally, or you might think that food cooked "a la plancha" is cooked on a plank! Actually, the term also refers to the flat, maybe boardlike surface of a hot griddle or skillet, on which relatively quick-cooking pieces of food—usually fish fillets, as well as shrimp, mussels, and sometimes thin fillets of meat or poultry—are seared in olive oil and seasoned with garlic and parsley.

**Romesco**

Throughout Catalan Spain, you'll find this spicy puree of hot and sweet peppers, tomatoes, almonds or hazelnuts, olive oil, and vinegar served as a condiment with meat, poultry, game, seafood, and vegetables, especially when any of those foods have been grilled.

**Serrano**

Spain's great ham, its name literally meaning "mountain-style," comes from lean, muscular pigs, their meat dry-salted and air-cured for many months. The thinly sliced raw ham may be used as a seasoning or enjoyed on its own as one of the classic tapas.

**Sopa seca**

The "dry soup" of northern Portugal, sharing a name with a signature dish of the Mexican kitchen, is made with layers of leftover bread, meats, and vegetables in a casserole. Then the whole construction is moistened with hot broth to make a satisfying, home-style main course.

## **Saffron:** Spain's fragrant gold

One of the signature seasonings of Spanish cooking, and also enjoyed in other kitchens around the world, saffron is the costliest spice in the world. To some it is as precious as gold. That's because it is derived through a labor-intensive, fastidious process, since the spice is harvested by hand-picking and then drying the tiny stamens of a variety of purple crocus flower. It takes the stamens of approximately five thousand blossoms to produce just one ounce of the spice.

Fortunately, just a tiny pinch of saffron threads—the thin, dried stamens—impart to any dish an intensely aromatic perfume and a deep golden color, which explains why the name derives from the Arabic word for "yellow." Beware of inexpensive saffron, which is probably ground turmeric masquerading as the higher priced, far more beautifully fragrant, but similarly colored spice. And always buy saffron in "thread" form, because powdered saffron can tend to lose its fragrance far more quickly, as well as possibly being adulterated.

**Tortilla**

Related to its Mexican cousin simply by its name, meaning "little cake," the *tortilla Española* is a flat potato-and-egg omelete cooked in olive oil. Cut into wedges or squares, it is enjoyed hot or cold as an appetizer or *tapa*, or as a simple lunch dish.

**Zarzuela**

Spain's lighthearted, often crazy-seeming form of operatic entertainment shares its name with a traditional seafood stew that, when properly made can seem like a veritable oceanic riot, brimming over with shrimp, crayfish, lobster, squid, clams, scallops, sole, and other denizens of the deep. Tying it all together, like the music rising from a theater's orchestra pit, is a broth liberally laced with white wine, tomatoes, peppers, onions, garlic, and saffron.

# Italy

It is all too easy to fall into the trap of thinking of Italian food as one cuisine. But consider that Europe's geographic high-topped boot united as a nation only as recently as the mid-19th century, and you'll come to realize that the country actually offers an incredible diversity of sub-cuisines now joined by a common language and a joy for life that pervades the entire Italian peninsula.

## FROM GENERATION TO GENERATION

*"To cook like your mother is good. To cook like your grandmother is even better."*

TUSCAN PROVERB

The northern Italian regions of Turin and the Piedmont are notable for robust, down-to-earth cooking, typified by *bollito misto*. Staple starches focus on cornmeal-based polenta and on the dumplings known as gnocchi. In the northwestern coastal provinces of Genoa and Liguria, you'll find seafood in abundance. You'll also thrill to try the fragrant garlic-and-herb sauce known as pesto. In the north-central and northeastern areas of Milan, Lombardy, and the Veneto, you'll find rice as a staple, starring in creamy risotto, a traditional accompaniment to the famed Milanese veal shank dish known as *osso buco*.

Some of Italy's most robust food may be found in its central provinces, from Bologna and Emilia-Romagna to Florence and Tuscany. You'll find pork and beef specialties in abundance, including Parma's famed *prosciutto*, simple but eloquent steaks cooked *alla Fiorentina*, and the famed bolognese sauce.

The farther south you go in Italy, the more olive oil predominates in the cooking. By Naples and other southern areas, it joins with sun-ripened tomatoes and pungent garlic to yield some of the dishes that understandably most define Italian cooking to the rest of the world, including bright-red *marinara* sauces. Sicilian cooking, too, captures the sun-kissed soul of Italy in every bite, adding touches of exotic Middle Eastern influence found in such dishes as the eggplant stew known as *caponata*.

**Aglio e olio, all'**

Often, simplest is best when it comes to food. Devotees of this way of saucing pasta would agree. Pronounced a tongue-twisting "ahl-ah-lee-oh-lee-oh," it means "with garlic and oil," and the preparation consists of briefly sautéing chopped garlic in extra-virgin olive oil until fragrant, then tossing it with freshly cooked pasta, usually spaghetti. The early-20th-century French artist Marcel Duchamp reputedly ate this for lunch almost daily, showing more common sense than you might expect from a leader of the absurdist Dada movement.

**Agrodolce**

A sour-sweet style of cooking, this term describes the way in which vegetables or meats are prepared using red wine, olive oil, vinegar, sugar or honey, and often raisins, citrus peel, or other dried or candied fruit.

**Alfredo**

This signature pasta sauce takes its name from the venerable Roman restaurant Alfredo all Scrofa, where anyone can enjoy it prepared tableside in a chafing dish, as I did long ago on my first visit to Rome. *Fettucine* is the featured noodle, tossed with lavish amounts of butter and freshly grated Parmesan, to which some also compound the cholesterol count with heavy cream.

**Amaretti**

These "little bitters" are small, light, crisp cookies resembling macaroons, made with egg whites, sugar, and the pleasantly bitter almondlike kernels extracted from apricot pits. Enjoy them with espresso at the end of a meal.

**Amatriciana, alla**

From Amatrice, near Rome, this pasta sauce features tomatoes, onions, olive oil, and bacon or salt pork, and is traditionally served with *bucatini*.

## **Amaretti wrappers** go up in flames

Some old-school Italian waiters might perform a favorite trick for you with the tissue-paper wrappers in which pairs of *amaretti* are packaged. They will roll one of these wrappers into a cylindrical chimney shape, stand it on end on a plate, and carefully touch a lighted match to its upper edge. As the paper burns downward, the air currents generated by the fire eventually lift the rapidly diminishing column upward like a tiny hot-air balloon. (Note: Do not try this trick yourself at home or in a restaurant dining room, and do not ever attempt to use it as a means of entertaining impressionable children!)

**Antipasto**

Some foodies misinterpret this term as "the course that comes before the pasta." In fact, it means "before the repast," a fairly sweeping reference to Italian appetizers. Sweeping is, indeed, the operative term, since a table of *antipasti* (the plural)—from which guests select those items that most appeal to them—can run the gamut from vegetables to cheeses to savory breads and pastries, seafood to poultry to meats.

**Arrabiata**

This tomato pasta sauce, meaning "enraged," is made with hot chili peppers, and usually served with *penne.*

**Bagna cauda**

A "hot bath" of olive oil, butter, garlic, and chopped salt-preserved anchovy fillets, this dish also contains the aromatic white truffles of the Piedmont, where this dip for vegetables, bread, or breadsticks originates. Cardoons, a local thistle in the region, are traditionally served for dipping. It's often brought to the table over a small burner that keeps it good and hot from first dip to last.

**Biscotti**

Literally "twice-cooked," these popular Italian cookies are formed by shaping a soft dough into a long, flattened loaf shape and baking it until fairly firm but still slightly soft. Then, the loaf is cut crosswise into slices, which are then arranged on their sides on the baking sheet and baked a second time until crisp and golden. *Biscotti* may be flavored or embellished in a wide variety of ways: with licorice-scented anise seed; with orange zest or lemon zest; with dried fruit; with hazelnuts or other nuts; or with chips or chunks of chocolate. In addition, they are sometimes dipped on one side in melted chocolate. The substantial, crunchy cookies are most often enjoyed with a cup of espresso or coffee, whether as a midmorning or midafternoon break or an after-dinner treat.

**Bistecca**

You can probably figure out what this means just by saying it and imagining that it's an English word spoken with a heavy Italian accent: yes, "beefsteak." But see *bistecca* in connection with the words *alla Fiorentina* on an Italian menu and you know you're likely in for one of the world's greatest meat treats, described a few pages ahead under that entry's explanation.

**Bollito misto**

Italy's "mixed boil" comes from the Piedmont region of the mountainous northwest. Beef, veal, chicken, ham, and tongue are slowly simmered together with carrots, onions, herbs, and spices until the meats are tender and a flavorful broth has formed. The broth is then served as a first course, elaborated with tiny pasta shapes such as *acini di pepe, annolini,* or *pulcini.* Then the meats are sliced and served, usually in the company of a separately cooked garlic sausage, and the broth is spooned over the meat to moisten it. *Salsa verde* is passed alongside as a condiment.

### Bolognese

In Bologna, where this meat sauce for pasta originates, you're more likely to find it referred to simply as *ragu*, an Italian spelling of the word *ragoût*, implying the rich, thick concoction it truly is. While many people outside of Italy might imagine a rather thin, anemic tomato-and-beef sauce when they hear the term, an authentic bolognese will be based on two or more different chopped meats—such as beef, pork, veal, chicken livers, *prosciutto*, or sausage—slowly simmered together for hours along with tomatoes, onions, garlic, mushrooms, wine, and herbs. In some of the most authentic versions, some milk is also stirred in during the last hour of slow simmering, which adds an elusive edge of sweetness and rounds off the rougher edges of the robust sauce.

### Bresaola

A specialty of Valtellina in northern Italy's Lombardy region, *bresaola* is to beef what fine ham is to pork. Lean fillets are salted and marinated with wine and spices, then air-dried. Cut into tissue-thin slices, the resulting meat is eaten most often as an appetizer, the better to savor its surprisingly subtle yet rich flavor and velvety texture.

### Buridda

Like the French *bourride*, this specialty from Liguria features a variety of fresh fish and squid or cuttlefish, layered together with tomatoes, onions, garlic, parsley, and oregano, then doused with white wine and olive oil and gently simmered until thick. The robust peasant-style dish is traditional ladled over crusty bread.

## **Italian cheeses:** some highlights

Italian cheeses are as varied as the nation's landscape, history, and people, with many tracing back for hundreds or even thousands of years. Keep your eyes—and mouth—open for these fine examples:

**ASIAGO** A nutty, tangy cow's-milk cheese from Vicenza in the northwest, reminiscent of Cheddar.

**BEL PAESE** Meaning "beautiful country," this mild cow's-milk cheese from Lombardy is smooth and creamy, with a hint of sweetness.

**FONTINA** From the Val d'Aosta in the northern Piedmont region, this cow's-milk cheese is distinguished by its firm texture, the small holes it is riddled with, and its mildly rich, slightly earthy flavor.

**GORGONZOLA** Italy's famed blue-veined cow's-milk cheese has a rich, tangy, almost spicy flavor to complement a texture that can range from soft and creamy when young to crumbly when aged.

**MASCARPONE** A tangy, lightly soured cream cheese made from cow's milk, this can range in consistency from as fluid as thick cream to as thick as freshly churned butter. Mascarpone is sometimes served as a garnish for fresh berries or other fruit; or it is used as an ingredient to enrich sauces and desserts.

## **Italian cheeses:** some highlights

**MOZZARELLA** This mild, stringy melting cheese may be made from cow's milk or, in its finest form, from the milk of water buffalo—the famed *bufalo mozzarella.* Mild, soft, fresh mozzarella may be found in Italian delis—and on the *antipasto* tables of good Italian restaurants—still floating in its whey, ready to be fished out and served alongside fresh tomatoes with fresh basil leaves, some fruity olive oil, salt, and pepper. Slightly drier, briefly aged *mozzarella* is a popular cheese for melting, appearing on pizzas and in other baked dishes.

**PARMESAN** Now referred to just as often by its Italian regional designation *Parmigiano-Reggiano,* this sharply tangy, salty, rich aged cow's-milk cheese is one of Italy's finest. Good Parmesan, freshly cut or grated, may be enjoyed on its own to end a meal; in thin shavings as an antipasto accompaniment; or grated as a flavoring and enrichment for pasta, risotto, and a wide range of other dishes.

**PECORINO** Similar to Parmesan in looks and flavor, this grating cheese from central and southern Italy has a distinctive tang that comes from sheep's milk.

**PROVOLONE** A smooth, soft-but-firm cow's-milk cheese from southern Italy, provolone ranges in flavor from mild to sharp, depending on how long it has been aged.

**RICOTTA** A fresh cow's-milk cheese enjoyed all over Italy, ricotta comes in soft, fluffy, mild curds that blend well with other ingredients in pasta fillings or stuffings. Look, also, for *ricotta salata,* a dried salted ricotta used as a grating cheese.

**Cacciatore, alla**

"Hunter-style" meat, poultry, or seafood generally means that the main course will be cooked and served in a sauce of tomatoes, wine, garlic, and rosemary, a treatment most popular in Italy's more southerly climes.

**Cannoli**

From Sicily, these tubes of deep-fried or baked wine-flavored pastry dough are filled with a sweet mixture of ricotta cheese, cream, candied fruit and chocolate chips. The pastries were introduced to the island in the 9th century by Saracen invaders who, referred to as "Turks" by the locals, gave rise to the old-fashioned name for cannoli: *cappelli di turco*, "Turk's hats."

**Caponata**

Sometimes referred to in the diminutive *caponatina* by those who feel particular fondness for this hot or cold *antipasto, caponata* is a sweet-and-sour stew of eggplant, tomatoes, celery, black olives, and capers, laced with vinegar and sugar. Other frequent embellishments include pine nuts and raisins. As one Sicilian devotee observed long ago, "He who has not eaten *caponatina* of eggplant has never reached the antechamber of the terrestrial paradise."

**Carbonara, alla**

According to the name, this is the way a charcoal-maker prefers to prepare spaghetti or other pasta strands. Freshly cooked, still-hot pasta is tossed with a mixture of bacon or salt pork, raw eggs, olive oil, Parmesan cheese, and freshly ground black pepper. The pasta's residual heat cooks the egg, which joins with its fellow ingredients to form a thick, creamy sauce.

## **The right way to** eat pasta strands

Non-Italians have long struggled with eating spaghetti and other pasta strands. A typical approach is to rake up some strands on the tines of a fork and lift them to the mouth, then attempt to gobble or slurp them up, leaving a trail of sauce all over the clothing and the table.

Some would-be sophisticates believe that the solution is to use a tablespoon or soup spoon in tandem, raking up the strands with the fork tines, then resting the tips of the tines in the bowl of the spoon, held in the other hand, and twirling the fork to wind the strands around its tine for easier popping into the mouth.

Alas, most Italians would frown on such a method. They accomplish the task in a far simpler fashion, facilitated by the fact that they serve pasta in shallow, curved-sided pasta bowls rather than on flat plates. The inner curve of the bowl's side is used much like the curve of the spoon, providing a niche in which to roll a few strands of pasta around the fork's tines. (Note that I said "a few." Many folks also mistakenly try to eat too many strands at a time, resulting in a too-big wad of rolled-up pasta strands on the fork.)

**Carpaccio**

Credit Harry's Bar in Venice for the creation of this now widely popular dish, in which the finest raw beef is sliced so paper-thin that it is translucent, then draped on a plate and served with piquant garnishes or sauces featuring anchovies, capers, roasted peppers, mustard, and herbs. The name pays tribute to Venice's renowned 15th-century painter, whose applied paint to canvas with similarly beguiling translucency.

**Cotechino**

This pork sausage from Emilia-Romagna gets its name from *cotenna,* "pig skin," the chopped pork rind it includes, which gives the usually mild-tasting, large links a succulent gelatinous consistency. You'll most often find *cotechino* served with pureed lentils, or in a *bollito misto.*

**Dente, al**

For many cooks and eaters, especially pasta lovers, this may well be the world's best known Italian cooking term. Literally "to the tooth," it refers to the consistency of properly cooked pasta: tender but still chewy. By extension, the term is now also used to describe vegetables that have been cooked correctly—tender but still with a pleasant hint of crispness.

**Fiorentina, alla**

"Florentine-style" refers to the straightforward, honest-to-goodness style of cooking found in this Tuscan city and its environs. Prime examples include *bistecca alla Fiorentina,* a beefsteak brushed with olive oil, charcoal-grilled, and then served with a squeeze of fresh lemon; and roast pork scented with rosemary and garlic.

**Focaccia**

Italy's famed flatbread is made by pressing out a yeast-leavened bread dough on a baking sheet, dimpling it by poking it at intervals with the fingertips, and generously lacing it with fruity olive oil before baking it into the oven until golden. The bread may be embellished in any number of ways by strewing it with fresh herbs such as rosemary or with thinly sliced onions or garlic; sprinkling it with coarse salt or grated Parmesan cheese; or even pressing whole grapes into the dough (an addition that goes remarkably well with the rosemary leaves). Focaccia may be served as an accompaniment to meals, or it can be cut into squares as the foundation for rustic sandwiches.

**Fonduta**

Like Switzerland's fondue, this popular northern Italian dish is a molten mixture of Fontina cheese enriched with egg yolks and milk. It is then topped with generous shavings of earthy, spicy white truffles.

**Frittata**

This skillet-fried flat omelet uses egg primarily as a binder for generous quantities of vegetables. Cut into wedges or squares, a frittata may be served as part of an *antipasto* table. Or the omelet can be served whole as a casual main course.

**Fritto misto**

A "mixed fried" assortment of foods, this popular appetizer is served all over Italy, varying with the local ingredients. Common versions feature squid, shrimp, thin onion rings, and sliced zucchini; but anything from zucchini blossoms to artichoke hearts to cauliflower florets, nuggets of calves' or lambs' brains or sweetbreads to slices of chicken breast to thin wafers of fresh lemon may also be included. The crisp coating may just be a dusting of seasoned flour, a light batter, or a crust of egg and bread crumbs, but it is usually fried in olive oil. Lemon wedges are served to season them and cut any oily edge.

**Frutti de mare**

Literally "fruits of the sea," this refers in general to seafood and more specifically to shellfish. On its own, this term might mean a platter of fresh raw shellfish. See it in partnership with other terms and you know what the featured ingredients are, as in *zuppa di frutti di mare* (seafood soup).

**Funghi**

Italians love their funguses—that is, mushrooms. See *ai funghi* on a menu and you know whatever it is will be smothered in earthy mushrooms, most likely sautéed with garlic and parsley and possibly slathered with cream. If you're lucky, the *funghi* in question will be *porcini*—no, not little pigs, but the famed *Boletus edulis*, fleshy, domed treat of spring and fall with a rich, meaty flavor.

## **Gnocchi** sayings

- **"Ridi, ridi che la mamma ha fatto i gnocchi."**
  (Old Italian saying, which translates, "Laugh, laugh because Mamma has made gnocchi.")

- **"Giovedí gnocchi."**
  (Typical sign in Italian pasta shops and trattorias: "Thursday gnocchi," the traditional day on which to make and serve gnocchi.)

**Gelato**

To define *gelato* simply as Italian ice cream is as much of a slight to its wonders as it would be to refer to pizza as a kind of Italian cheese toast. Typical non-Italian ice cream is generally made with cream as much as 30 percent higher in butterfat than that used for *gelato*, meaning that the authentic Italian product tastes cleaner and lighter on the tongue. But don't think it's a less rich experience. On the contrary, only about one-third as much air by volume is beaten into *gelato*, which is typically produced in small batches; so the frozen dessert is far denser. Add the wide range of pure flavors, from chocolate to sweet spices, fruits to nuts, and the result is an intensely satisfying treat typically enjoyed in small scoops. When in Italy, look for small *gelato* shops and stands in the business districts of cities and towns. Choose your flavors, take a tiny spoon, stroll, and savor this most Italian of sweets.

**Gnocchi**

Literally meaning "lump," it's an apt description for these generally thumbnail-size dumplings (pronounced "nyoh-kee"). Usually made from a dough of mashed potatoes, wheat flour, and water, they are sometimes colored and flavored with other vegetables such as pureed spinach or pumpkin. Gnocchi are usually boiled first, then served with butter, a cream or cheese sauce, or tomato-based sauce. Or, after boiling, they may also be baked in a sauce. The term is also used to refer to an idiot or knucklehead, something you'd have to be to overlook this humble but delicious specialty. (See also **A pasta shapes glossary**.)

**Granita**

This "grainy" iced dessert, distant kin to sorbets and ices, is typically made by preparing a mixture of pure fruit juice and sugar syrup, pouring it into a metal pan, putting it into the freezer, and repeatedly scraping the partially frozen mixture with a fork or spoon until it eventually forms of mass of crystals. Only then is the *granita* scooped into chilled dishes for serving. Nothing cools and refreshes on a hot summer's day quite like a sweet, snowy granita.

**Gremolata**

Think of *gremolata* as an explosion of flavor Italian cooks add to savory dishes. Finely chopped garlic and parsley are tossed together with grated orange zest and lemon zest, and these powerfully aromatic ingredients are activated the instant they encounter a hot, just-cooked dish. Most often, you'll find gremolata scattered over *osso buco* just before serving.

**Livornese, alla**

Livorno, Tuscany's coastal province, gives its name to seafood dishes cooked with the region's familiar ingredients: olive oil, tomatoes, onions, garlic, and anchovies.

**Marinara, alla**

You might wonder, at first, why a sauce named for a sailor would contain not a trace of seafood? The answer lies in the geographic origin of this simple but delicious combination of fresh or canned tomatoes, garlic, olive oil, and basil or oregano: the seafaring town of Naples. Indeed, pasta served with this sauce—usually spaghetti, though it works well with other strands, too—may also be referred to as *alla Napolitana*.

**Marsala, alla**

The noble name of Sicily's sweet, raisiny-tasting fortified wine, Marsala also describes any recipe in which it figures prominently in the sauce. A perfect example, which you're likely to find on menus most often, is veal *alla Marsala*, breaded (or naked) cutlets of tender veal, pan-fried in butter and then finished with a syrupy reduction of the wine enriched with a splash of broth and another dollop of butter. Chicken or turkey breast cutlets may also be done in this way.

**Mortadella**

A 17th-century Italian gourmet referred to this sausage from Bologna as "the noblest of all pork products," an air-dried link of smooth-textured, finely ground pork and mild spices, served thinly sliced. The name reputedly comes from the heavy mortar in which the meat was originally prepared: *mortaio della carne di maiale* (mortar for pork). Some scholars, however, would like to have you believe that it derives from a flavor and texture so sublime that one could die from (*morta-della*) a single bite.

**Osso buco**

The "hollow bone" to which the name of this great Milanese main course refers is a meaty cross-section of veal shank, which contains a bone at its center packed with marrow. The pieces of shank are lightly floured, browned in olive oil, and then

## A slice of pizza history

For centuries, people in Mediterranean climes ate flatbreads of various kinds. These rolled out scraps of leftover yeast-leavened dough would be informally drizzled with oil, sprinkled with herbs and other seasonings, and baked until crisp, to be eaten as a snack.

The first true pizza of the modern era is generally believed to have been created in 1889 by Neapolitan baker Rafaele Esposito, who topped a bit of thinly rolled dough with tomatoes and mozzarella cheese, then named it in tribute to Queen Margherita. The pizza Margherita remains a classic to this day, though pizzas today may carry a wide range of toppings, from tomato sauce to pesto to a Parmesan-cream sauce resembling *Alfredo,* many different kinds of cheeses, and elaborations from sausage to ham to anchovies, as well as all manner of fresh or roasted vegetables.

slowly simmered in wine, broth, and tomatoes along with onions, garlic, carrots, celery, and herbs. When the meat is falling-off-the-bone tender and the sauce is thick, the *osso buco* is served alongside a simple Milanese-style risotto and topped with *gremolata* (a mixture of chopped parsley, garlic, and orange and lemon zests that adds a final burst of aromatic flavor on contact with the heat). When guests have finished the meat on their plates, they traditionally spoon the rich yet delicate-tasting marrow out of the bones as a final treat.

**Panettone**

A holiday-season specialty of Milan since the 15th century, this tall, cupola-shaped, sweet, yeast-leavened, butter-and-egg-enriched bread is generously enhanced with bits of candied fruit. Enjoy it sliced at breakfast, with midmorning or afternoon coffee or tea, or for dessert along with a glass of sweet Marsala wine or brandy.

## **A pasta shapes** glossary

Where folks in other parts of the Western world might think of pasta largely as spaghetti, Italians have many, many different imaginative names for the differently shaped noodles formed from a fresh dough of flour and eggs or a dried flour-and-water dough. Here are some of the most common, with a scattering of the less so:

**ACINI DI PEPE** Tiny balls for soup, reminiscent of "peppercorns."
**AGNOLOTTI** "Fat little lambs," describing small, round shapes stuffed with meat- or cheese-based fillings.
**AMORINI** "Little loves," small cube shapes for soup.
**ANELLINI** Small, ring shapes for soup.
**ANOLINI** Small, semicircular, stuffed shapes.
**BAVETTE** Strands like slightly flattened spaghetti, oval in cross-section.
**BUCATINI** "Little holes," describing long hollow noodles.
**CANNELLONI** "Big pipes," meaning large tubes for stuffing and baking.
**CANOLICCHI** Short, ridged tubes.
**CAPPALETTI** Stuffed "little hat" shapes.
**CAPPELLI D'ANGELO** "Angel hair," describing long, wispy spaghetti.
**CONCHIGLIE** "Conch-shell" shapes.
**DITALINI** "Little thimbles," tubes just big enough to fit on a fingertip.
**ELICOIDALI** Straight tubes covered in curved ridges reminiscent of "helixes."
**FARFALLE** "Butterflies," bite-size shapes also called "bowties" in English.
**FETTUCELLE** Narrow *fettucine.*
**FETTUCINE** "Ribbons," most popularly enjoyed with *Alfredo* sauce.

# **A pasta shapes** glossary

**FUSILLI** "Fuses" or "spindles," resembling squiggly strands.
**GEMELLI** "Twins," describing two short strands twisted around each other.
**GIGLI** "Lilies," ruffle-edged bite-size shapes resembling blossoms.
**GNOCCHI** "Lumps," resembling small, roughly made cups shaped on a thumbtip, sharing a name with the popular dumplings.
**GRAMIGNA** Small, ridged tubes.
**LASAGNE** Probably derived from the Latin *lasanum,* a large cooking pot sufficiently sized to boil these long, wide ribbons, which are then layered and baked with sauce and cheese to make the popular homestyle dish lasagna. To quote the 13th-century Bolognese nobleman, monk, and poet Iacopone da Todi, "He who regards greatness often deceives himself. A grain of pepper conquers lasagna with its virtue."
**LASAGNETTE** Wavy-edged *lasagne* noodles.
**LINGUE DE PÀSSERO** "Sparrow's tongues," describing long, thin ribbons.
**LINGUINE** "Small tongues," describing thin, flat strands.
**LUMACHE** Small curved shells resembling "snails."
**MACCHERONI** Short tubes, spelled "macaroni" in English.
**MAFALDE** Long ribbons with fluted edges.
**MALTAGLIATI** "Badly cut" little rough sheets of pasta.
**MANICHE** Short tubes.
**MANICOTTI** "Muffs," describing large tubes similar to *cannelloni.*
**MOSTACCIOLI** Slender tubes reminiscent of "little mustaches."
**ORECCHIETTE** "Little ears," describing bite-size, indented round shapes.

## **A pasta shapes** glossary

**PAPPARDELLE** Wide, short ribbons.

**PENNE** Slender tubes with their ends cut on the bias, resembling old-fashioned quill "pens."

**PERCIATELLI** Long, thin, hollow tubes.

**PULCINI** Tiny pasta for soups, shaped like "little chicks."

**RADIATORE** Bite-size, ridged shapes reminiscent of "radiators."

**RAVIOLI** Bite-size, square "wraps" of stuffed pasta, with a wide range of savory fillings, the most common of which are based on ricotta cheese.

**RIGATONI** Long, "ridged" tubes.

**ROTELLE** "Little wheels" resembling bite-size corkscrews.

**RUOTE** Bite-size pasta shaped like "wagon wheels."

**SPAGHETTI** "Strings," describing the familiar long, slender pasta strands, round in cross-section.

**STROZAPRETTI** You can only imagine what the mind of the first cook must have been like to name these curled bite-size ribbons "priest stranglers."

**TAGLIARINI** Small, narrow *tagliatelli*.

**TAGLIATELLI** Egg pasta ribbons slightly wider than *fettuccine*.

**TORTELLINI** "Little pies"—stuffed pasta shapes twisted around to form bite-size circles that resemble plump belly buttons, leading Italians to sometimes refer to them poetically as "navels of Venus." Ah, those Italians!

**TORTIGLIONE** Corkscrew-shaped short spirals.

**TRENETE** Flattened spaghetti.

**VERMICELLI** "Little worms," describing thin spaghetti.

**ZITI** "Bridegrooms," a fanciful (or smutty) word for curved slender *maccheroni* tubes.

**Pesto**

A specialty of the northwestern city of Genoa, this glorious sauce is made by pounding together (the name comes from the word for "pestle") or otherwise pureeing fresh, fragrant basil leaves, toasted pine nuts, olive oil, garlic, and freshly grated Parmesan or pecorino cheese. The thick but fluid, deep-green sauce may be stirred into vegetable soups or used to flavor dressings. It's grandest manifestation, however, is as a sauce for pasta or gnocchi when, upon contact with the hot, just-cooked-and-drained pasta or dumplings, the pesto bursts forth with wondrously aromatic flavor.

**Polenta**

The ancient Etruscan porridge the Romans called *pulmentum* has come a long way, becoming so much of a staple in northern Italy that citizens of Venice are sometimes referred to as "polenta eaters." Ground dried cornmeal is slowly simmered with water or broth and salt until it forms a thick mixture that may then be enriched with butter and grated cheese. Spooned straight from the pot, polenta may be served alongside stews or roasts, a perfect way to soak up flavorful juices. Or it can be spread on a greased baking sheet or a cutting board, left to cool, and cut into shapes that may then be either sautéed in butter until crisp on the surface and golden; or baked with butter and cheese.

**Prosciutto**

Parma's famous ham comes from pigs fattened on the whey left over from the process of making Parmesan cheese. The flavorful meat of the animal's rear leg is then seasoned, cured with salt for a month, and then hung in huge sheds to cure further in the cool air for six months or longer. The meat develops an intense flavor and an almost satiny texture that are best appreciated in paper-thin slices. *Prosciutto* stars on many *antipasto* tables, from which it may be enjoyed on its own or as the perfect companion to juicy melon, pears, or figs. You'll also find it served in sandwiches, as well as used sparingly to flavor stuffings, pasta sauces, or pizzas.

**Risotto** Only short, plump grains of rice from such evocatively named varieties as Arborio, Carnaroli, or Vialone Nano qualify for use in this preeminent Italian rice dish. When cooked in a combination of broth and wine and stirred continuously, they give up their abundant surface starch to form a creamy sauce that enrobes every grain of the pleasantly chewy rice. Finished with a little butter and some freshly grated Parmesan, simple risotto makes the classic companion to *osso buco*, and may also be served alongside other meat, poultry, or seafood dishes. Or risotto may become a featured dish in its own right, with small pieces of vegetables, fish, fowl, or meat folded into the rice when it is almost finished.

**Salsa verde** "Green sauce," a pungent cold condiment most commonly found served alongside *bollito misto*, is made by pureeing together capers, garlic, shallots, anchovies, olive oil, and lemon juice.

**Saltimbocca** Literally "jump in the mouth," this Roman specialty delights the taste buds. Paper-thin slices of *prosciutto* and fresh sage leaves are rolled inside thinly sliced and pounded scallops of veal, or sometimes turkey. They are then sautéed in butter. Dissolving the pan juices with white wine provides a simple sauce. The finished rolls are sometimes topped with a sharp cheese such as Parmesan, pecorino, or provolone.

## Italy's *aceto balsamico*

From the town of Modena in Italy's Emiglia-Romagna region comes this king among vinegars. Unlike most grape-based vinegars, it is made not from wine but from the unfermented juice of white Trebbiano grapes, which is aged in a series of casks of diminishing size made of various types of wood, each of which imparts its own flavor to the complex profile of the ever-more-concentrated vinegar.

The final product, which may be anywhere from one to 75 or more years old, is an almost syrupy elixir with a powerful sweet-sour flavor. Balsamic vinegar need be used only sparingly, as a condiment, to lend flavor to dressings and sauces, or on its own sprinkled over berries or other fresh fruit.

When choosing a balsamic vinegar, look for products with a seal indicating they were made in Modena following *tradizionale* methods.

**Vongole**

Italian for "clams" in their many forms, *vongole* are most often enjoyed in a red (tomato-based) or white (wine-and-butter-based) sauce for pasta.

**Zabaglione**

To make this frothy custard dessert, egg yolks, sugar, and Marsala are whisked briskly over very low heat until they form a thick, voluptuous foam. (In restaurants with fancy pretensions, this might be done by a waiter with great flourishes tableside over a portable burner.) Then, the mixture is spooned into glasses, to be enjoyed hot. Sometimes, *zabaglione* is served over fresh fruit such as seasonal berries, or it may be chilled or even used as the base for an ice cream.

**Zuppa Inglese**

"English soup," this is the Italian term for the British dessert known as trifle.

# Greece and Turkey

Historically, Greece and Turkey may well have been inimical. And they may bristle at the notion I'm about to present. But the evidence is irrefutable: their cuisines are so similar that they demand to be covered in the same chapter.

## TOUGH LOVE

*"Choose your friends by the taste of their food."*

TURKISH PROVERB

Of course, the same history that supports their desire to be treated separately also supports the need for joint coverage. Many of Greece's definitive dishes from *dolmathes* to *moussaka* to *baklava,* trace their history back to the country's rule under Turkey's Ottoman Empire. That influence may well have been for the best when you consider that the ancient Greeks routinely feasted on such main courses as dogs, donkeys, horses, hedgehogs, and foxes. Of course, Greek cooking improved down through the ages, with the people of the peninsula and its many islands developing a wide range of seafood specialties and baked goods. The Greek kitchen can proudly present its own creations to set it apart among the world's cuisines today, from creamy dips like *hummus* and *taramasalata* to the rich soup and sauce called *avgolemono* to the fragrant meatballs called *keftedes.*

Turkish cuisine itself benefited from outside influences, most notably the exotic culinary traits of Persian cooks who emigrated westward. Turkish cuisine also boasts dishes that, having not traveled across the Aegean Sea, remain uniquely its own. From *Çerkez tavugu* to *imam bayildi* to *kadayif,* such sumptuous specialties show the important geographic role Turkey has always played as the crossroads between Europe and Asia.

**Avgolemono** Its name derived from the Greek words for egg (*avgo*) and lemon (*lemono*), this term refers to a soup made with chicken stock and *orzo*, or a sauce enriched and zestily seasoned with a whisked mixture of eggs and lemon juice. Look for *avgolemono* sauce bathing warm *dolmathes* or gracing *keftedes* or roast chicken.

**Baklava** Its roots reaching back to the Byzantine Empire, this lavish pastry layers thin sheets of *filo* dough with chopped nuts, sweet spices, and butter. After baking until golden brown and crisp, an entire pan of *baklava* will be drenched with honey syrup, sometimes scented with such sweet floral essences as rosewater or orange flower water.

**Börek** Like Greece's *spanakopita*, this savory Turkish pastry has a crispy wrapping of *filo*, rolled up around a filling of spiced ground meat, chopped vegetables, or garlic-scented goat cheese. You'll often find these in the form of "cigars," *cigara börek*, which are shaped into thin tubes to serve as appetizers. Larger *börek* may be served as a main course.

**Cacik** This cold Turkish soup is a combination of plain yogurt, shredded cucumber, garlic, mint, and enough ice water to bring it to a fluid, spoonable consistency. It's a close cousin of the Greek dip or sauce *tzatziki*.

**Çerkez Tavugu** Don't miss a chance to try this classic Turkish appetizer, Circassian chicken, a cool salad of shredded chicken bathed in a thick pureed sauce of toasted walnuts, bread crumbs, onions, garlic, and seasonings including paprika. So the story goes, slaves from Georgia introduced the dish to the Turkish royal court.

**Cilbir**

Try this Turkish morning or luncheon dish and you may never go back to eggs Benedict! Eggs are gently poached in water, then topped with creamy plain yogurt and onions and garlic that have been fried in butter and seasoned with hot red pepper. Scoop up the glorious mess with toasted bread.

**Dolmathes**

These Greek "rolls" (or, in Turkey, *dolmas*) are made by folding grapevine leaves around a filling of rice (embellished with dried currants) or rice mixed with chopped lamb, forming a bite-size morsel generally served as an appetizer. The stuffed leaves are poached in water or broth and lemon juice, then drained and served either cold with olive oil, or hot with an *avgolemono* sauce.

**Feta**

Greek's best known cheese, crumbly, salty, tangy white feta is made from the milk of goats or sheep, and is generally bought still afloat in its salty whey. You'll find crumbles of feta garnishing many Greek dishes, even though most of the feta in the world is now produced in other countries, including the U.S., Argentina, France, Romania, Bulgaria, and Israel. Feta varies in strength of flavor and consistency from maker to maker, country to country, and region to region. Some feta is also now made from cow's milk, and has a firmer consistency and milder taste.

**Gyro**

The name comes from the same word as "gyrate," describing the way this large spit covered in a roast-size mass of seasoned ground lamb rotates in front of a heat source. The cooked, crisped meat on the surface is then sliced off to serve in or with pita, to be sauced with yogurt and garnished with onions, cucumbers, and tomatoes. A favorite street food, *gyro* becomes elegant when transformed into *yogurtlu kebab.*

**Horiatiki**

Meaning "country-style," this Greek term most often refers to a popular salad, served as an appetizer or side dish, composed of crisp lettuces, tomato, cucumber, black olives, sliced onion, and the crumbled sheep's-milk cheese called feta. It is dressed with olive oil, lemon juice or vinegar, and a generous sprinkling of aromatic dried oregano.

**Hummus**

This popular Greek appetizer is made by pureeing cooked chick peas and then enriching them with *tahini* (sesame seed paste), olive oil, garlic, lemon juice, and spices. Triangles of warm pita are the ideal scoopers for savoring the dip.

**Imam bayildi**

According to the name of this classic Turkish side dish, "the holy man swooned" upon tasting this mixture of eggplant roasted in olive oil with tomatoes, onions, and garlic. Scholars still debate whether the fainting spell was actually brought on by the luscious taste of the dish or its profligate use of olive oil.

**Kadayif**

Spelled in various ways, including *katayifa* and *cataif*, these popular Turkish pastries resemble biscuits of breakfast-time shredded wheat. The shredded-looking part is actually a fine, wispy Arabic pastry called *konafa*, which is wrapped around sweet fillings of cream, cheese, or chopped nuts, then soaked in a citrus-scented syrup straight out of the oven. It is served at room temperature and cut into individual pieces.

**Keftedes**

Fragrant with mint, onion, and garlic, Greece's meatballs of lamb or beef may be deep-fried, baked, simmered, or grilled before serving as an appetizer or main course.

## *Filo*: thin leaves of pastry

Whether you spell it *filo* or *phyllo* in the English alphabet, the word translates from the Greek root for "leaf"—the perfect description for the tissue-thin layers of this very typical, highly popular pastry in Greece, Turkey, and other neighboring countries. Ultra-thin sheets of a flour-and-water dough are stacked one atop the other and, brushed with butter or oil, are used to enclose both savory and sweet fillings, from *börek* to *spanakopita* and back to *baklava*. Baking transforms the pastry to golden crispness, yet the leaves remain so delicate that they virtually disintegrate with a bite.

**Moussaka**

Sometimes it may seem as if every Greek restaurant includes *moussaka* on the menu, and with good reason. No dish seems to distill in a more satisfying way the homespun flavors of that country's heartland. Ground lamb, seasoned with garlic, oregano, cinnamon, and tomatoes, is layered with slices of fried eggplant and topped with a custardy sauce enriched with sheep's-milk cheese and a hint of nutmeg, then baked in the oven. You'll also find versions of *moussaka* in Turkey, where potatoes are sometimes included among the layers.

**Orzo**

This rice-shaped Greek pasta is often served as rice would be, seasoned and steamed as a side dish.

**Pastitsio**

Greece's answer to mac-and-cheese combines thick pasta tubes or macaroni in a baking dish with grated cheese, eggs, and a thick meat-and-tomato sauce spiced with cinnamon and nutmeg. The whole assembly is covered with a custard of egg yolks and more sweet spices, and baked to a rich, appetizing golden hue.

**Pita**

These oval- or round-shaped individual flatbreads of yeast-leavened dough are the most common appetizer and sandwich bread of Greece and Turkey. Properly prepared, each pita develops an air pocket in its center—source of the nickname "pocket bread"—that makes a pita ideal for stuffing as a sandwich. Wedges of hot pita are also served for scooping up dips like *hummus* and *taramasalata*.

**Saganaki**

This popular Greek appetizer, named for the pan in which it cooks, starts with a thick slice of *kasseri*, a firm, mild-but-tangy cheese made from sheep's milk. The cheese is first browned on both sides in the pan in hot olive oil or butter. Then, it is generally presented to guests at the table, where the waiter adds a shot of brandy and ignites the spirit's fumes to a dramatic finish. Finally, the flames are doused with fresh lemon juice, which also shifts the combination of flavors into perfect balance. Warm pita is an ideal accompaniment.

**Skordalia**

Greeks serve this creamy sauce of garlic pureed with bread and almonds or potatoes, olive oil, and vinegar or lemon juice as a dressing for vegetables.

**Souvlakia**

These traditional Greek kebabs of lamb, usually cubes of boneless leg meat, are marinated in a mixture of olive oil, lemon juice, white wine, garlic, oregano, and other seasonings before they're skewered and grilled over an open fire. The meat may be eaten with a rice pilaf or slid off the skewer and folded into pita.

**Spanakopita**

Literally "spinach pie," this popular Greek appetizer or luncheon dish has a seasoned mixture of spinach and feta cheese either enclosed between layers of *filo* dough in a baking dish or placed inside long strips of the same dough, which are folded around it like a flag to make bite-size triangles. The construction is then baked until the filling is hot and the pastry has turned a deep golden brown.

**Stifado**

The Greek term refers in general to stews. More specifically, however, it is taken to mean Greece's signature beef stew made from bite-size boneless cubes of meat, browned in olive oil and then slowly simmered with onions, tomatoes, red wine, oregano, bay leaves, and other herbs. Bread must be served alongside to soak up the rich juices left on the plate.

**Tarama**

In Greece, the flavorful eggs of carp or mullet fish are preserved by salting them and then, sometimes, immersing them in olive oil, becoming *tarama*. When blended to a smooth paste with olive oil, garlic, bread crumbs, onion, and lemon juice, the pink roe becomes one of Greece's most popular appetizers, *taramasalata*, which is scooped up with triangles of warm pita.

**Tzatziki**

Similar to Turkey's *cacik*, this mixture of yogurt, cucumbers, garlic, onion, and dill is served as a dip along with hot pita.

**Yogurtlu kebab**

This is the most lavish presentation of grilled meats to be found in Turkey and Greece. Chunks of skewer-grilled lamb or slices of *gyro* are scattered atop a bed of bite-size pieces pita and then covered with a hot, spicy fresh tomato sauce and another hot sauce of garlicky yogurt.

# Dining in Africa and the Middle East

# Africa

Why confine a whole continent to a single section entry in this book? If time and space allowed, I'd love to devote an entire book to the food of Africa. But this book is, first and foremost, a guide to the foods you'll find in restaurants—not just when you travel to their countries of origin but, more importantly, that you come across in your daily life. And, alas, African cooking has not yet emerged sufficiently to make a major impact on the international dining scene, in large part because many countries in that continent are still emerging nations pulling themselves from poverty—hardly the conditions to foster engaging cuisines of worldwide interest.

Nevertheless, you will find culinary accomplishments worthy of interest and exploration throughout the continent. North Africa has a complex and ancient cuisine of its own, typified by such specialties as couscous and tagine. In Ethiopia, you'll find preparations like *injera* and *wot* that form the foundation of a wonderfully down-to-earth approach to eating. And South Africa reflects its prosperity in a cuisine grown from a fascinating amalgam of cultures—indigenous African, Dutch, and English settlers, and the immigrant workers from India and other parts of southwestern Asia who helped build the nation.

## A RECIPE FOR PEACE?

*"Those who eat from the same plate will not betray each other."*

ETHIOPIAN PROVERB

**Biltong**

To define biltong as South African beef jerky is both glib and inaccurate. Like biltong, American jerky is a strip of meat prerserved in salt and seasoning and then dried in the open air. But biltong, developed by early trekkers as a way of preserving their meat in their covered wagons, is distinctively flavored with vinegar and such spices as coriander seed, along with the coarse salt that helps concentrate its flavor. While beef is the most common meat, you'll find biltong made from game animals as exotic as springbok, impala, or ostrich as well. The word itself is derived from the Dutch *bil*, meaning "rump," and *tong*, for "tongue," capturing the range of cuts that could be used. Biltong is usually chewed as a snack, and especially beloved by the spectators at rugby games, perhaps for its natural affinity with beer.

**Bobotie**

This home-style South African casserole, reflecting the influence of Malaysian and Indian laborers who were brought to the country in its early days, is made by filling the bottom of a casserole with a sautéed mixture of ground beef or lamb and onions, seasoned with Indian-style curry spices along with almonds, raisins and other dried fruit, and a little sugar and lemon juice. Raw eggs beaten with milk are poured over the meat, forming a light custardlike topping when the *bobotie* is baked. Spooned from the casserole onto plates, it's eaten with steamed rice and such garnishes as shredded coconut, chopped nuts, and Indian chutney.

**Boerwurst**

Also spelled *boerewors,* this plump, succulent fresh South African sausage, literally "Boer sausage," is usually made with beef or pork and gets its tantalizing flavor from such East Indian spices as nutmeg and cloves. It is usually the starring item at a South African barbecue or *braai.*

**Brik**

Popular in Tunisia and across North Africa, this triangular turnover, also sometimes spelled *bric,* is a savory, generously spiced filling that often includes such ingredients as ground lamb or beef, spinach, potatoes, and whole raw egg inside tissue-thin sheets of pastry called *malsouqua,* similar to *crêpes* or Greek *filo* pastry, made by quickly griddle-cooking an elastic batter. Part of the fun of eating a *brik* is the surprise of finding hot, runny egg yolk inside, which becomes almost a sauce for the other filling ingredients.

**B'stilla**

The Moroccan tradition of eating with your fingers may be experienced at its most sensuous with the serving of this savory pie, often prepared in communal-size portions. Thin, flaky pastry dough is layered with tender boneless chunks of chicken, squab, finely ground nuts such as almonds or pistachios, beaten eggs, and generous and surprisingly sweet seasonings of sugar and cinnamon. As you gingerly break through the crust to pick up bite-size pieces of pastry and poultry, your fingertips experience the hot, crisp sensations before your lips and mouth enjoy the succulence. The thrill of eating this way is only heightened if you're sharing the *b'stilla* (a name occasionally, less accurately transliterated "bistilla" or even "pastilla") with someone with whom you're romantically involved and begin to feed it to each other, fingertips to lips.

**Chakchouka**

This Tunisian vegetable dish is widely versatile. Sliced or chopped bell peppers, chili peppers, garlic, onions, and tomatoes are sautéed in olive oil with *harissa*. At its most basic, there you have it, ready to serve alongside a main course. But *chakchouka* may also be mixed with eggs for a luncheon omelet, or enhanced with chick peas, and I've also seen it sautéed with chicken livers.

**Couscous**

Many people mistakenly think that the Moroccan dish known as couscous is based on a steamed whole grain, perhaps fine cracked wheat. In fact, couscous is a very fine form of dried semolina wheat pasta, no different in substance from those of Italy, and its name comes from the Arabic words rac keskes, "crushed small." The dried pasta is put in the top half of a cooking vessel with a perforated bottom called, appropriately enough, a couscousière. Here it steams to fluffy tenderness atop a spicy lamb or chicken stew abounding in chick peas, carrots, potatoes, and onions, and often raisins or other dried fruit. When finished, the grains are mounded on a large serving platter, and the stew is ladled around it. Guests help themselves, seasoning individual servings to taste with harissa. Steamed over water or simmered in milk or cream, then sweetened with sugar or honey and enhanced with nuts and raisins, couscous also becomes a wonderful dessert similar to rice pudding.

**Harira**

Moroccans traditionally break their fast each day during the Muslim holy month of Ramadan by eating this hearty main-course soup of lamb, onions, tomatoes, chick peas, lentils, and noodles, generously seasoned with pungent and sweet spices such as saffron, black pepper, ginger, and cinnamon. Before serving, the soup, which already includes butter in which the meat and vegetables were browned, is enriched further by stirring in a mixture of beaten eggs and lemon juice. The resulting broth, according to proverb, should be "smooth as silk." It's customary to enjoy plates of dried figs or dates along with the soup.

**Harissa**

You might call this the ketchup of North Africa—except for the fact that you'd get a rude awakening if you spread *harissa* on your hamburger! Ground dried red chilies, paprika, roasted red bell pepper, ground caraway and coriander seeds, garlic, and salt are combined with olive oil to form a thick, reddish-brown paste that is a ubiquitous table condiment, as well as a kitchen seasoning that is generously massaged into meats, poultry, or seafood before cooking. Come to think of it, spicy though it is, *harissa* would be delicious on a hamburger…

**Mealiepap**

Also spelled *mealie pap* and *mealie-pap,* or simply referred to as *pap,* this is the ultimate South African nursery food. A mush made of dried ground cornmeal, it is similar to America's grits or Italy's polenta. (The name may be loosely translated as "soft corn," the word "pap" meaning "soft.") Traditionally eaten for breakfast, it's also delicious as a side dish, and my South African cousins have served it to me as a side dish at a *braai,* or barbecue, to be eaten with grilled *boerwurst.* The most traditional way to make it requires that you combine cold water and cornmeal the night before you cook them. This causes a slight fermentation, which gives the *mealiepap* a distinctive sour edge of flavor.

## A RECIPE FOR HAPPINESS

*"A shining face goes with a full belly."*

WEST AFRICAN PROVERB

**Mechoui** This traditional North African way of cooking a whole lamb—or, on a more reasonable scale, a leg or shoulder of lamb—starts by marinating the meat overnight slathered with an intense seasoning paste that may include such ingredients as ground hot and sweet peppers, garlic, mint, cumin, saffron, butter, olive oil, and lemon juice. The lamb is then oven-roasted or grilled slowly over an open fire.

**Pap** See **Mealiepap**.

**Pastilla** See **B'stilla**.

**Ras el hanout** The name, literally "head of the shop," captures the idiosyncratic way in which this traditional Moroccan seasoning mixture is composed. You can almost imagine the owner of a spice shop throwing together his own secret blend of ingredients, which can number fewer than a dozen or as many as several dozen different seasonings. Typical elements will include ground hot chilies, cinnamon, nutmeg, cloves, allspice, cardamom, aniseed, black and white pepper, saffron, turmeric, and dried ginger, along with more exotic items like dried rose petals and lavender buds.

**Snoek**

Oh, how South Africans, particularly those who grew up in the Cape region, love their snoek! A distant relative of the barracuda, this bony fish of the waters was once considered too lowly to be served in restaurants, reserved for grilling at home or eating in its smoked or canned forms. Nowadays, creative South African chefs are finally acknowledging the downright goodness of the fish. The snoek is so much a part of local culture that, as American food writer extraordinaire Calvin Trillin observed in a September 2004 article about snoek in *The New Yorker*, a popular old expression of surprise there is, "*Slaat my dood met 'n pap snoek*," which translates, "Hit me dead with a soft snoek."

**Tagine**

Also spelled *tajine*, the word refers both to an earthenware cooking vessel used all over North Africa and to the generous stews of lamb, mutton, goat, or chicken cooked in them. Expect a tagine (softly pronounced "tah-ZHEEN") to include onions, tomatoes, chick peas, and other vegetables, beans, or pulses; sometimes lemons preserved in salt, a distinctive flavoring of the region; plus robust seasonings similar to those you might find simmering beneath a couscous.

Tagine

**Wot**

Seasoned with crushed red peppers, ginger, cumin, cardamom, and coriander seed, the spicy Ethiopian sauce known as *wot* becomes the cooking medium for a wide variety of ingredients, from lentils to vegetables, poultry to meat to seafood. The resulting stews are usually heaped atop *injera* on each guest's plate.

# The Middle East

Although they are often defined by rivers, mountain ranges, coasts, or other natural features, international borders are really artificial things. That fact is dramatized most boldly in the daily news headlines emerging from all across the Middle East.

## SAFETY IN NUMBERS

*"He who eats alone, chokes alone."*

ARABIC PROVERB

Food, however, seldom follows borders, which is why I group the countries of the Middle East together despite the strife that seems always threatening to tear apart that region of the world. Read just a little bit about foods of the Middle East and you soon discover a fascinating phenomenon: specialty after specialty, from *baba ghanoush* to *felafel, shawarma* to *tahini* is likely to be claimed as a definitive native dish by more than one culture. This bespeaks the region's ancient roots, and the influence of the traders who crisscrossed this land for centuries on their journeys between Asia, Africa, and Europe.

What are the culinary characteristics that unite this diverse and often unsettled part of the world? You'll find an abundance of sun-ripened vegetables, including eggplants, bell peppers, and tomatoes; the pungent flavors of onion and garlic, tantalizing spices such as cumin and chili peppers, and lively herbs such as oregano and mint; luscious lashings of fruity olive oil and smooth, rich sesame paste; and generous servings of lamb from the fields and fresh fish from the surrounding seas. Close your eyes, take a bite of the cuisine, and you'll be instantly transported to the Middle East.

**Baba ghanoush** "Harem girl," as it's called in Lebanese, captures the voluptuous, seductive nature of this popular dish, a cold puree of smoky-tasting roasted eggplant, garlic, lemon juice, olive oil (extra-virgin, of course!), *tahini*, and sometimes a touch of yogurt. You'll find it served as a dip to start meals throughout the Middle East.

**Falafel** This dish is widely popular in the Middle East, regardless of political boundaries. It is so often consumed tucked inside pita bread along with salad greens and a peppery *tahini* sauce that I've seen it referred to as an "Israeli hot dog." Still, *falafel* seems more an authentically Arabic phenomenon to me. A puree of boiled chick peas, *burghul* (cracked wheat), garlic, onion, cumin, parsley, and other seasonings is shaped into bite-size balls and deep-fried, resulting in a treat that is temptingly crunchy on the outside, tender and steaming within. You can enjoy *falafel* as a finger-food appetizer, too.

**Fattoush** Literally "moistened bread," this popular Lebanese salad consists of cubes of toasted bread tossed with chopped summer vegetables—tomatoes, bell peppers, cucumbers, and green onions—along with lots of chopped fresh mint and parsley. Olive oil and lemon juice form the dressing that provides the moisture.

**Felafel** See **Falafel**.

**F'ul medammes**

Egypt's national dish is loved, and eaten regularly, by people of humble and exalted means alike, and you'll find it on breakfast tables, hawked by street vendors, and featured on the menus of fine restaurants. What could have such broad appeal? Only an earthy, sustaining, and flavorful preparation that starts with a small, purple-hued variety of broad beans, which are boiled with lentils until tender and then mashed with olive oil, lemon juice, and garlic.

**Kibbeh**

I must thank my dear friend Suad (the most cosmopolitan person I know, since she was born in Bogota, Colombia to Lebanese immigrant parents, then came to New York after college and married Irish-American John McCoy) for not just giving me my first taste of this classic Lebanese meat-and-grain appetizer or entrée but also teaching me how to make it. High-quality raw lamb (I like to use tenderloin) is pounded together with *burghul* (cracked wheat), onion, lots of fresh mint, olive oil, and other seasonings. Eat the paste raw (scoop it into little lettuce leaves) and you have *kibbeh nayyeh*. Or cook the *kibbeh*, either by shaping it into balls and patties destined for the deep-fryer or by layering it with a mixture of ground lamb and pine nuts, then baking it. Similar dishes with similar names may also be found in the region, including Jordanian *kobbah* and Iraqui *kubbah*. I've also seen cooked forms of *kibbeh* made, though infrequently, with beef, chicken, or fish.

## **Eating** by hand

One of the great pleasures of traditional family-style dining in Arab countries is that food is often served and eaten communally from a platter in the center of the table, covered with flatbread, mounded with rice, and heaped with fragrant roasts or stews of lamb. Individual eating utensils aren't used. Rather, each person picks up bites of food by hand, conveying them from fingers directly to mouth. If you ever have the opportunity to eat this way, remember that in Arab culture the left hand is considered unclean so you should only use your right hand for eating.

**Shawarma**

*Shawarma* stands are easy to spot wherever hungry people gather in public in the Middle East. In fact, you're just as likely to smell them before you see them, as the scent of well seasoned cooked beef or lamb fills the air. Mixtures of ground beef and lamb, seasoned with garlic and spices, are packed in prodigious quantities around a large vertical spit to form a giant column-shaped roast. It slowly revolves in front of a glowing gas or electric heating element that cooks the outermost layer, which the stand's attendant shaves off with a sharp knife onto waiting pita bread. The customer's garnishes of choice—including chopped tomato, onion, cucumber, *tabbouleh*, and garlicky yogurt sauce—are added, and the whole gloriously messy sandwich is then eaten. Some stands might also offer chicken *shawarma*.

**Shishlik**

This is the widely popular, very simple Israeli style of kebab. Cubes of beef or lamb are seasoned with garlic, salt, pepper, and olive oil, threaded onto skewers, and then cooked over a hot fire.

## Sufganiyot

Their name derived from a Greek word meaning "fried and puffed," these Israeli jelly-filled doughnuts are a staple of Hanukkah, since that holiday's celebrations center on dishes cooked with oil. This tradition commemorates the one-day's supply of oil that burned miraculously for eight days and nights when the ancient temple in Jerusalem was rededicated.

## Tabbouleh

Thanks go again to Suad McCoy, who also taught me to make *kibbeh,* for introducing me to this classic Lebanese salad. Earthy, nutty-tasting steamed *burghul* (cracked wheat) is tossed with plenty of chopped fresh parsley and mint, onions, green onions, tomatoes, olive oil, and lemon juice. Especially the way Suad makes it, *tabbouleh* is one of the simplest-tasting, healthiest, most addictive dishes I know, a perfect appetizer or accompaniment to roast or grilled meat, poultry, or seafood.

## Tahini

Pulverize toasted sesame seeds and they release their rich oils, which combine with the fine solid particles to form luxuriously smooth *tahini* paste. Throughout the Middle East, you'll find it used on its own or combined with other ingredients as a condiment, a dip, or a dressing. Without it, dishes like *baba ghanoush* or *hummus* (see **Greece and Turkey** chapter) would be nowhere near as voluptuous. Its contribution is recognized in Middle Eastern restaurants by the fact that the latter of those two appetizers is often called *hummus bi tahini.* Take the sesame paste on its own, season it with garlic, salt, and lemon juice, thin it with a little water, and you have a wonderful dip called *tahini taratoor.*

## "They tried to kill us. We won. Let's eat!"

**The title may puzzle you, until you learn the joke to which it's a perfect punch line: "How do you summarize every Jewish holiday?" Jewish holidays do, indeed, seem to center on food to inordinate extremes—as do Jewish gatherings of any kind.**

Truth be told, this sidebar could almost more accurately be included in the European chapter, since so many of today's definitive Jewish foods developed among the religion's communities in central and Eastern Europe. Yet, Jewish cooking is also a phenomenon unto itself, and although many of its dishes are similar to German, Russian, or other traditional European cuisines, they are also distinct from those, and have comfortably made the trek to restaurants in the Middle East along with settlers in the Jewish homeland. So why not include it near modern-day Middle Eastern specialties of Israel?

**BAGEL** This central European bread is roughly the size and shape of a doughnut—an individual-portion ring-shaped roll with a hole in the middle. What gives the bagel its distinctive glossy surface and chewy texture is the fact that after the yeast-leavened wheat dough has been shaped, it is boiled before baking. The popularity of bagels today owes much to the incredibly varied way in which they can be flavored. Most traditional are plain "water" bagels and richer tasting egg bagels. Brown pumpernickel-dough bagels are also popular. Before baking, the dough may be crusted with sesame seeds, poppy seeds, coarse salt, or slivered onion. Modern bagels can travel much further afield, into flavors such as blueberry or pizza, which can sometimes seem like aberrations to traditionalists.

**BLINTZ** Derived from the Russian word *blini*, this favorite Sunday brunch dish starts with a thin egg-batter *crêpe*, generally wrapped around a filling of sweetened curd cheese to form a tidy bundle that may be either pan-fried in butter or baked in the oven. Sometimes fruit or jam, such as seedless raisins or cherry preserves, are included in the

## "They tried to kill us.
We won. Let's eat!"

filling, and the finished *blintzes* are traditionally served with a dollop of sour cream. Inventive modern cooks often get creative with their *blintz* fillings, including savory versions that might incorporate potatoes, fish, meat, or poultry. For that reason, lots of diners have gotten into the habit of specifying "cheese *blintzes*." But doing so, observed Jewish-American humorist Leo Rosten in his classic *The Joys of Yiddish*, "once would have sounded as redundant as 'wet water.'"

**CHOLENT** Late on Friday afternoon, before the Jewish Sabbath begins, Orthodox homemakers assemble the ingredients for this traditional casserole: dried beans, chunks of lamb, beef, or chicken; broth; and seasonings. On the way to Sabbath eve services, they would customarily drop off their covered casseroles at the town bakery, where the *cholent* would slowly cook in the oven's dying embers, leaving a rich, satisfying, savory dish that could be picked up on the way home and eaten without having violated the restriction against doing any work on the Sabbath.

**GEFILTE FISH** When I got my first-ever goldfish as a child, I very responsibly put the miniature castle and colored gravel in the bottom of its new bowl and filled it with tap water. Moments before I was about to pour the fish from its plastic bag into the bowl, my mom dipped her fingers into the water. "This is too warm!" she exclaimed. "You want to turn it into *gefilte* fish?" The name stuck, and Gefilte the goldfish lived a long, happy life in cool waters. I share this story because it dramatizes first that *gefilte* fish is a poached dish, and second that it's a commonly held point of reference for most Jews. The Yiddish term comes from the German *gefült*, meaning stuffed,

# "They tried to kill us.
We won. Let's eat!"

describing how in early forms of the dish, a fish fillet was filled with a coarsely pureed mixture of white-fleshed fish (such as pike or carp, the latter a distant cousin to my Gefilte), matzo meal, egg, onions, and seasonings. Today's version, however, does away with the fish fillets. The fish puree mixture alone is shaped into single appetizer-portion oblongs. These are poached or baked, then eaten hot or, more often, cold along with a pungent sauce of grated horseradish mixed with vinegar, salt, pepper, and often beet juice to give it a bright red color. *Gefilte* fish is the appetizer most commonly served at a Passover *seder.*

**GRIBINIS** One of my fondest childhood memories of my father's mother, my *Bubbe* Zelda, was when she'd take over the kitchen in our home when she and my grandfather visited from Chicago. She'd make chopped liver, which called for copious amounts of rendered chicken fat (*schmaltz*). She'd prepare this by slowly cooking in a pot the lumps of solid fat from chickens along with a chopped onion. When all the fat had melted and was sizzling hot, she'd strain it through cheesecloth. What was left behind was *gribinis,* crispy golden-brown little cracklings of connective tissue and onion that we'd eat as a snack.

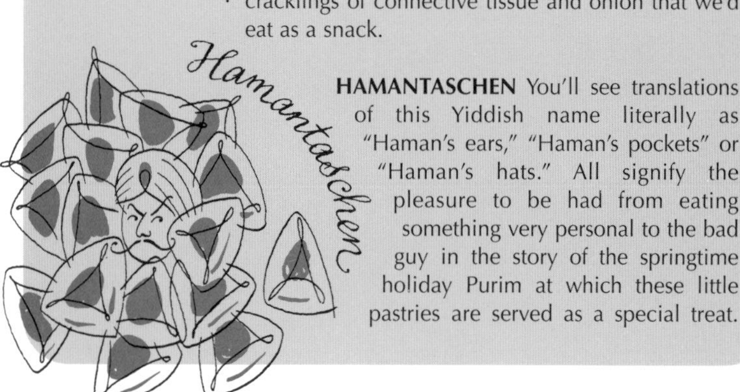


**HAMANTASCHEN** You'll see translations of this Yiddish name literally as "Haman's ears," "Haman's pockets" or "Haman's hats." All signify the pleasure to be had from eating something very personal to the bad guy in the story of the springtime holiday Purim at which these little pastries are served as a special treat.

## "They tried to kill us.
## We won. Let's eat!"

Resembling a triangular shortbread cookie or yeast-leavened sweet Danish dough, they are shaped into a triangle with an open pocket at the center containing a sweet filling. Haman, incidentally, was an evil adviser to the king of ancient Persia who tried to persuade that ruler to exterminate the Jews before the king's Jewish wife, Esther, tipped him off to Haman's plot and saved her people. Typical fillings for *hamantaschen* include a sweet poppyseed paste, pureed prunes, and various fruit jams.

**KASHA VARNISHKES** Popular among Jews of Russian heritage, this "*kasha* with bowties" consists of the earthy, pleasantly sour-tasting buckwheat groats known as *kasha,* cooked with egg, sautéed onion, chicken broth, and bowtie-shaped pasta. Robust and satisfying, the dish may be eaten on its own as a humble meal or served alongside roast or braised meat or poultry.

**KISHKE** Also spelled *kishka,* and sometimes more delicately referred to as "stuffed derma," this name literally means "intestines." Originally, intestine casings (often replaced nowadays by baking paper) used to hold and shape a very flavorful, satisfying stuffing-like mixture of mashed barley, flour, rendered chicken fat, onions, garlic, minced carrot, and seasonings. First boiled and then baked, the *kishke* is served in slices as a side dish to roasts or, less often, as a very filling appetizer. And you don't have to eat the casing.

**KNISH** The ultimate Jewish dumpling, this can be as big as a baseball or softball. A knish is a rolled-out piece of wheat dough wrapped around a filling of oniony mashed potatoes, meat, or *kasha. Knishes* may be baked or deep-fried.

## "They tried to kill us.
We won. Let's eat!"

**KREPLACH** Resembling a giant, malformed *ravioli*, this popular dumpling is usually found floating in a bowl of chicken soup. It is made of a simple wheat-flour dough filled with a peppery, oniony stuffing of finely chopped beef or corned beef, which is simmered until chewy and tender.

**KUGEL** This casserole-like oven-baked pudding comes in both sweet and savory forms, both of which are generally cut into squares and served as a side dish along with roast or braised meat or poultry. The most common form is a noodle, or *lockshen, kugel,* in which wide egg noodles are combined with beaten eggs, raisins, sugar or honey, and sweet spices before baking. Savory potato *kugel* combines shredded potato with eggs, flour, onion, and salt. During the Passover holiday, when unleavened bread and other flour products are forbidden, you'll find both sweet and savory *kugels* prepared with matzo. There's something comforting about eating any kind of *kugel,* which has a dear, almost precious quality. This probably explains why spoiled girl children in the Jewish community of South Africa are referred to as "kugels."

**LATKES** Since the celebration of Hanukkah features food fried in oil (including *sufganiyot*), symbolizing the one night's worth of oil that, in a central part of the Hanukkah story, kept the eternal light burning for eight nights in the rededicated temple of Jerusalem, this shallow-fried or deep-fried potato pancake is traditionally associated with that late-fall/early-winter holiday. But the central European Jewish specialty is actually available in delis year-round, as an accompaniment to main courses or as a filling lunch (or even breakfast or brunch) dish in its own right. You'll find three basic kinds, all bound by

## **"They tried to kill us.** We won. Let's eat!"

beaten egg, maybe a little matzo meal, and seasoned with chopped or grated onion, salt, and pepper. Those based on mashed potato have the most tender exterior. Those based on finely grated raw potato have a little more substance to them. My favorites are those made with shredded potato. The liquid given off by shredding is drained away and mixed with the other ingredients. This yields ultra-crisp pancakes full of rich flavor and texture. Traditional accompaniments are sour cream and apple sauce.

**LOX** This Jewish type of smoked salmon tends to be more thickly sliced and somewhat oilier than the paper-thin sliced smoked salmon you might find in some high-end restaurants. Which is just the way it should be: a much less refined, more primal cured fish experience. *Lox* (the name comes from the German *lachs,* for "salmon") may be chopped and mixed with scrambled eggs and sautéed onions to make a popular deli breakfast dish called, prosaically, *lox,* eggs, and onions. But its apotheosis is found when it tops a toasted bagel half (onion, poppy seed, or sesame seed for me, please, toasted well, and give me both halves) that has first been generously *schmeared* with cream cheese. Add a squeeze of lemon, maybe some slivered red onion or chopped chives, a grind of black pepper, and you have one of the great brunch treats. You also have the makings of one of the most cornball puns imaginable, uttered in Jewish delis wherever English is spoken: "How do you keep your bagels from being stolen? Put *lox* on them!"

**MATZO** Turn to *Exodus 12:30-39* for the story of how the children of Israel were expelled so quickly from ancient Egypt that they didn't have time for their bread dough to rise, sweeping it up unleavened

## "They tried to kill us. We won. Let's eat!"

in their haste to leave. Having escaped, they baked that unleavened dough to make the first matzo. The thin, crisp wheat crackers are still enjoyed year-round but are the only bread to be eaten during the Passover holiday that commemorates the exodus from Egypt.

**MATZO BALL SOUP** The ultimate Jewish comfort food, so-called matzo ball soup is actually rich chicken broth featuring one or more matzo balls, spherical dumplings made by mixing crushed matzo meal with beaten egg, salt, chicken fat or oil, and a little water. The mixture is chilled until firm, then shaped into balls that are simmered in water to cook them before being added to the soup. The eternal debate among lovers of matzo ball soup is "fluffy" versus "chewy," that is, whether the matzo balls are light as air (well, figuratively speaking) or so dense that they have their own gravitational pull. My son and I opt for the latter, my wife for the former. Fortunately, I'm the one who makes the matzo balls in my family.

**MATZO BREI** An old college friend of mine once overheard a famous orchestra conductor order this in a deli as "*matzo brie*," as if it combined matzo and the creamy French cheese pronounced "bree" instead of the popular pronunciation, "bry." Whatever you call it, think of it as Jewish French toast, a mixture of broken matzo pieces, beaten egg, salt, and pepper, pan-fried in melted butter and served for breakfast in heaping platefuls. Some delis will get all frou-frou on you and give you cinnamon sugar or apple sauce to garnish each bite to taste. I've even seen some get too literal with my analogy and offer (gag) maple syrup with it. For my money, the best accompaniment is a good preserve such as strawberry jam or orange marmalade.

## **"They tried to kill us.**
## We won. Let's eat!"

**PASTRAMI** This popular Jewish deli meat is made from beef brisket cured with coarse salt, garlic, black pepper, juniper berries, and other spices before being steamed to tenderness and sliced for sandwiches on rye bread. Good pastrami should pack a powerful punch of flavor, not least from the garlic, which allows me to quote one of my favorite old New York Jewish sayings: "A nickel will get you on the subway, but garlic will get you a seat."

**RUGELACH** One of the most popular treats from the Jewish pastry kitchen consists of bite-size, roughly crescent-shaped pastries made from a dough enriched with cream cheese or sour cream and filled with a mixture of nuts, raisins, and cinnamon, or with chocolate chips or jam.

**TSIMMES** "Don't make such a *tsimmes*!" You might hear a Jewish grandmother speak those words forthrightly in response to needless fuss, bother, or a messy situation. The term comes from these delightfully jumbled sweet-and-sour vegetable side dish, the most common of which combines carrots and dried apricots, moistened with such liquids as wine, orange juice, or lemon juice. (I once made what I called a "tropical *tsimmes*" for Passover, replacing the apricots with chunks of dried pineapple and papaya, adding shredded coconut and chopped macadamia nuts, and moistening the whole thing with pineapple juice.) Like many Yiddish words, this one is derived from German: *zum* ("to the") and *essen* ("eating"), perhaps touching on the humble contribution *tsimmes* makes to the pleasures of consuming the beef brisket or roast chicken it often accompanies.

# Dining in Asia and the Pacific

# China

Gone are the days when phrases like "going out for chop suey" or "getting a plate of chow mein" summed up the experience of dining Chinese style. A combination of increasing emigration from China, greater freedom for foreign visitors to journey within China, and ever-growing sophistication among fearless gourmets everywhere has led to a vast array of Chinese dining options, waiting for you to experience.

## DEMIGODS OF THE KITCHEN?

*"Our lives are not in the laps of the gods, but in the laps of our cooks."*

LIN YUTANG (1895-1976)

The following entries highlight some signature dishes found both in Chinese restaurants everywhere and also in those featuring the cuisines of specific Chinese regions. To help you navigate your way through any Chinese meal, however, it helps to have a grasp of the basic characteristics of that nation's regional cuisines.

China's southern regions are the home of some of the nation's best known cooking, particularly Cantonese style from the city of Canton, thanks to the simple geographic fact that the city was an easy port of embarkation, far from the capital of Beijing, for people heading off to seek better lives elsewhere. Cantonese cooking is light, simple, and flavorful, known for such specialties as *char siu*, steamed seafood dishes, and stir-fries such as monk's vegetables. You'll also find in this part of China, as well as elsewhere in the country, some of the world's best noodle shops, where skillful cooks cook noodle dishes—and sometimes make the actual noodles fresh before your eyes, pulling and folding, pulling and folding an elastic ball of dough until it miraculously transforms into a skein of slender strands—as well as plump meat-stuffed dumplings for hungry lunchtime crowds. Another one of the most popular of Cantonese styles of eating is the morning-to-midday snack known as dim sum, a treat particularly popular in palatial restaurants floating on barges docked in Hong Kong's harbor.

The coastal provinces of Shanghai and Fukien both feature soy sauce as a seasoning in many of their dishes, along with rice-wine vinegar and sugar in the former and fermented shrimp paste in the latter. Soy's mahogany-brown color leads to the designation red-cooked, applied to many such dishes, including the ample seafood featured along the coast. Meat dishes tend to be satisfyingly rustic; witness beggar's chicken and lion's head as two fine examples.

Inland China gives the world two of the fieriest versions of Chinese cooking, both featuring hot red chili peppers: the cuisines of Hunan and Szechwan provinces. Joining that distinctive seasoning are others which create a medley of bold seasonings that make the cuisines of inland China such crowd-pleasers: garlic, ginger, and onions. You'll find them all at work in such signature dishes as hot-and-sour soup and *kung pao*.

Northern Chinese cooking is generally regarded as the nation's most aristocratic, centered as it is on the Mandarin dishes of the old imperial court of Beijing. You'll find dishes that gain their distinctive, subtle-yet-rich character from rare delicacies, such as bird's nest soup and shark's fin soup. When it comes to starchy staples, wheat comes into play almost as much as rice, most notably in the thin pancakes that accompany dishes presented with great ceremony, particularly Beijing duck. Further north still in Mongolia, you'll find food reflecting the traditionally rugged outdoor life of the region, with distinctive communal dishes like fire pot and Mongolian barbecue.

Whichever of China's diverse regions you choose to explore through food, you'll find one truth prevails: In this part of the world, meals however grand or humble are meant to be shared—the more people the merrier—reflecting a fundamental joy of living in human society.

**Ants climbing a tree**

How can you resist a dish so charmingly named, especially once you know that no insects are involved? The "ants" in question are actually bits of stir-fried ground pork, in a sauce seasoned with garlic, soy sauce, ginger, and often Chinese salted black beans. The barklike section of tree is, in fact, a bed of tender bean threads or rice sticks. It's real comfort food, and you can almost imagine some Chinese parent long ago coaxing a child with a sense of macabre humor to eat by describing dinner in just this way.

**Beggar's chicken**

Imagine someone so poor he can't even afford a pot in which to cook his meals. So he scrounges a scrawny chicken; or, more desperate still, he purloins one—hence the oft-repeated opening line of the traditional recipe, "First, steal a chicken." Then he smears it with wet clay scooped up from the ground, and roasts it in an open fire. That's how folklore from the Hangzhou province would have you believe this regional specialty got its start. Despite such humble origins, beggar's chicken today starts with a plump hen marinated in rice wine and fragrant spices, stuffed with mushrooms, bacon, and bamboo shoots, then wrapped in aromatic lotus leaves and clay and roasted in the oven until the bird is done and the clay has formed a hard pottery shell. At table, the pottery is broken with a mallet to reveal the most tender, succulent chicken imaginable.

**Bird's nest soup**

Unlike ants climbing a tree or lion's head, there's no poetic metaphor intended in the name of this classic dish. It really is made from the nests of swiftlets, which the small birds compose from delicate strands of saliva-dissolved seaweed. Simmered in chicken broth with finely chopped chicken, the nests dissolve, contributing sublime body and subtle flavor to the finished soup. It is considered a delicacy by gourmets and is recommended for the delicate stomachs of children and the elderly.

**Bok choy**

Literally "white vegetable," this loose-leafed Chinese cabbage is a popular ingredient in both steamed and stir-fried dishes.

**Char siu**

Chinese roast pork is made by marinating tender pork loin in a mixture of rice wine or sherry, soy sauce, garlic, five-spice powder, and other seasonings. Then the meat is glazed with honey and oven-roasted hanging vertically on hooks. You'll find the meat served cut into thick bite-size slices in many restaurants, as well as appearing in stir-fries, fried rice and noodle dishes, and as the most popular of the fillings for the dim sum known as *bao*.

**Chop suey**

An American-Chinese invention dating back to the mid-19th century, its name meaning "chopped bits," this is a rather bland stir-fry of inexpensive vegetables, especially bean sprouts, mixed with beef, chicken, pork, or shrimp, which most likely evolved as a way for entrepreneurial immigrants to introduce their foreign cuisine to wary Americans. You won't find it in restaurants in China; and, fortunately, it's becoming harder and harder to find in Chinese restaurants in the United States nowadays.

## **Duck in** all its glory

For more than a millennium, Beijing duck, prepared in the grand style of the imperial capital, has been one of the great glories of the Chinese kitchen. A special type of duck was eventually bred specifically for the dish, with plump, meaty breasts and thin skin.

Before a duck is roasted, air is pumped underneath its skin to separate it from the meat, after which the skin is doused with boiling water, glazed with a malt-sugar syrup, and left to dry. While the duck hangs in a hot oven to roast, its body cavity is filled with water. The result is ultra-tender, moist meat complemented by mahogany-brown, crispy skin.

Traditionally, squares of that skin are served first to diners, who wrap it at the table in thin wheat pancakes along with bean paste and thin strips of cucumber and green onion. Then the carved meat is presented, to be eaten with the same garnishes either in the pancakes or in small baked sesame-crusted buns. Nowadays, however, most restaurants serve skin and meat together, the crispy skin making a perfect companion to the succulent meat and other accompaniments.

Only the grandest restaurants specializing in Beijing duck will also still offer one or both final courses of the traditional presentation. This includes a stir-fry of the remaining duck meat with vegetables first, and lastly a fragrant soup made from the duck's bones, afloat with the final fine scraps of meat from its carcass.

**Chow mein**

Literally "fried noodles," this is a stir-fry of Chinese egg noodles (see **Notable Chinese noodles**) and thin strips of vegetable and meat, poultry, or seafood. Chow mein may be served either as a starchy side dish in a Chinese menu, or eaten on its own as a casual one-dish meal.

**Cloud ear fungus**

Found growing on trees, and also known as "tree ear fungus," these delicate dark mushrooms do indeed look like tiny ears. You'll usually find them dried and packaged in plastic bags. They're reconstituted in water before cooking in such dishes as monk's vegetables, hot and sour soup, or *mushu,* in which they add more texture—at once slightly crunchy and slippery—than flavor.

**Congee**

Also sometimes called *jook,* this thick, savory porridge is made from ground rice. You'll find it offered in the morning and at midday along with dim sum in many Chinese restaurants, garnished with pungent morsels like ham, dried shrimp, salted fish, or thousand-year egg.

**Drunken prawns**

In this popular preparation, fresh steamed shrimp are served simmering in a fragrant broth based on Chinese rice wine, flavored with ginger, soy sauce, dried scallop, sesame oil, and other seasonings. Some traditional recipes, a touch brutal for some diners, begin with shrimp meeting their fate with a preliminary swim in the wine.

**Egg foo yung**

This is one of those dishes that stands as a cliché of Westernized Cantonese restaurants. A giant deep-fried or pan-fried pancake-style omelet of beaten eggs, soy sauce, and a little cornstarch, it is shot through with bean sprouts, onions, and bits of Chinese barbecued pork, shrimp, or chicken, then served topped with a gloppy cornstarch-thickened brown sauce. In fact, the dish has authentic roots in a traditional Shanghai preparation featuring egg whites and finely chopped ham or chicken. The name, incidentally, roughly translates as "blossomed eggs," perhaps a reference to the floral appearance of the original dish so named.

**Fire pot**

A specialty of Mongolia, and sometimes preceded by that regional name, this main-course soup is named for the utensil in which its is both cooked and served at table: a small brazier heated with charcoal or some other fuel, with a central funnel-shaped chimney encircled by a ring-shaped basin filled with simmering broth. Presented alongside it are various platters covered in thinly sliced meats, poultry, or seafood and vegetables. Guests pluck food items of their choosing from the platters and immerse them in the broth to cook, then retrieve them, dip them into one or more of various soy-salty, sweet, tangy, or spicy sauces, and eat them. Finally, cellophane noodles or bean threads are put into the pot to soften, and the broth and noodles are served as a soup course.

**Five-spice powder**

If you see this term connected with a Chinese dish, you'll know it features a traditional Szechwan seasoning made by combining ground cinnamon, cloves, fennel seeds, star anise, and spicy red Szechwan peppercorns. The resulting flavor will present a complex combination of spicy and sweet savors.

**Hoisin**

Soybeans are the basis for this widely used condiment and seasoning, which looks like a slightly runny paste, with a dark brown color and a salty, savory, sweet taste.

# **Little bites** that touch the heart

**You'll find the Chinese term dim sum translated variously as "touch the heart," "delight the heart," or similar such phrases. All aim to capture the simple fact that this morning or midday Cantonese-style meal composed of myriad small dumplings served with tea is one of the most pleasurable ways to start the day with family and friends.**

In its most traditional form, dim sum are enjoyed in a large restaurant with tables spaced far enough apart to allow servers to steer large carts filled with food back and forth, stopping when guests hail them. Some heated carts carry stack upon stack of small interlocking baskets containing just-cooked morsels of steamed dim sum such as *bao, har kow,* or *siu mai.* Others might be devoted to a single specialty still sizzling on a built-in griddle, such as pot stickers. Still others carry shelves displaying individual plates of hot-from-the-kitchen items like sliced *char siu,* deep-fried *wontons* or spring rolls, or just-baked *dan taat.*

The procedure for enjoying such a meal to the maximum is simple. First, gather together as many family members or friends to come along as you can, because the more people you have, the greater variety you'll get to enjoy. Dim sum restaurants tend to have lots of large tables to accommodate just such ample parties. Once everyone is assembled and tea has been delivered to the table (along with hot mustard and chili sauce for dipping to taste), just flag the next cart down and ask to see what's available. The classics mentioned below are a good starting point, but don't be shy; ask to see what's available, and the server will uncover and display the top basket in each stack, usually offering explanations of what fillings contain. You might find an odd surprise, too, such as braised chicken feet or steamed tripe; try them if you're so inclined. Most baskets or plates contain three or four pieces, so order enough of each dish that appeals to give each person at your table a taste or two. Then, wait for the next cart and repeat the process until everyone is satisfied.

And don't worry about your table being buried in an ever-increasing clutter of plates. Each cart-pusher will usually make a mark on an order form that stays on your table, on which columns or rows signify differently priced dim sum (they're all amazingly inexpensive). As baskets and dishes are emptied, runners will generally clear them away, while the record of how many you took remains on the table, ready to be totted up when your meal is over.

**BAO** Sometimes referred to by the plural *baozi*, these are steamed fist-size buns of ever-so-slightly sweet, fluffy white, yeast-leavened wheat dough, stuffed with either chopped pieces of the barbecued pork called *char siu* bound with a thick mixture of hoisin sauce, oyster sauce, and soy sauce, or with chopped roasted or braised chicken meat, sometimes mixed with mushrooms. Before eating a *bao* (also sometimes spelled *bow*), be sure to peel off the small square of paper that keeps its bottom from sticking to the steamer. Occasionally, you'll find baked versions.

**CHEUNG FUN** Served on small oval platters covered with metal lids, these are long rolls of soft steamed rice noodle wrapped around a filling of *char siu*, shrimp, or beef. Just before serving, they're splashed with some soy sauce and a little sesame oil.

**DAN TAAT** Even if you're just starting your dim sum meal, snare a plate of these if you see them going by before they get snatched up by others! A sweet, tender egg custard is baked inside bite-size, ultra-flaky, rich-tasting, light pastry shells, to make a traditional Chinese dessert surprisingly reminiscent of fine European pastry.

**HAR KOW** Translucent, pleated white noodles made of wheat starch enclose these crescent-shaped steamed dumplings filled with chopped shrimp, pork fat, and bamboo shoots.

## **Little bites** that touch the heart

**JIAO ZI** A favorite to celebrate spring but available year-round, these tiny crescent-shaped steamed or boiled dumplings, a specialty of northern China, have a filling of minced pork, ginger, green onion, shredded cabbage, soy sauce, and sesame oil. As an old saying goes, "Nothing is more delicious than *jiao zi*." See also **Pot stickers**.

**NOR MI GAI** Generous fist-size portions of sticky rice are mixed with delicious tidbits—including bits of sausage and ham, shrimp, chicken, and mushrooms—then wrapped inside individual lotus leaves and steamed in a basket. Unwrap a hot leaf and enjoy the tender, steaming mixture, scented with the essence of the lotus leaf; but don't eat the leaf!

**POT STICKERS** Take a basic *jiao zi* dumpling and, instead of boiling or steaming it, put it in a heavy skillet and cook it first with oil to brown it on one side; then add water or broth and cover the pan to let the dumplings finish cooking by steaming. The result is a morsel at once crispy and juicy, with the descriptive name of "pot stickers" (despite the fact that the oil actually keeps them from sticking most of the time).

**SIU MAI** Sometimes spelled *shao mai*, these bite-size steamed dumplings are generally filled with a minced mixture of shrimp and pork, enclosed in an open drum-shaped noodle wrapper and crowned with a sprinkle of tiny carrot dice.

**WONTON** Small, square, thin wrappers of wheat flour dough are wrapped around a filling of minced pork, chicken, or shrimp. For dim sum, *wonton* are usually deep-fried and served with a sweet-and-sour sauce. You'll also find simmered *wonton* afloat in chicken broth to make *wonton* soup.

## **California invents** the Chinese fortune cookie

For many Westerners, the fortune cookie—a thin sweet wafer folded twice into a shape resembling a small coin purse, thus enclosing a slip of paper containing a whimsical fortune or saying—epitomizes the Chinese dining experience as a special little treat to end the meal. Few folks know, however, that the fortune cookie is not really Chinese. Depending on which source you choose to believe, a decision that most likely depends on whether you favor southern California or northern California, the treat was invented either in 1920 by Los Angeles Chinatown restaurateur David Jung; or not by someone Chinese at all but rather Japanese designer Makoto Hagiwara, who reputedly served them at his teahouse at the 1915 Panama-Pacific Exhibition in San Francisco.

So, don't be surprised by the fact that you're unlikely to be served fortune cookies to end your meal when traveling and dining in China. Almost anywhere else in the world, however, you're likely to enjoy them, especially in Chinese restaurants in the cookies' true homeland, the United States.

**Hot and sour soup**

A specialty of the Szechwan province, where it's known as *suan la tang*, this robust soup combines all of that region's signature flavors: spicy red or green chilies and black pepper (the "hot") and tangy white vinegar (the "sour"), along with rich chicken broth, shredded roast duck and pork meat, sliced mushrooms including a crinkly variety known as "cloud ears", bean curd, bamboo shoots, soy sauce, and sesame oil, plus sliced green onions floating atop each bowlful.

**Kung pao**

The hot dried red chilies of Szechwan province lend a hint of fire to this stir-fry. The name pays tribute to Ting Pao Ts'en, governor of the province in the final years of the Qing Dynasty, during the late 19th and early 20th century. Chili paste, bean paste, vinegar, and roasted peanuts complete the flavor profile, and the featured protein could be chicken (a favorite), shrimp, meat, or even tofu. Beware of eating the pieces of dried chili themselves. They can unexpectedly take your breath away with a single bite.

**Lion's head**

From Shanghai, these large pork meatballs fragrant with ginger, green onions, rice wine, and soy sauce are typically served atop a bed of shredded Chinese or Napa cabbage. Let your eyes go unfocussed, apply a generous dose of whimsy, and you just might think that a meatball resembles the noble head of the King of the Beasts, and the cabbage its mane.

**Ma po dofu**

One of the great bean curd preparations of China, this dish has spread to other Asian countries as well, particularly Japan, where you'll find it served as a topping for plates of rice or bowls of noodles. Small cubes of soft bean curd (*dofu*) are quickly cooked in a sauce of ground pork or beef, onions, garlic, ginger, black beans, chilies, green onions, soy sauce, bean paste, and hot peppercorns. The humble dish carries a humble name, the "*ma po*" referring to a pockmarked street-vendor grandmother who reputedly first created the dish hundreds of years ago.

**Mongolian barbecue**

In a variation on stir-fry (see **Stir-fry: Chinese fast food**), thinly sliced meat, poultry, or seafood and copious amounts of vegetables are quickly cooked together on a large, flat iron or steel griddle, then served with sesame-crusted buns, noodles, or rice. Mongolian barbecue restaurants are now widely popular outside of China, enjoyed for the casual, buffet-style service, in which guests pile their own selections of raw vegetables and proteins into bowls, add their seasonings of choice, including soy sauce, sesame oil, hot chili oil and paste, garlic, ginger, rice vinegar, lemon juice, green onions, cilantro, and other assertive flavors. They then behold the spectacle of their individual creations being cooked before their eyes and whisked back into a clean bowl.

**Monk's vegetables**

Also sometimes referred to as "Buddha's Delight," this dish gets both of its names from the fact that Buddhist monks are vegetarians. A wide assortment of stir-fried or braised vegetables such as this—the contents may vary, but are likely to include broccoli, cabbage, carrots, snow peas, bean sprouts, bamboo shoots, various mushrooms, onions, and whole ears of baby corn, along with cubes of plain or fried tofu for the requisite protein—ensures a well balanced diet. Non-vegetarians known that, ordered as part of a Chinese meal, this provides a wonderfully varied side dish.

**Mushu**

Also spelled *moo shu*, this specialty from northern China has its origins in economic necessity. It is a great way to stretch small scraps of precious protein. Today, fine restaurants routinely feature it because, well, it's delicious and fun to eat. Shredded pork, chicken, or beef (or chunks of shrimp or, for vegetarians, cubes of tofu or no protein at all) are stir-fried with shredded cabbage, cloud ear fungus, tiger-lily buds, green onions, beaten egg, soy sauce, and rice wine. The steaming mixture is presented along with a separate platter of warm, thin wheat-flour pancakes and a bowl of hoisin sauce. Guests prepare individual servings, smearing a pancake with hoisin before spooning in the *mushu* mixture, then fold them closed and eat them by hand. Beware: these do tend to drip, so eat them leaning forward over your plate, not reclining with the bundle over your clothing.

**Red-cooked**

This term describes a coastal-style dish cooked slowly with a plenty of soy sauce, which imbues the seafood, meat, or poultry with a deep reddish-brown color and an earthy sweet savor.

**Shark's fin soup**

Let's make one thing clear: you're unlikely to think, "Hmm, so this is what shark tastes like," when eating this popular soup. In fact, you'll think you're eating a particularly rich, gelatinous chicken soup seasoned with ginger, onion, and rice wine, then garnished with bits of chicken, crabmeat, or ham. That suave, gelatinous quality resembling thin transparent noodles in every spoonful: there's your shark's fin. You'll find the soup on the menus of upscale restaurants, but it's most commonly found as part of special banquets, especially for Chinese weddings.

**Sizzling rice soup**

Ingenious Chinese cooks long ago found the perfect way to make use of the browned, crispy crust that forms on the bottom of a potful of rice left on the heat too long. Indeed, they now prepare the recipe expressly for this recipe by spreading cooked rice on baking pans and crisping it up in the oven. The roughly broken-up cakes of rice then go in the bottom of a tureen or individual serving bowls, into which hot soup—usually based on chicken broth with meat,

## **Notable** Chinese noodles

The Chinese may not, in fact, have introduced the Venetian merchant adventurer Marco Polo (1254–1324) to pasta. Evidence suggests it evolved in Italy as well. Nevertheless, for millennia the Chinese have enjoyed and developed noodles in many forms. Keep an eye open for opportunities to enjoy these three notable forms of Chinese noodles.

**BEAN THREADS** Also known by such descriptive names as "cellophane noodles" or "glass noodles," and called *fun see* in Cantonese, these delicate, transparent strands are in fact made from a dough of mung-bean starch. Sold dry, they are soaked in warm or hot water to soften them before use in soups, braises, and stir-fries.

**EGG NOODLES** The *mein* of *chow mein* refers to long, fresh noodles. They range from the thinness of Italian angel hair to the thickness of fat spaghetti. They are made from a dough of wheat flour and eggs.

**RICE STICKS** Referred to phonetically in Chinese as some variation on *mee fun,* these noodles are made from rice flour. Varying in size from thin threadlike strands to narrow or wide ribbons, they are cooked either by boiling, which turns them snowy white; or by deep-frying, becoming a golden-brown, crispy nest for stir-fries or braises.

seafood, and vegetables, although hot and sour soup may also be used—is ladled. When the soup makes contact with the hot, crispy rice, a loud sizzling noise issues from the bowls—usually making every head in the restaurant turn, and causing guests to decide that they want the sizzling rice soup, too.

**Thousand-year eggs**

Timorous diners who fear a seafood equivalent of road kill should rest reassured that, though the cooks of Shanghai might believe this dish looks like the popular tree-scampering rodent, there is no resemblance whatsoever in looks or taste. A whole fish, usually sea bass, is cleaned, and its head is removed but reserved. The fish's filets are cut from the bone and deeply scored but left attached to the tail. The entire fish is dusted with flour and deep-fried. Arranged on a platter along with the cooked head, the fish is then doused with a sweet-pungent sauce and served.

**Tiger-lily buds**

Also known as "golden needles," these slender little yellow-orange strips barely bigger than a needle are the dried buds of the tiger-lily flower. They're a traditional ingredient in hot-and-sour soup and in other dishes, including the stir-fried mixture wrapped up in pancakes to make *mushu*, in which they contribute mostly pleasantly chewy texture along with just a hint of pleasantly sour, tangy flavor.

**Velvet**

See this term applied to a main ingredient—usually chicken or shrimp—in a Chinese menu description and you'll know it means the ingredient has been finely ground, mixed with egg whites, cornstarch, and ice water to form a soft paste, and then gently cooked, usually by steaming. Served with a mild sauce usually based on broth and seasoned with ginger, the resulting ingredient will, indeed, be as soft as velvet on the palate.

## **Fill it up,** please!

Many guests in Chinese restaurants feel lost when the time comes to request a refill on their pot of tea, especially during the swirl of dim sum service (see **Little bites that touch the heart**). Pay attention, however, to Chinese guests dining nearby, as I did years ago but way too long after my first-ever dim sum experience, and you'll notice that there's a simple system to signal for a refill. Just lift off the lid of your teapot and replace it sitting at a jaunty angle across the opening. Chinese waiters are trained to notice this indication that your teapot is empty. You'll be surprised by how quickly action is usually taken.

## **Stir-fry:** Chinese fast food

Without a doubt China's most-used cooking method, stir-frying is a technique born of humble origins. For the poor, cooking fuel was usually scarce; so, too, was protein. Inventive cooks many centuries ago, then, devised a way to maximize minimal fuel and protein. A hemispherical iron or steel pan, known as a *wok*, could heat up quickly and evenly over the most meager of fires. Small pieces of food cooked very quickly by being rapidly stirred around inside the capacious cooking surface. Meanwhile, finely sliced, diced, or minced to cook quickly along with its accompanying less expensive vegetables, a small amount of meat, poultry, or seafood could be stretched creatively to feed a large family.

# Japan

It is amazing to consider that a cuisine as subtle and complex as that of Japan should come from such a small island crowded with so many people. Shift your perspective, however, and you realize that, just as they have for art, poetry, performance, and so many other aspects of the culture, Japan's almost claustrophobic geographical and historical conditions have led its chefs to turn inward. They have found beauty in foods prepared and presented with exquisite austerity and have a deeply philosophical regard for the changing seasons and for using ingredients at their absolute freshest.

That emphasis on freshness can be seen in its greatest glory in the category of food preparation now most revered by lovers of Japanese food worldwide: the raw seafood dishes called sushi and *sashimi*. You'll also find it in the ceremonial precision of a Japanese meal, as seen in the many carefully defined categories of Japanese menu items, from *aemono* to *menrui*, *nimono* to *yakimono*. At its ultimate, you can witness it in the ceremonial meal known as *kaiseki* (see **Kaiseki: Japan's tasting menu**).

Whether you enjoy such exalted and refined cuisine, or just a quick meal of *udon* or *soba* noodles or a *donburi*, you'll find good Japanese food an almost contemplative experience, one well rewarding of exploration.

## FOOD AS FOUNTAIN OF YOUTH?

*"For each new food you sample, your life will be 75 days longer."*

JAPANESE PROVERB

## **Japanese** chopsticks etiquette

Most Japanese restaurants, including sushi bars, provide guests with disposable wooden chopsticks in narrow paper envelopes. These eating utensils lead to an unwitting breach of etiquette for many Westerners, who invariably split the sticks apart and immediately start rubbing them vigorously against each other (as if trying to start a fire) to remove any splinters. Doing so is actually a mild insult to restaurateurs, implying they offer inferior-quality utensils, and Japanese parents routinely scold children who commit such gaffes. The polite thing to do after splitting the sticks is to pick off any visible splinters discreetly with your fingertips.

**Aemono** The general category of salads in a Japanese meal, usually vegetable or seafood with a dressing based on *miso, tofu,* or sesame seed paste.

**Agemono** The general category of deep-fried foods, among which *tempura* is the best-known example.

**Chawan-mushi** Steamed in individual bowls, this mixture of *dashi* broth and eggs forms a delicate, savory custard in which each spoonful reveals a delicious tidbit: shrimp, chicken breast, or slices of *shiitake* mushroom. A slice of lemon usually tops each serving, adding an extra nuance of pleasing flavor.

**Daikon** This giant white radish appears again and again in Japanese meals: grated and stirred into soy sauce to use as a dip for *tempura*; sliced and marinated with vinegar, soy sauce, and sugar to make delectable pickles; or cut into chunks and simmered in all kinds of braises and stews. When cooked, the radish tastes surprisingly mild; raw or pickled, it has a pleasant, not-too-spicy bite.

**Dashi**

The basic cooking broth of Japanese kitchens is made by briefly simmering together flaked dried bonito fish and dried kelp, then straining the liquid to yield a slightly briny, rich, clean-tasting essence. *Dashi* is used as the foundation for braises such as *sukiyaki* and is encountered most frequently as part of the dipping sauce served with *tempura*.

**Donburi**

In this broad category of casual lunchtime meals based on a large bowl of rice with an assortment of toppings, the name of the topping with the suffix *don* (for bowl) composing the designation for the particular dish you order. Thus a rice bowl topped with the deep-fried pork cutlet called *katsu* becomes a *katsudon*.

**Gohanmono**

The category for all rice-based Japanese dishes.

**Menrui**

The Japanese culinary category covering all noodle-based dishes.

**Miso**

Soybeans and rice are fermented to produce the fundamental sour, salty, sweet source of flavor and body in Japanese cooking. The type of soybeans used and their proportion to the rice results in two basic *miso* categories: milder *shiru* or white *miso*, which is actually tan colored; and stronger-tasting *aka* or black or red *miso*, which is reddish-brown in color. Dissolve a spoonful of either in hot water and you have *miso* soup at its most basic. A soothing bowlful is often served at the start of a meal garnished with cubes of tofu, bits of seaweed, green onions, and other garnishes. It is used as a pickling agent, too; or slathered on eggplant, mushrooms, seafood, meat, or poultry before cooking.

**Nimono**

This term refers to all manner of simmered dishes in Japanese cooking.

## **It's okay to slurp:** Japanese noodles

Walk into any of the many noodle shops you'll see in Japanese cities and towns, especially in areas around train stations where commuters like to grab a quick meal, and you'll witness—or, rather, hear—a deafening array of loud slurping noises, as diners suck up large bowlfuls of hot noodles. For those of us in the West who were long ago taught by our parents to eat *quietly*, this phenomenon can bring about a feeling of remarkable unease at first. But soon it begins to make perfect sense.

Making noise while eating noodles is not frowned upon in Japanese society. For one thing, it shows true enjoyment of the gustatory sensations offered by hot meat broth, chewy and earthy-tasting noodles, and assorted toppings ranging from roast pork to *wontons* to sliced fish cake, sautéed bamboo shoots to sweet corn to diced tofu. On a more practical level, slurping also cools the steaming-hot noodles as they're being eaten. The generous amount of air taken in with each mouthful prevents painful burning of the lips and mouth.

Frankly, I've tried slurping noodles to cool them, and it may be a skill best acquired in childhood, because the noodles are still generally too hot for me and require that I blow on them before inserting them into my mouth. But the flavors of a good bowl of noodles in broth do make me eat with more audible gusto than usual.

When ordering noodles in a Japanese restaurant or noodle shop, look for these basic choices:

**RAMEN** These long, thin wheat noodles are prized for their chewy texture, mild earthy flavor, and an attractive yellow color. This traditionally comes from potassium carbonate or sodium carbonate but also may be due to some egg yolk combined with the wheat, water, and salt that make up the dough.

## **It's okay to slurp:** Japanese noodles

Good freshly made ramen served up in a restaurant are a world away from the dry, sometimes cardboardlike noodles sold under that name in just-add-water instant *ramen* packets. The name *ramen,* by the way, evolved from one of the Chinese words for wheat noodles, *mein.*

**SOBA** With a rich, earthy, ever-so-slightly sour flavor, these buckwheat noodles are about as thick as spaghetti. They're served either hot in broth or cold with a soy-based dipping sauce. Look, also, for green-tinted soba flavored with tea, an especially refreshing-tasting treat.

**SOMEN** These thin wheat noodles are more of a summertime delicacy and are usually served cold or even iced, with a dipping sauce.

**UDON** Thick and chewy, these pale white wheat noodles, which can be round or square in cross-section (if hand-cut) may be eaten hot in broth or cold with a dipping sauce.

**Shabu-shabu**

The onomatopoeic name for this cooked-at-the-table specialty suggests the sound made as guests (or a server) swish thin slices of meat or chicken, or pieces of seafood, back and forth in a pan of simmering water to cook them quickly before dipping them in a choice of sauces and eating them. Most restaurants specializing in *shabu-shabu* feature adjustable burners set into the table for each group of guests. Vegetables, noodles, and tofu also typically simmer in the liquid, to be plucked out and enjoyed as accompaniments.

**Shioyaki**

In this traditional cooking method, seafood or other ingredients are completely enclosed in coarse sea salt, then broiled or grilled before the now-hardened crust is broken free and discarded. The food inside turns out moist and, surprisingly, seasoned to perfection.

**Shirumono**

This broad category of Japanese soups ranges from simple creations such as *dashi* and *miso* soup to more elaborately creative bowlfuls.

**Sukiyaki**

This widely popular dish is actually inaccurately named. The *suki* part of its name (pronounced "skee") refers to the iron blade of a traditional plow, the *yaki* to broiling, an easy-to-imagine primitive way for a farmer to cook beef. Today, however, the dish is actually composed of thinly sliced beef, vegetables, tofu, and noodles simmered together in a soy sauce-based broth, simmered at the table or in the kitchen.

**Sunomono**

Literally "vinegared foods," this category of bright-tasting little salads is served as a refreshing accompaniment to other savory dishes, or as an appetizer. The most common form features thinly sliced cucumber, sometimes spiked with bits of shrimp or crab.

**Tempura**

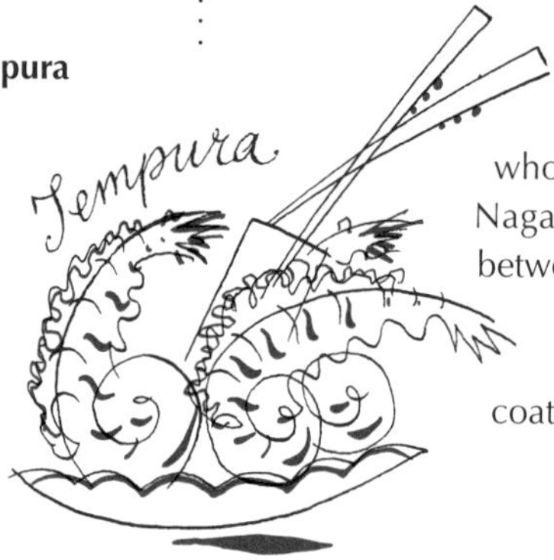

Tempura

Give credit to the Spanish and Portuguese traders who came to the port of Nagasaki after trade opened between Japan and the West in the 19th century for Japan's unique variation on batter-coated, deep-fried shrimp.

## **Kaiseki:** Japan's tasting menu

So the story goes, centuries ago Japanese Buddhist monks would carry a hot stone (*seki*) inside the kimono pocket (*kai*) as a meditative object to help them endure fasting. That term came to refer poetically to a contemplative meal originally served ceremonially with tea but now evolved into Japan's most exalted of dining occasions.

A *kaiseki* meal strictly adheres to seasonality, starring the freshest vegetables (in its original form, it was strictly vegetarian) and seafood, often garnished with other seasonal objects such as leaves, blossoms, or seedpods. The better to highlight their just-harvested, peak-of-season perfection, *kaiseki* ingredients are simply prepared in small portions, with the progression of perfect little bite-size, artfully presented dishes forming a sort of edible poetry akin to a Japanese *haiku.*

Today, top Japanese restaurants and chefs will often showcase their talent by offering special *kaiseki* menus. These can be pricey, but the meal can be one of the most exquisite dining experiences imaginable.

**Tsukemono**

This refers to the wondrous world of Japanese pickles, which may be cured in salt or in vinegar with a range of seasonings including chili flakes and soy sauce. You could almost compose a satisfying meal from Japanese pickles alone, choosing from fresh cucumber slices; sliced carrot or *daikon*; shredded cabbage or ginger; and even tiny whole pickled plums or apricots. (I was once served just such a meal by a Moroccan artist who lived in London and was, for some obscure reason, possibly an old romance, obsessed with Japanese pickles.)

# **At the** sushi bar

**Absolutely fresh raw fish, artfully cut into bite-sized pieces that highlights the color, flavor, and texture, and then served on its own as *sashimi* or combined with a small cylinder of cold seasoned rice as sushi, is one of the pinnacles of Japanese style dining. But few non-Japanese know how to get the best out of their local sushi restaurant.**

Don't succumb to the Western habit of ordering a platter of assorted sushi, all brought to your table at once. For the most authentic, highest-quality experience, sit at the sushi bar and communicate directly with the sushi chef. Ask him what is best today, and start by requesting whatever mild white fish he recommends. Then order each new item only after you've finished the previous one: Eating sushi and *sashimi* is a logical progression of artful tastes, not a buffet for grazing.

To show you know what you're doing, keep a few tips in mind. Eat each piece in a single bite: that's the way the chef designs it to be eaten, to highlight the particular fish's color, texture, and taste. Don't dissolve the fiery green horseradish paste called *wasabi* in your little bowl of soy sauce for dipping, a move that overamplifies its flavor. Instead, dab a little onto your food with the tip of a chopstick. And eat the thinly sliced *gari*, pink pickled ginger, only to cleanse your palate between bites, not as a condiment for the sushi or *sashimi*.

A good sushi bar will offer many choices on any given day, always varying with what's in the market. Use the following as a guide to some of the basic choices; but always strike up a chat with your sushi chef to learn more!

**ABURAGE** Chewy little brown pouches of tofu skin that has been boiled in sweet sake and soy sauce before being filled with rice balls.

**AJI** Spanish mackerel.

**AMA-EBI** Sweet (meaning raw) shrimp.

**ANAGO** Cooked saltwater conger eel.

**CHIRASHI SUSHI** A bed of sushi rice topped with sashimi or other ingredients.

## **At the** sushi bar

**EBI** Cooked shrimp.

**FUGU** Blowfish. A delicacy in Japan, this requires strict licensing by chefs who prepare it because the fish's liver contains a neurotoxin that adds a thrilling tingle to the tongue when traces of it are present, but can be deadly if improperly prepared. This danger led to near-fatal consequences for Homer in the episode of *The Simpsons* entitled "One Fish, Two Fish, Blowfish, Blue Fish."

**FUTOMAKI** A large seaweed-wrapped roll, often containing an assortment of colorful Japanese pickles plus slices of *tamago.*

**HAMACHI** Yellowtail.

**HIRAME** Halibut.

**IKA** Squid.

**IKURA** Big pearly orange-pink beads of salmon roe.

**MAGURO** Tuna.

**MIRUGAI** Long-necked clam.

**NIGIRI SUSHI** Your basic sushi, consisting of sliced fish on an oblong of seasoned sticky rice.

**NORIMAKI** Sushi rolls, made by enclosing sticky rice and fish or some other filling in a wrapper of *nori,* dried seaweed. Popular choices include cucumber, pickled radish, spicy tuna, spicy yellowtail, larger rolls known as *futomaki* or *tazuna sushi,* and such Westernized combos as the Philadelphia roll (smoked salmon and cream cheese) and the California roll (tuna and avocado). After rolling, *norimaki* are cut crosswise into bite-size slices.

## **At the** sushi bar

**ONIGIRI** Big bite-size balls of steamed rice containing assorted stuffings.

**OTORO** Extra-rich fatty tuna.

**SABA** Mackerel.

**SAKE** Salmon. (Note that in the Western alphabet, the word "sake" refers to both salmon and Japanese rice wine. But those letters represent two different words, pronounced slightly differently in Japanese.)

**SHIRO MAGURO** Albacore tuna, often served slightly seared on the outside but raw in the middle.

**TAI** Sea bream.

**TAMAGO** Slices of cold, slightly sweet rolled omelet, served on sushi rice or plain, *sashimi*-style.

**TAZUNA SUSHI** Rainbow roll, a form of *norimaki* filled with multiple colors and flavors of raw fish.

**TEMAKI** Cone-shaped hand rolls, similar in ingredients to *norimaki* but served in single pieces resembling miniature ice cream cones.

**TOBIKO** Flying fish roe, tiny pink eggs that add a sweet flavor and pleasantly grainy texture.

**TORO** Fatty tuna.

**UNAGI** Cooked freshwater eel.

**UNI** Sea urchin roe, in clusters resembling small tongues the color of brown mustard, usually served atop an oblong of rice and wrapped in a collar of *nori*, dried seaweed. An acquired taste, it puts off many people with by its sometimes funky aroma and flavor. But the best sushi restaurants get absolutely fresh *uni* that has a bracing, sweet ocean flavor with hints of brine, nuts, and iodine.

## **Tofu:** the ultimate vegetarian protein

Whether you call it tofu as they do in Japan or *dofu* as the Chinese do, bean curd is a high-protein custardlike substance manufactured from soybeans and enjoyed as a primary source of protein throughout Asia. Widely available in supermarkets today, the cream-colored, water-packed blocks come five different consistencies, ranging from ultra-soft "silken" tofu to soft, medium, firm, and extrafirm. Different types are used for different cooking purposes, with harder tofus standing up to longer simmering or to stir-fry techniques, while the softer types might be seasoned lightly and cooked gently on their own.

Tofu doesn't have much of a flavor on its own. (A friend of mine once referred to it as "edible air.") That makes it a perfect vehicle of sauces and seasonings, which it absorbs readily, or a soothing counterpoint to spicier dishes in any Asian meal.

Beyond its culinary benefits, tofu—like all soy-based food products—is being proven by modern Western medical research to have health benefits as well. Not only is it rich in protein, low in fat, low in sodium, and completely lacking in cholesterol, but it also contains micronutrients that are being shown by study after study to help prevent or even reverse certain forms of cancer. But that's no news to Asians. As an old Chinese proverb goes, "Eating vegetables and *dofu* will keep you safe and well."

**Yakimono**

This general Japanese culinary category literally means "grilled things," though it also includes any meat, poultry, seafood, or vegetable seared in a pan or cooked under a broiler as well as cooked on a grill over a heat source.

**Yakitori**

Bite-size pieces of boneless chicken marinated in sweetened, ginger-scented soy sauce are threaded on skewers for this popular grilled Japanese snack food.

# India

First, you must know one thing about the foods of the Indian subcontent, which includes not only India but also Bangladesh, Pakistan, and the island of Sri Lanka. There is no such thing as a "curry" sauce. That term and concept arose from the era of the British Empire, when Western colonists used it in a relatively feeble attempt to grasp, with one word, the vast complexity of Indian cuisine.

**WHERE PRAISE IS DUE**

*"Sing their praises, those who give you food."*

INDIAN PROVERB

That which we in the West persist in calling "curry" is, in fact, a vast repertory of complexly seasoned stews, braises, and sauces from India's various regions. Each features its own particular blend of many different spices and herbs, such as (in no particular order other than alphabetical) cardamom, chilies, cinnamon, cloves, coconut, coriander, cumin, fennel, garlic, ginger, mint, mustard, nutmeg, saffron, tamarind, and turmeric. In addition, those same seasonings bring character to a wide range of other preparations, anything from the delicate *biriani* and other rice dishes to the fire-grilled category of foods known as tandoori.

A tour of India's regional kitchens reveals remarkable variety, ready to be sampled at various Indian restaurants worldwide. From the north come the aforementioned tandoori specialties. Western India and Pakistan is best known for foods that show the influence of the Portuguese and Middle Eastern Parsees who settled here, including the rich and fragrant braise referred to by the term *dhansak*. Vegetarian dishes abound in the Hindu regions of the south, where you'll find incredible variety in the various forms of *dhal* that are the primary protein sources, and be wowed by the single-person buffet-style presentation known as the *thali* (see **Thali: a meal on a platter**). Here, as in the island of Sri Lanka, seasonings can reach fiery hotness, epitomized by the non-vegetarian *vindaloo*. Seasonings in Bangladesh can be hot as well, with mustard seed and chilies bringing distinction.

More and more outside of India, you'll find restaurants that specialize in the foods of a single region of the subcontinent. Seek these out as opportunities to explore, in depth, a world of exciting, subtly yet boldly spiced, widely varied cooking styles far removed from generic "curry."

**Bhaji**

These bite-size, deep-fried appetizer fritters are made from a spiced batter of chickpea flour and usually feature slivered onions or sometimes other vegetables. They're served accompanied by chutney for dipping.

**Bhelpuri**

Stroll along the beach in Bombay, or through market streets of any Indian city or town, and you're likely to spot *bhelpuri* vendors. They toss together crispy puffed rice, crunchy chickpea-flour noodles, toasted lentils, roasted peanuts, chopped onion, cilantro, and sweet chutney to make one of the most satisfying snacks imaginable—a mind-boggling combination of snappy textures and salty, sweet, and sour flavors.

**Biriani**

India's main-course rice pilaf traces its history back to the Moguls of the 16th century. Saffron-scented basmati rice—with long, fluffy, nutty-tasting grains—is combined with tender pieces of lamb or other meat, chicken, shrimp or other seafood, eggs, and vegetables. The grandest *birianis* of them all will also be gloriously garnished, mounded on a platter and decorated with sliced hard-cooked egg, wedges of tomato, raisins, crispy fried onions and garlic, and—a true extravagance rarely found—strips of tissue-thin edible silver or gold foil. If your *biriani* doesn't come with a side sauce to moisten it, be sure to order a vegetable curry or *dhal* or a *raita* to spoon over or alongside each serving.

**Chapati**

The daily bread of India is an unleavened flatbread made from whole-wheat dough, rolled into thin pancakes and cooked on a hot griddle. Scraps are torn by hand to use as edible utensils or to eat alongside food forked or spooned into the mouth.

**Chutney**

Not so much one dish as a category of different preparations, this term applies to the many condiments served alongside—or sometimes used to season—Indian meals. You'll find dozens of them in restaurants, snack stands, and home kitchens: jamlike sweet ripe mango chutney or spicy green mango chutney; grated coconut-and-spice chutney; fresh mint chutney flavored with chilies, onion, ginger, and sugar; fluid sweet-sour tamarind chutney; chopped onion with chilies and cilantro; and many more. Presented at table in separate dishes or jars, the chutneys are spooned by guests onto individual plates to season each bite to taste, or for use as a dip for Indian breads such as *chapati* or naan.

**Dhansak**

Its name derived from the word *dhan*, meaning "wealth," in Parsee, the language of Indians of Persian ancestry, this rich-tasting, mildly spiced main dish features lamb or chicken chunks bathed in a puree of lentils with such vegetables as tomato, eggplant, onions, squash, and spinach, seasoned with cilantro and fresh green chilies and topped with crisply fried onion strings.

**Ghee**

One of the primary cooking fats of India, *ghee* is a close cousin to what cooks in the West call clarified butter, that is, butter which has been heated until it melts and the clear liquid butterfat separates from the milk solids. With those solids discarded, the remaining liquid fat will keep longer and can be used to cook foods at higher temperatures without burning. The difference between *ghee* and clarified butter, however, is that the *ghee* is cooked longer in the clarification process, acquiring a pleasantly nutty flavor and darker color.

**Hopper**

When I lived in London in the 1970s, this Ceylonese specialty became one of my favorite quick meals, perhaps because it strangely reminded me of the Mexican *huevos rancheros* I'd loved growing up in Southern California. A crispy, deep-fried, cup-shaped pancake is made from a batter of rice flour and coconut milk. Into the cup goes a poached or fried whole egg, over which you spoon your choice of sweet or, even better, spicy chutney. Break the yolk and start forking up bits of crispy pancake, rich and tender egg, and sinus-clearing garnish. Heaven!

**Idli**

A vegetarian specialty of southern India, this dish consists of little, spongy dumplinglike cakes made from rice and lentils that are soaked from several hours, ground to form a pasty dough, and then left to ferment overnight. Usually steamed, the *idli* may be served on their own with chutney or doused with a mild curry sauce.

**Keema**

This term refers in general to ground meat, usually lamb or beef, mixed with spices. *Keema* appears most often on menus as a filling for naan, though you'll also find it in richly spiced sauces, sometimes with vegetables added, to be spooned over rice as a main dish.

**Korma**

Also spelled *kurma*, this Mogul version of a curry is made by marinating and then gently simmering lamb fillet or chicken breast in a thick sauce of cream, yogurt, ground almonds or cashews, and sometimes pureed fruit. The result is an incredibly rich-tasting, tantalizingly spiced, ultra-tender main course with a thick gravy.

## **India's** best-loved kababs

**Whether grilled, broiled, or fried, cooked individually or on skewers, India's small pieces of meat find favor as both appetizers and main courses. Look for these popular menu choices.**

**BOTI KABAB** Lamb cubes marinated with yogurt and spices, then charcoal-grilled on skewers.

**NARGIS KABAB** Similar to an English Scotch egg, this starts with a whole peeled hard-cooked egg, which is completely enclosed in a spiced mixture of ground lamb, dipped in egg white, and deep-fried. Cut it open and, if you know the language, you understand why the dish is named *nargis*: It resembles the cup-shaped corona of a narcissus flower.

**PASANDA KABAB** Similar to Southeast Asian *satay*, this is prepared by cutting strips of lamb tenderloin, pounding them until thin, then marinating them with Indian spices before threading them on skewers and charcoal-grilling them.

**SEEK KABAB** A mixture of ground lamb, cooked yellow split peas, and seasonings is shaped into appetizer-size patties and shallow-fried in *ghee* or oil.

**TIKKA KABAB** Bite-size pieces of chicken, lamb, or seafood are marinated with yogurt, ginger, and spices, then slipped onto skewers and cooked in a tandoori oven.

**Lassi**

As thick as a milkshake, this yogurt-based drink is sometimes offered alongside an Indian meal, providing a cooling and soothing counterpoint to the spices. *Lassi* may be sweet, combined with pureed mango or other fruit; or salty, seasoned with a little salt and possibly some spices.

**Naan**

One of Indian cooking's most delicious breads is made from a soft dough combining wheat flour, eggs, *ghee*, sugar, salt, milk, and fresh cheese curds or yogurt. The dough is left to ferment, becoming puffy and developing a mild, pleasantly sour flavor. Generous single-portion flattened ovals of the dough are then slapped onto the inside wall of a tandoori oven, where they quickly bake up crusty and brown on one side, pale and puffy on the other, while gravity stretches them out to teardrop shape. Always try to order a naan alongside your main course, tearing off pieces to pick up bites of food or swab up sauce or chutney. Also watch for stuffed naans—especially those filled with caramelized onions or garlic, or with *keema*—which make excellent appetizers.

**Paneer**

This soft, mild fresh cow's-milk cheese is used in a wide range of Indian dishes. Cubed or crumbled and cooked on its own or with vegetables such as spinach or peas and spices, it makes a delicious side dish or, in vegetarian kitchens, a protein-rich main dish. You'll also sometimes find it mixed with spices as a stuffing for naan.

**Papadum**

Sometimes referred to by Westerners as the potato chips of India, these thin, crispy wafers contain not a jot of potato. Rather, they're made in factories from a paste of lentil flour, sometimes combined with chilies, pepper, or other seasonings. They are sold packaged as brittle disks about the size and thickness of a DVD or CD. Drop them in hot oil, however, and seconds later they've puffed up to two or three times their original diameter and are ready to eat. Many people enjoy them as a snack to start an Indian meal, dipping them into chutney or *raita*. Others eat them as a sort of cracker-bread alongside the main course. I sometimes take a third sybaritic option and crumble them into bite-size shards over a plate of curry and rice, adding a wonderfully crunchy texture to each bite.

**Paratha**

This rich, flaky, earthy-tasting Indian unleavened flatbread is made from whole-wheat flour. The dough is repeatedly rolled out into a small circle, brushed with *ghee*, folded, and rolled out again until it is composed of multiple tissue-thin layers. Slapped onto a hot griddle slicked with *ghee* or oil, the bread is cooked on both sides until brown, to be served for breakfast (where it's a favorite in northern India) or with lunch or dinner. Look, too, for *parathas* that, before cooking, are stuffed with a thin layer of spiced pureed potato, spinach, or cauliflower.

**Raita**

Now I can finally share this pun in print rather than boring my wife with it yet again: I've always wanted to publish a softcover book on Indian cooking and title it *Paperback Raita*. Okay. I feel better now. Actually, *raita* is one of the standard dishes of almost any Indian meal. In its most basic form, it's plain, tangy yogurt combined with enough shredded cucumber and sometimes chopped onion to become almost a loose salad, then seasoned with maybe a hint of salt, pepper, and ground coriander or cumin. More elaborate *raitas* may include tomato or other raw or cooked vegetable, and you'll even find *raitas* based on such fruit as pineapple, banana, or grapes. However it's composed, *raita* sort of serves as the fire brigade of an Indian meal, offering a cooling (sometimes fire-extinguishing) counterpoint to hotter dishes on the table.

## **Tandoori:** barbecue, Indian-style

One of the most accessible styles of Indian cooking, instantly appreciable to any Western lover of barbecue, tandoori gets its name from a giant jar-shaped oven of northern India known as a tandoor. Foods to be cooked are first marinated in spiced yogurt. An intense fire is then built in the bottom of the oven and and the food is suspended on long hooks from the top lip of the tandoor (or, in the case of the bread called naan, simply slapped against the oven's side, to which it adheres). The intense ambient heat combined with the live fire simultaneously and quickly roast and barbecue the food, giving it a pleasant charred, smoky surface while maintaining a juicy interior.

**Samosa**

Served as an appetizer or snack, these small triangular pies are made from a fine wheat-flour pastrydough folded around a spiced filling. Usually based on potatoes or other vegetables they sometimes also feature meat or chicken.

**Tikka**

Describing one of the most popular forms of tandoori treats, this refers to any boneless kebabs cooked on skewers in the tandoor. Most popular of these is chicken *tikka*, consisting of plump cubes of skinless chicken breast meat. Lamb *tikka* is also widely enjoyed, and so are *tikkas* of fish fillet or whole shelled jumbo shrimp. I've also enjoyed chunks of succulent lobster tail cooked *tikka*-style; and one year, when I was on my own in London at Christmas, I even had turkey *tikka* in an Indian restaurant I found open.

**Vindaloo**

When I lived in Britain in the 1970s, I sometimes witnessed a peculiar spectacle of British manhood. After the pubs closed on Friday or

## **Thali:** a meal on a platter

If you're in an Indian restaurant and having trouble deciding what you'd like to order, opt for a *thali* if the menu offers it. The term applies both to the serving platter—a wide, circular, rimmed tray (usually made of stainless steel), companioned by half a dozen or more little palm-size bowls that fit neatly inside it along its rim—and the meal served with it.

While a *thali* will most often be vegetarian, you'll sometimes find it offered in non-vegetarian versions as well. In either case, each of the individual bowls is filled with a small serving of a different specialty from the kitchen—different kinds of *dhal* and various vegetable (or meat, chicken, or seafood) dishes, variously seasoned, some saucy, some more dry. Once filled, these are arranged around the inside of the tray. In the tray's center, the chef will mound a generous serving of rice—whether plain steamed fragrant long-grain basmati rice or a mildly spiced pilaf made from it.

A bread such as *chapati, roti,* or naan comes alongside, as do assorted chutneys. Then you go to town on this single-platter tasting menu, trying each dish in turn and then combining forkfuls in however many different ways bring you contentment.

Saturday nights, packs of blokes out for an evening would head for the nearest Indian restaurant. There they would order the hottest *vindaloo* and see who could eat an entire order without breaking a sweat or reaching for the beer or water glass. At once searingly hot and mouth-puckeringly sour, a *vindaloo* sauce—whether it features shrimp, chicken, or meat—is prominently seasoned with hot mustard seeds, garlic, onions, vinegar, and tamarind. Properly prepared, it can be as subtle as it is bold.

# Other Asian Cuisines

At the risk of not giving them the due they so richly deserve, space restrains me from providing separate, extensive listings for other Asian cuisines. China, Japan, and India have so dramatically taken hold of the world's fascination with Asian food that those of other countries in that part of the world have an uphill battle in gaining territory in the public's consciousness, retail space, and kitchens.

**COULDN'T PUT IT BETTER!**

*"Eating is a heavenly thing."*

KOREAN PROVERB

Clearly, the situation is changing. Thai restaurants have sprung up everywhere in the past few decades; so, too, are restaurants featuring Korean and Vietnamese cooking, including outstanding Korean-style tabletop barbecue places filled with fragrant smoke from marinated meats, poultry, and seafood; and Vietnamese noodle shops where you can enjoy big, steaming bowls filled with *pho* from morning to night.

No doubt Filipino and Indonesian will be the next big things; indeed, in my home city of Los Angeles, you can find outstanding Filipino restaurants now, catering to the large and prospering immigrant community, and I know of Indonesian *rijstaffel* restaurants that serve feasts almost as impressive as those you might find in Amsterdam. All such progress reflects waves of emigration from those countries to the West, as well as increased travel by Westerners to those parts of Asia.

For fearless gourmets, then, the cuisines of these countries are ripe territory for happy exploration. Please use the capsule descriptions of keynote cuisines in the listings that follow, along with more detailed explanations of some of their signature dishes, as a pathway by which you can begin your own gustatory or culinary journeys.

**Achar**

The Indonesian word for "salad," also found in Indian cuisine to describe a chutney pickle, refers to dishes many Westerners might view as pickles: mixtures of raw or cooked onion, carrot, cabbage, bell peppers, potatoes, and string beans mixed with vinegar, sugar, salt, fresh ginger root, and garlic, then left to steep for several hours. These are often served as side dishes or condiments alongside appetizers and main dishes.

**Adobo**

A signature dish of the Philippines, this stew of pork or chicken is liberally laced with vinegar, soy sauce, garlic, and black pepper, giving it a pleasantly sharp and pungent taste. In certain parts of the country, coconut milk might round its rough edges, and seafood or even beef might be the star ingredient.

**Banh chung**

These Vietnamese rice cakes are traditionally made by families to celebrate Tet, the new year. To make one portion, a generous helping of soaked sticky rice is filled with seasoned pork and green mung-bean paste, then snugly wrapped into a square parcel enclosed in bamboo leaves. Then the parcels are boiled until the rice is tender. The bamboo gives the rice inside a subtle green hue and pleasantly herbaceous flavor.

**Banh mi**

These are the signature sandwiches of the Vietnamese kitchen, a charming and delicious reflection of the nation's French colonial era. A large, soft French roll is split and spread with butter, mayonnaise, or pâté and sprinkled with *nuoc cham*, then stuffed with sliced ham or other cold cuts, fresh cucumber slices and carrot shreds, pickled daikon, slivered green onion, thinly sliced fresh chili peppers, and fresh basil and mint leaves.

**Bee bim bap**

This Korean one-dish meal features an oven-heated stoneware bowl filled with sticky rice and bits of meat or poultry and vegetables. A raw egg goes on top, and each guest stirs it into the bowl's contents, the heat of the food and the bowl serving to cook the egg. The result is like a cooked-at-the-table fried rice and is immensely satisfying.

**Bulgogi**

Sometimes referred to as Korea's national dish, these thin strips of beef marinated with soy sauce, garlic, ginger, sugar, green onion, and sesame oil are barbecued on tabletop grills in a style of service referred to as "Korean barbecue."

**Cha gio**

These slender Vietnamese egg rolls, about the size of an index finger, feature fillings of chicken or seafood, rice stick noodles, and shredded vegetables, rolled up compactly in an edible rice paper wrapper and then deep-fried. They're served accompanied by *nuoc cham,* a lively dipping sauce combining *nuoc mam,* lime juice, sugar, water, minced hot red chili, shredded carrots, and chopped peanuts.

**Chao tom**

One of Vietnam's most beguiling treats, this starts with a mixture of finely minced raw shrimp and raw egg whites, seasoned with *nuoc mam* and chopped green onions. The resulting paste is then molded around peeled lengths of fresh sugar cane and then grilled over a charcoal fire, to be nibbled right off the sweet-tasting stalks.

**Chap chae**

This simple stir-fry of finely shredded vegetables and meats tossed with noodles is a popular side dish in Korean meals.

## **Durian:** the world's most prized—and reviled—fruit.

If you count yourself among the most fearless of gourmets and you encounter "durian" on a menu, order it. But be prepared. It smells so horrible that some governments in Southeast Asia actually ban its transportation across international borders.

Why? Because, to many people durian, a tropical fruit that looks like a green football or rugby ball covered in spikes, bearing a remarkable resemblance to a medieval weapon, has the foulest smell imaginable. It is something akin to the ripest of cheeses or the sweatiest of athletic clothing left unwashed and untended in an unventilated storage locker for weeks. Try though durian aficionados might to disguise the fruit's aroma, wrapping it airtight in multiple layers of plastic and sealable bags, that aroma cannot fail to seep through, sending passengers and customs officials running for cover—and fresh air.

If that's the case, why does durian inspire such intense devotion? Some of it is attributable, no doubt, to the thrill that comes of getting past the funk just to eat it. But those who do (and, fearless though I may claim to be, I am not one who has) claim that durian has a sublime flavor. Others, though, have described the flavor as something akin to rotting flesh!

Durian

Be that as it may, you *will* find durian on some Southeast Asian menus. Its fans like the fruit fresh, but it can also be simmered with spices and coconut milk, or pureed and mixed with cream and sugar to make durian ice cream.

**Gado gado** Long ago, when I first tasted this as it was prepared for me by the adventurer/cooking teacher Copeland Marks (alas, now long departed), I started twisting the name of this Indonesian salad to call it "Oh God! Oh God!" That's how sublimely delicious it can be. An assortment of

## **Just call it** "fish sauce"

Used throughout Southeast Asia, the commercial condiment and seasoning known in English as "fish sauce," a term by which you'll see it labeled in ethnic markets and referred to on some menus, is known variously by such names as the Vietnamese *nuoc mam*, the Thai *nam pla*, and *patis* in the Philippines. Whatever term you use, and however slightly one might differ from the other, the sauce is fundamentally the same and used in similar ways.

Fresh anchovies or other seafood (in some versions, shrimp are used) are layered with salt in large barrels and left to ferment for about six months. During this time, they transform into a pungent, briny essence that is then drained off and bottled. Much like soy sauce, the fish sauce may be used as a seasoning for cooked dishes or as a table condiment to garnish individual servings to taste.

To those unfamiliar with fish sauce, it may seem unpleasant at first. Remember, though, that it's not intended to be eaten on its own, just as you wouldn't likely relish a straight spoonful of mustard or salt. Blended in with the other elements of a dish, it adds a pleasant, exotic extra dimension of flavor. For the best examples of this, witness the subtle impact in such widely loved dishes as Thai *tom yum* or the *nuoc cham* dipping sauce for Vietnamese *cha gio*.

raw or lightly cooked vegetables—including lettuces, spinach, carrots, string beans, cabbage, cucumbers, bean sprouts, and potatoes—are garnished with raw or fried bean-curd cubes, sliced or quartered hard-cooked eggs, *krupuk*, and crisply fried bits of onion and garlic. Then the whole thing is tossed with a warm dressing of peanut butter, coconut milk, chilies, and sugar. The overall effect is delicious, and not to be missed in any Indonesian restaurant.

**Goi Cuon**

These popular Vietnamese "salad rolls" consist of soft, edible rice-paper squares briefly soaked and rolled up around a filling of rice noodles, shredded carrots, cucumbers, and cabbage, bean sprouts, cubes of tofu, fresh mint and basil leaves, and cooked shrimp, pork, or chicken. The cold rolls are then generally cut in halves and served as a cool, refreshing appetizer along with a dish of Chinese hoisin sauce and *nuoc cham* for dipping.

**Guisado**

A Spanish word for "disguised" charmingly describes the transformation that takes place in the Filipino kitchen when chunks of beef or other meat or poultry are slowly braised with tomatoes, onions, garlic, ginger, and soy sauce. This is a true blending of East and West that reflects the history of the Philippines.

**Kaeng**

When you spot this term (also *gaeng*) on a Thai menu, you know it's a curry, usually made with red or green Thai curry paste.

**Kimchi**

Koreans dote on their pickles, and restaurants seem to vie to outdo each other in the number and variety they present as part of *panchan*, the array of small dishes accompanying rice and main courses. The best known of these is the pickle most often referred to by the term *kimchi*: mild white loose-leafed cabbage cut into squares and layered with salt, garlic, and red chili paste until it ferments slightly, almost like German *sauerkraut*, developing a tender-crisp texture and pleasing tang. Such *kimchi* can range from only slightly spicy to explosively hot, depending on the time of year and the cook, so sample with caution. You'll also find a wide array of other pickle offerings, including cucumbers, squashes, onions, radishes, carrots, and chilies, sometimes barely vinegary, sometimes heavily salted, sometimes made suave with Japanese-style *miso* paste, sometimes barely spiced, sometimes incendiary. Such more-robust winter-style *kimchis* are also complemented, in turn, by lighter, less salty, vinegary and even slightly sweet summer *kimchi* featuring such ingredients as cucumber, white radishes, beansprouts, and tender greens. A fearless gourmet samples them all before deciding on those that beckon to be finished off completely.

**Korean cooking**

Chilies, garlic, ginger, and soy sauce are four of the ingredients that set the bold taste parameters of cooking from the Korean peninsula. This cuisine shows the influence of nearby northern China and Japan but has its own distinctive character, evident in such robustly flavorful specialties as *bulgogi, bee bim bap,* and *kimchi.*

**Krupuk**

Buy a box of these in an Indonesian ethnic market and you might thing you'd stumbled upon poker chips: hard, brittle, and dull-looking, they are nowhere near being edible. But carefully drop a handle of *krupuk* in hot oil and in an instant they miraculously transform, puffing up and dramatically expanding into crisp, light, snack chips. A mixture of *manioc* flour and dried shrimp, they have a pleasant flavor that's like a slightly ocean-scented potato chip. You'll find them served with drinks, as an appetizer, or as a garnish for dishes such as *gado gado.*

**Kung jung shinsulro**

This Korean-style hotpot is a slowly simmered mixture of beef, seafood, and vegetables, traditionally presented at table in a heavy brass or cast-iron pot with rice and *kimchi.*

**Laksa**

This popular dish of Malaysia and Singapore features thin rice noodles in a lightly spiced sauce enriched with coconut milk and embellished with bite-size pieces of meat, poultry, or seafood, vegetables, and tofu.

**Larb**

A Thai salad of lettuce leaves topped with stir-fried minced poultry or meat seasoned with lime juice and chilies, this is also spelled *lab*.

**Lechon**

Crispy-skinned whole roasted pig, Filipino-style, shows the influence both in language and cuisine of the country's Spanish colonial past. It is generally served with a vinegary dipping sauce to counterpoint the rich meat and skin.

**Lemon grass**

Many people new to Thai cooking marvel at how much lemon is used in the cuisine, not knowing that what they're in fact tasting is a refreshingly acidic-tasting herb with a flavor remarkably close to that of lemon. The slender, tough green stalks of the lemon grass, which look similar to small, slender canes of bamboo, are peeled to reveal their more tender, pale-colored inner stalks, which are then crushed, sliced, or chopped to release their essence and added to simmering liquids or stir-fried mixtures. Generally, when you find pieces of lemon grass in a dish—they're likely to turn up, for example, afloat in a bowl of *tom yum*—you put them to one side rather than chew on them. This is especially the case if the cook started with dried pieces of lemon grass, which, though more widely available, do not deliver the same bright flavor as the fresh herb.

**Lontong**

Looking almost like cubes of snowy white tofu, this Indonesian rice cake is made by cooking white rice inside a closed cylindrical container.

As the rice grains expand and become tender, they compact into a solid cylinder. Unmolded, the *lontong* may be eaten hot or cold, whole or sliced, on its own or with chili sauce or peanut sauce, or even as a garnish for skewers of *satay*.

**Lumpia**

Filipino-style egg rolls, these are crisp little deep-fried cigar shapes in wheat-dough wrappers, filled with a peppery mixture of thin rice noodles and shredded vegetables and meats.

**Masaman**

Whatever the spelling, this refers to a particular type of Thai curry (see **Kaeng**) enriched by great lashings of coconut milk. Also spelled variously *massaman, musaman,* or *musman,* all are references to the Muslim influences in the dish.

**Mee krob**

One of the must-have dishes on any Thai menu, this consists of thin rice noodles fried until they're as crispy as breakfast cereal, then tossed with a sticky sweet-and-sour sauce and bits of meat and usually shrimp. Also sometimes spelled *mee grob*.

**Mie goreng**

Only slightly less common than *nasi goreng,* this popular Indonesian dish features small lengths of fresh wheat noodles in place of the rice.

**Nasi goreng**

While Indonesian restaurants in the West may feature this on their lunch and dinner menus, this popular version of fried rice is typically served for breakfast in the islands. It makes sense, too, since the dish employs leftover steamed rice and other ingredients from the night before. The rice is stir-fried in oil with generous amounts of minced garlic; chopped up chicken, meat, or shrimp; shredded cabbage; beaten egg; spicy tomato ketchup; hot chilies; and crispy fried shallots. Recipes vary, of course, from cook to cook.

**Pad See You**

This simple Thai dish of stir-fried noodles is simpler than the very popular *pad Thai,* but nonetheless deserving of respect. Fresh rice noodles are tossed with slices of meat, poultry, or seafood (marinaded in garlic, sesame, soy, and black pepper); maybe some broccoli; and a sweet-salty mixture of sugar, soy sauce, oyster sauce, and fish sauce. The resulting tangle has a deep brown color and a soothing yet complex flavor. The name is also sometimes spelled *pad siew*—though the former spelling always tempts me to punningly say, "Peekaboo, pad see you!"

**Pad Thai**

Literally "Thai fry," this is considered by many to be an essential on any Thai menu and, although it's a fairly basic dish, many Thai food aficionados consider it a bellwether of a restaurant's quality. Narrow ribbon-shaped rice noodles resembling Italian *linguine* are pan-fried in an aromatic soy-based sauce with chicken, pork, shrimp, beaten egg, and fried tofu cubes (vegetarian versions are also sometimes available), then garnished with fresh bean sprouts, chopped peanuts, and lime wedges to be squeezed over just before all the components are tossed together at table.

**Pancit**

This Filipino dish of fried rice noodles, shredded cabbage, carrots, and green onion, egg, and a mixture of such proteins as pork, chicken, and shrimp gets distinctive flavor from its combination of soy sauce, liberal freshly ground black pepper, and a squeeze of fresh lemon.

**Philippine cooking**

You'll find Spanish, Chinese, and Southeast Asian influences combining in the complex dishes of the Filipino kitchen, most evident in aromatic stews like *guisado* and the distinctive rice noodle dish known as *pancit.*

**Pho**

One way I can make sure you never forget the name of this Vietnamese main-dish soup is to share with you, in as G-rated a way as possible, the pronunciation guidelines given to me by a student of mine who'd lived and traveled extensively in Southeast Asia. "Say it like you would say...(and here, he spoke a very popular four-letter obscenity)...but without the 'k' sound at the end." There you have it: a mundane aide-mémoire for a soup of otherworldly goodness. First, a rich, clear meat broth is prepared using beef, vegetables, and such seasonings as star anise, ginger, cilantro, and *nuoc cham*. Then softened rice sticks are heaped in a large bowl. On top of it go proteins ordered by the guest, which can range from slices of cooked anise-scented stewing beef to tender bits of beef tendon or tripe to shreds of chicken or slices of fish cake or whole cooked shrimp or rings of squid; but, most prized of all, are tissue-thin slices of raw beefsteak. Finally, the steaming-hot broth is ladled in—which, in the case of the raw beef, cooks the ingredient in a flash. Sometimes sliced green onions, thinly sliced onion, or fried garlic may be floated in the broth as well. But that's not all. The bowl is presented to the guest along with add-it-yourself garnishes: bean sprouts to pile in, fresh mint and basil leaves to tear up and strew over the soup, and wedges of fresh lime to squeeze in; plus, condiment jars of hot chili paste and oil, chopped peanuts, chili-laced vinegar, soy sauce, and *nuoc cham*. In effect, you customize your serving to taste, then slurp it all up with a big soup spoon and a pair of chopsticks. The capital city of Hanoi is thought by many people to prepare the best versions of *pho*, which is why you'll sometimes still see this dish referred to as "Hanoi soup" rather than by the "ph" word.

## **Rijstaffel:** Indonesia's rice table feast

Why, you may ask, does an Indonesian feast go by a distinctively Dutch name? The answer traces back to Indonesia's past as a Dutch colony, and to the perfect understated name those European traders and settlers came up with to describe a feast of epic proportions: "rice table."

A typical *rijstaffel* consists, first, of bowls of steamed rice, presented to guests at the table, the more people the merrier. Then the other elements start arriving: platter after platter, filled with one flavorful specialty after another, from *satay, krupuk,* and *gado gado* to all manner of intriguingly spiced dishes of seafood, chicken, lamb, beef, pork, and vegetables, many of them laced with coconut milk, chilies, and peanuts.

The dishes keep coming long after you think the feast has ended—a veritable culinary bacchanalia. This may explain why, long after the end of the colonial era, it seems as if there are as many *rijstaffel* restaurants in Holland as there are in Indonesia. Who, you might wonder, finally colonized whom?

**Prik king**

Many a smutty witticism has been uttered upon finding this dish on a Thai menu. Get over it and enjoy this chili-spiked stir-fry of fresh string beans, often enjoyed as a vegetarian side dish and also elaborated to main-course status with the addition of meats, poultry, seafood, or tofu.

**Satay**

These skewers of marinated seafood, chicken, lamb, pork, or beef are served as an appetizer in Indonesia, Thailand (where you're more likely to see them spelled *sate* on a menu), and other Southeast Asian countries. Traditionally, they're served with a creamy, mildly spiced dipping sauce of peanut butter and coconut milk, as well as a small dish of cucumber-and-onion *achar*.

**Thai cooking**

If you aren't familiar with Thai food, think of it as a sort of light, clean-tasting version of southern Chinese cooking crossbred with that of India, only featuring fresh chilies, lemon grass, cilantro, garlic, shallots, basil, and mint in place of the latter's mostly dried spice blends. Look for such signature Thai dishes as *tom yum, pad Thai, prik king,* and *mee krob.*

## DON'T STOP

*"Eat until your lips protrude!"*

FILIPINO PROVERB

**Tom yum**

Thailand's popular "hot and sour" soup is a clear broth distilling the essences of lemon grass, lime juice, fresh green or red chili peppers, and fish sauce. Typical ingredients are whole fresh shrimp or bite-size pieces of boneless chicken, and small mushrooms or other vegetables.

**Vietnamese cooking**

Like that of Thailand, this nation's cuisine bears some resemblance to light southern Chinese cooking, only Vietnam has an even greater reliance on *nuoc mam* and lemon grass. Signature dishes include *goi cuon, chao tom,* and the huge bowls of steaming noodle soup called *pho.* You'll also see lingering influences of the French colonial past, most evident in the sandwiches called *banh mi.*

# Australia and New Zealand

In the early 1980s, American and British tourism to Australia skyrocketed thanks to a series of ads in which stereotypical Aussie male Paul Hogan, who went on to achieve Hollywood stardom as the character Crocodile Dundee, invited folks to come visit "the land down under," promising to "throw another shrimp on the barbie."

## MULTICULTURAL HERITAGE

*"Australian cooking...has strong roots in French technique, a little bit of a nod to our British heritage now and then with a bit of steak or kidney pie, but generally, it is a mixture of the Asian, the Greek, the Italian, and other influences."*

HELEN GREENWOOD, *Sydney Morning Herald*

Coming from the same twangy voice that had previously propelled sales of Foster's Lager, it further solidified stereotypes of Australian cuisine as a beer-fueled marathon of outdoor cooking.When you get right down to it, many a cuisine would be only too glad to suffer from such stereotyping, particularly in the wake of a culinary heritage—shared with New Zealand to the north—based on the worst clichés about the cooking of the mother country, Great Britain: soggy vegetables, stodgy baked goods, and meats cooked far beyond any lingering traces of juicy pink rareness. Add jokes about kangaroo steaks and bush tucker—typified by the roasted fat, plump whole ghost moth larvae known as witchitty grubs—and you have a formula ready to strike fear, and dyspepsia, into the heart of the most fearless gourmet.

When approaching food in Australia and New Zealand today, however, remember that the aforesaid are all clichés bandied about largely for the sake of humor. And more and more, the joke is actually on the self-proclaimed wits who continue to toss about quips about eating kangaroo or emu. In fact, when prepared in the kitchens of expert chefs, the meats of both the hopping marsupial and the big, gawky bird are proving to be not only deliciously flavorful and well suited to gourmet preparation but also surprisingly outstanding, low-fat sources of protein. Even cooks beyond the continent-nation are beginning to experiment with such native Down-Under meats, too, winning rave reviews for their innovations.

When considering the cooking of Australia and New Zealand, it's far more important to remember two key truths about the cooking of these southern hemisphere Pacific island nations. First, their old-fashioned traditional cooking, when done well, can be some of the most generous-hearted and satisfying comfort food imaginable, represented below in specialties from carpetbag steak to meat pies (remember, I said "when done *well*") to treats such as ANZAC biscuits and Pavlova.

What you won't see listed in the following entries, however, is actually what you'll find most exciting about the food of Australia and, to a lesser but nonetheless significant extent, New Zealand. Australia in particular is one of the world's leaders in so-called fusion cuisine, which takes the best of the world's culinary influences and marries them to the finest seasonal produce. Indeed, articles and books have been published (by Australian food experts, of course) making the claim that modern fusion cuisine was nothing less than an Australian innovation that chefs in other parts of the world subsequently emulated and called their own.

Whether or not such claims are strictly accurate, in Australia and New Zealand you will indisputably find outstanding examples of the cuisines of nearby Asia, especially Thailand and Vietnam, as well as the cooking of European immigrants, particularly from Portugal and from countries bordering the Mediterranean like Greece and Italy. Add the fresh produce of a fertile land, and abundant fresh seafood from waters surrounding the island nation, and you have some of the most exciting and innovative cooking to be found in the world today.

**ANZAC biscuits**

Named after the acronym for the Australia New Zealand Army Corps that fought heroically at Gallipoli and in other battles during World War I, these hearty oatmeal cookies were developed from an old Scottish recipe by women who wanted to send to their loved ones serving overseas treats that were not only as nourishing as possible but also capable of withstanding the long journey to them on supply ships. Before ANZAC was formed, they were known as soldier cookies, and to this day they're a sentimental staple.

**Carpetbag steak**

Taking its name from big old-fashioned valises sewn from squares of carpet, this Australian favorite starts with a thick raw beefsteak of excellent quality. A small, sharp knife is inserted horizontally along one edge to cut a pocket in its center, into which freshly shucked oysters are stuffed. Then the steak is grilled over a live fire. If you've got appetite enough, try to finish a whole one, though the steak is often cut crosswise into thick slices to serve several people.

**Damper**

The daily bread of Australia's pioneers and Outback ranchers (stockmen), this simple dough of white wheat flour, baking powder, and water was traditionally cooked on the glowing coals of an open fire, or only slightly more fastidiously in a cast-iron camp oven heated on the coals. The resulting bread, crusty on the outside and puffy and tender within, is best eaten soon after baking because it turns hard and dry very quickly.

**Hokey pokey** Let other nations have their chocolate, strawberry, or vanilla ice cream. In New Zealand, home to arguably the world's greatest consumers of ice cream, hokey pokey is the national flavor of choice. (Well, okay, boring old vanilla might maintain a slight edge.) Wacky though the name may sound, this mid-20th-century development by the Tip Top ice cream company is simply vanilla ice cream shot through with bits of buttery toffee candy.

**Kitchener bun** Patriotically renamed after Australian war hero Lord Kitchener between the 20th century's two World Wars, this is actually a version of the German-style jam- or cream-filled yeast-leavened doughnut known in central Europe as a Berliner.

**Lamington** Lord Lamington, who served as Governor of Queensland from 1896 to 1901, was honored with the creation of this popular Australian treat: big cubes of buttery sponge cake, coated with rich chocolate icing and then rolled in sugar and sweet shredded coconut. Reputedly, the cake came about when a young cook working for Lamington accidentally dropped some plain cake into a pan of chocolate, at which point the Governor suggested that she roll it in coconut to help keep the fingers clean when a piece was picked up and eaten.

**Meat pies** According to conservative estimates, each Aussie eats approximately 260 meat pies a year, whether made at home, bought hot from a bakery, picked up at a convenience store, ordered at the local pub, or consumed in the stands at a sporting event. A rich but simple pastry of flour, beef fat, and water encloses a mixture of cubed or minced meat, usually beef, generously seasoned with broth, onion, maybe a dash of Worcestershire

## **An Aussie food** slang lexicon

Some show the influence of London's Cockney rhyming slang. Herewith, a translation guide.

| | |
|---|---|
| **BARBIE** | Barbecue or outdoor grill |
| **BIKKIE** | Biscuit or cookie |
| **BREKKIE** | Breakfast |
| **BUG** | Short for Balmain bug or Moreton Bay bug, both species of small clawless crustaceans resemble small lobsters |
| **CHOKKIE** | Chocolate |
| **CHOOK** | Chicken |
| **CUT LUNCH** | Sandwich |
| **DEAD HORSE** | Tomato sauce |
| **DOG'S EYE** | Meat pie |
| **FLAKE** | Deep-fried shark fillet |
| **LOLLIES** | Candy or sweets |
| **MYSTERY BAG** | Sausage |
| **PAV** | Pavlova |
| **SANDO** | Sandwich |
| **SANGA** | Sandwich or sausage |
| **SNAG** | Sausage |
| **SPAG BOL** | Spaghetti with Bolognese sauce |
| **TUCKER** | Food |
| **YABBIE** | A species of freshwater crayfish |

**Talk to any Australian about food, and you might soon feel you're listening to a foreign language. The colorful style of speech found in the land down under can make it hard to decipher references to even the most familiar of foodstuffs.**

sauce, and some flour to thicken the gravy. This wholesome pie can be transformed into what is known as a "meat pie floater," especially in South Australia, where it's a customary offering of pie carts that ply the streets of Adelaide. Fill a bowl with thick, hot soup—split pea generally being the choice. Then, carefully float a freshly baked meat pie in the center, like a raft at sea. Finally, drizzle tomato sauce (a.k.a., tomato ketchup) over the pie. Ah, Australian culinary heaven!

**Pasties**

Close cousin to the meat pie, these are Australia's own version of the Cornish pasty, a half-circle-shaped turnover filled with minced meat and vegetables.

**Pavlova**

When Russian prima ballerina Anna Pavlova came to perform in Perth in the late 1920s, Herbert Sachse, chef of the Hotel Esplanade, reputedly created this glorious dessert. A giant meringue shell, baked from beaten and sweetened egg whites, it is filled with berries or other fresh fruit and whipped cream. That's all well and good, except for the fact that a hotel chef in Wellington, New Zealand, is also said to have created the same dessert when Pavlova came to that nation's capital on the same world tour. Of course, that version included kiwifruit. Quickly closing in on a century later, the two countries are still duking it out over who can claim to have originated the Pavlova, which is now claimed as the national dessert of both New Zealand and Australia.

**Tim Tams**

Made by Arnott's, these finger-shaped chocolate-covered cookies are beloved by Australian children of all ages. Over the years, the original version has been joined on store shelves by dark chocolate, caramel, chocolate fudge, double-coated, chili-chocolate, mocha, white chocolate, hazelnut, and even alcohol-enhanced varieties. The name of the cookies, first launched in 1963, pays tribute to a horse that ran in the 1958 Kentucky Derby, which a member of the Arnott family happened to attended. Nearly 300 million individual cookies are sold and consumed in

Australia each year. Aficionados use the biscuit to perform a feat known variously as the Tim Tam Slam, Tim Tam Suck, or Tim Tam Bomb, biting both ends off of the chocolate-covered cookie and then using its porous interior as a straw for sipping milk, coffee, tea, or something more intoxicating, then quickly stuffing the saturated cookie in the mouth just before it disintegrates.

**Vegemite**

Proof that favorite tastes are often formed in early childhood, this popular commercial product made from brewer's yeast, usually eaten thinly spread on bread or toast, is considered the ultimate comfort food by many Australians—and a funky abomination by foreigners who come to it in adulthood. Rich, aromatic, salty, and almost beefy, though it's strictly vegetarian, Vegemite has been around since the 1920s, originally developed as a nutritious source of B vitamins by a food chemist for the Fred Walker Company. The extract can also be used to add depth of flavor and body to sauces, much as a bouillon cube might. If you ask, many Australians will happily launch into a rendition of the traditional advertising jingle, "The Happy Little Vegemite Song," which begins: "We are happy little Vegemites, as bright as bright can be."

**Yiros**

Leave it to South Australians and their countrymen to apply their own English-language spelling to gyros, the popular Middle Eastern meat dish of highly seasoned minced lamb or beef, carved layer by layer off a large rotating vertical spit, served folded into pita bread.

# Dining in the Americas

# United States

In 1908, British-born playwright Israel Zangwill took Broadway by storm with his drama about the New York immigrant experience, which he entitled "The Melting Pot." That metaphor for America stuck, describing the way in which people of many different nations, cultures, and faiths have come together to form a new culture that is uniquely American.

## DEVILISH AMERICAN COOKING?

*"The English will agree with me that there are plenty of good things for the table in America; but the old proverb says: 'God sends meat and the devil sends cooks.'"*

CAPTAIN FREDERICK MARRYAT,
*Diary in America* (1837)

"Melting pot" also begins to describe American cuisine, as those dishes you might consider unique to the country more often than not combine influences of many cuisines that were once "foreign" to the continent. But the metaphor doesn't quite capture the truth about gourmet experiences offered in America today, implying a a blend, much as a Swiss *fondue* becomes one homogeneous mass into which diners hungrily dip. Culinarily (and probably culturally) speaking, America is more like a great big stew pot, brimming with big, distinct chunks. The stew is waiting for a hungry diner's enjoyment, and each chunk represents a different cuisine that contributes to the dining experience in the United States.

Truth be told, you can get just about any cuisine from anywhere in the world somewhere in the United States. On any American street you might find Chinese, Indian, Japanese, Ethiopian, German, Swedish, English, Irish, Italian, Turkish, Greek, Russian, Mexican, Brazilian, Argentine, Korean, Salvadoran...you get the idea.

All these assorted heritages have come to America through wave after wave of immigration over the course of more than half a millennium (dating back to soon after the journeys of Columbus). The world's cuisines have intermingled with the cooking of Native Americans and with indigenous ingredients to produce dishes that are uniquely, regionally American.

American cooking began to be defined in New England, with its rare bounty of lobsters, clams, cod, and other seafood; wild turkeys; corn, beans, and pumpkins; tart red cranberries; and amber-hued maple syrup. Specialties here include such dishes as chowder, Boston baked beans, New England boiled dinner, and

Indian pudding; but the sine qua non of the region may be found in the makings of a traditional all-American Thanksgiving dinner (see "The First Thanksgiving.")

The Mid-Atlantic States make the most of what the ocean has to offer, particular in the famed crabmeat of Maryland. Another distinctive cuisine of the region is that of the Amish and the so-called "Pennsylvania Dutch," who in fact descend from German and Swiss immigrants, a heritage visible in dishes like smoked hams, chicken pot pies, scrapple, and shoofly pie.

In the South, cooking has a comforting homespun style, typified by such dishes as fried chicken, chicken-fried steak, and grits. Louisiana and its major city, New Orleans, boast a cuisine to themselves, or rather two: Cajun, with big flavors and bold spicing evident in such preparations as gumbo and jambalaya, as well as the recent blackened cooking craze; and the more refined by no less vibrant French-influenced Creole cooking of dishes like oysters *Bienville*, bananas Foster, and *beignets*.

The Midwest, also referred to as the Heartland, abounds in images that capture the broad appeal of the nation's culinary identity: the "amber waves of grain" sung of in "The Star-Spangled Banner," and vast stretches of dairy farms and cattle ranches. This is meat-and-potatoes country, with great slabs of cheese and fruit-filled pies thrown in for good measure. You'll find many dishes that hark back generations to the Scandinavian and middle-European settlers who came here, perhaps most quirkily represented by *runza*, the German-style meat pies.

In the Southwest, you'll find an distinctive Latino-influenced cuisine with its own character separate from but richly influenced by that of Mexico to the south, as well as by the Native American peoples of the region. The nation's westernmost lands, the Pacific Coast and Hawaii, gain great inspiration from Asia as well, blending influences from Japan, China, Korea, and other nations with a wealth of seafood and abundant produce grown from the state of Washington south to California and throughout the Hawaiian Islands.

## HARSH WORDS!

*"A man accustomed to American food and American domestic cookery would not starve to death suddenly in Europe, but I think he would gradually waste away, and eventually die."*

MARK TWAIN,
*A Tramp Abroad* (1880)

**Anadama bread**

A rich, dense, pleasantly yeast-leavened bread made with wheat flour, cornmeal, and molasses. The name most likely evolved from some now lost Native American words for the ingredients. But popular lore holds that long ago, a Massachusetts fisherman, fed up with his lazy wife's refusal to bake for him, made a loaf of the bread himself, declaring, "Anna, damn her!"

**Andouille**

It's hard to get away from this spicy, garlicky pork sausage in New Orleans kitchens, so prevalent is it in such dishes as gumbo, red beans and rice, and jambalaya. But why would you want to avoid such a succulent treat?

**Bananas Foster**

New Orleans restaurateur Owen Brennan created this dish in tribute to his friend Dick Foster, a leader of a Vice Committee responsible for bringing order to the French Quarter in the 1950s. Who knows if the featured fruit was a punning part of said tribute? The bananas in question are cooked at table in a skillet with butter, brown sugar, sweet spices, and rum that is set alight in a glorious display before the hot, sweet fruit is spooned over vanilla ice cream.

**Beignets**

There's no better place in the world to savor these hot-from-the-oil square doughnuts than late at night or early in the morning at the Café du Monde in the French Quarter of New Orleans.

**Bienville, oysters**

A signature New Orleans Creole preparation claimed to have originated both at Arnaud's and at Antoine's restaurants, both highly esteemed establishments, this appetizer starts with freshly opened oysters on the half shell, nestled in a bed of rock salt. Each mollusk is bathed in a sauce based on a classic French *béchamel*, enhanced with a sautéed mixture of garlic, onions, bell peppers, and minced shrimp, plus white wine, lemon juice, hot pepper sauce, and bitters; then topped with bread crumbs and grated cheese. A hot oven lightly cooks the oysters and browns their topping. Jean Baptiste le Moyne, the Sieur de Bienville, French governor of Louisiana and the founder of New Orleans in 1718, would no doubt have been proud of such an honor.

**Bizcochitos**

These "little biscuits" of the Southwest are butter cookies, usually flavored with whole anise seeds that give them a mild licorice flavor. Home cooks making them by the dozens in the holiday season.

**Blackened**

A cooking style made popular in top New Orleans restaurants, most notably in the 1980s by the famed chef Paul Prudhomme, this involves coating a seafood fillet, originally the local flaky redfish, with a blend of seasonings prominently featuring hot paprika, then cooking it quickly in a smoking-hot skillet with oil or clarified butter. The spice mixture chars on the surface to form a slightly bitter, smoky, spicy crust for the succulent flesh inside. The rocketing popularity of Cajun cooking and of this dish in particular actually led to a redfish shortage and restrictions on its fishing. As a result, creative chefs began to blacken other types of fish, as well as chicken breasts, chops, steaks, and prime rib, and even tofu!

**Boston baked beans**

A definitive home-style dish, traditionally served as a main course but also as a side dish for roast ham, pork, or other meats, this is made by gently baking for many hours boiled dried pea beans or other mild white beans with onion, molasses, brown sugar, powdered mustard, salt, pepper, and a generous hunk of pork fat or bacon. The result is incredibly rich tasting, earthy, and satisfying.

# **American** barbecue styles

Other cultures may love to cook outdoors over an open fire, but Americans have made barbecuing their own particularly proud contribution to the world's culinary wonders.

The term "barbecue," however, means different things in different parts of the country. Most loosely, the term is used to refer to basic outdoor grilling, cooking hamburgers or hotdogs, chicken, steak, or seafood over a wood, charcoal, or gas fire on an outdoor grill. But barbecue as an art form, involving marinades, liquid bastes or "mops," dry seasoning rubs, and fragrant smoke, varies from region to region. Depending on where you order it in America, or what part of the country the cook hails from, here's what you're likely to get:

**CALIFORNIA** The state's most memorable barbecue is found in and around the rural town of Santa Maria, north of Santa Barbara. It utilizes oak fires, and the featured meat is beef tri-tip, a large, flavorful, triangular piece of sirloin seasoned with salt and pepper. The thinly sliced, juicy, smoky meat comes either on a plate with beans and tomato salsa or heaped into sandwich rolls.

**KANSAS CITY** From Missouri, this Midwestern style of barbecue consists of great slabs of meat seasoned with a dry spice rub, cooked slowly with sweet hickory smoke, and slathered with a thick, sweet sauce of tomatoes, molasses, vinegar, and hot peppers. Beef brisket and ribs are the meats of choice.

**KENTUCKY** This Southern state's slow-cooked barbecue style features lamb accompanied by a mild barbecue sauce based on either tomatoes or spicy hot black pepper.

## **American** barbecue styles

**MEMPHIS, TENNESSEE** A great place for pork barbecues, featuring a well balanced, flavorful sauce seasoned with vinegar, mustard, and tomatoes.

**NORTH CAROLINA** A thin "mop" of vinegar seasoned with black pepper, cayenne, and salt is basted frequently over pork shoulder or ribs as they slowly cook over fragrant wood. The finished pork shoulder may then be served "pulled" (shredded with a fork), and piled high in sandwiches.

**TEXAS** Always remember that Texas is beef country, and you'll understand why flavorful brisket is barbecue king here. Depending on which place you hit, you'll find a wide range of sauces, from thin and vinegary to thick with tomatoes and sugar, reflecting the diversity of the state that was the nation's biggest until that upstart Alaska joined up.

**Boston brown bread**

Similar in flavor to Anadama bread, this humble loaf generally has a higher proportion of cornmeal to wheat flour, along with the molasses that produces its color. However, Boston brown bread is leavened with baking soda rather than yeast, so it's made more quickly, and it is traditionally steamed in a large tin can set on a trivet inside a large pot over simmering water. Prized for its moist tenderness, the resulting loaf is often served as a companion to main-course Boston baked beans for a supper whose homespun goodness likely explains a common old saying among New England's Puritans: "Brown bread and the Gospel is good fare."

**Brownies**

Certainly other nations boast their own little chocolate cakes. But nothing compares to the American brownie. A cross between a cake and fudge, this "bar cookie" contains a high proportion of chocolate, sugar, and butter to its flour and eggs, resulting in a dense, smooth texture and rich, intense flavor. True decadents will eat their brownies warmed, topped with good vanilla ice cream and drizzled with hot fudge sauce.

**Brunswick stew**

Step on up for a steaming bowlful of squirrelly goodness! (And if it tastes like chicken, the reason is probably that you're enjoying the more acceptable modern version, made with everyone's favorite farmyard poultry.) This old Virginia favorite was reputedly first cooked up back in Brunswick County in 1828 by camp cook "Uncle" Jimmy Matthews with squirrels bagged on a hunting trip by state legislator Dr. Creed Haskins. Using ingredients at hand, he cooked the rodents with onions and potatoes, thickening up the stew with dried bread. Today, Brunswick stew has evolved into a rich concoction of chicken, smoked ham, potatoes, onions, and other favorite Southern vegetables like tomatoes, peas, corn, and lima beans, and the cooking liquid is more likely to be rich chicken broth than clear water from the river or lake closest to the campsite.

**Burgoo**

A stew of old Kentucky, burgoo gets its name most likely from the bowls of thick *burghul* (or bulgur) wheat eaten by American sailors. Traditionally cooked in huge cast-iron cauldrons for a day or longer, the stew may include any or all of a wide range of meats, poultry, or game, along with vegetables from the larder or garden, including such Southern staples as corn, lima beans, and okra. Before serving, the stew's ample juices are thickened up with a *roux* of flour and butter. Back in the 19th century, burgoo was a popular dish served to the crowds at the region's political rallies, which themselves came to be nicknamed burgoos.

**Caesar salad**

What is most likely America's favorite salad has an Italian name and a Mexican origin. It was invented in 1924 in the border town of Tijuana, south of San Diego, California, by Caesar Cardini, an Italian restaurateur there. He concocted the salad with ingredients on hand in his refrigerator one evening to feed some late-night revelers. The salad—crisp Romaine lettuce leaves, torn and tossed with a thick dressing of olive oil, garlic, coddled egg (lightly boiled in its shell), anchovies, mustard, and grated Parmesan cheese—quickly caught on. Though Cardini's restaurant closed long ago, several establishments in Tijuana claim to this day to prepare and serve the original Caesar salad.

**Chess pie**

The first time I ordered a slice of this pie, I imagined its top crisscrossed with a latticework of pastry evocative of the squares on a chessboard. Nope! This delicious Southern specialty dating back to the mid-19th century is simply a form of pecan pie in which the nuts and syrup for the open-face filling are combined with beaten egg to give the results a lighter consistency. The most plausible explanation for the name, then? It may well come from a humble reply given by a Southern cook (imagine the accent when you read it) who was asked enthusiastically what it was: "It's jus' pie."

**Chicken-fried steak**

The name of this Southern down-home specialty concisely sums up precisely what it is. A thin slice of inexpensive beefsteak is breaded and pan-fried in fat or oil just as you would ordinarily do to a piece of fried chicken. To enjoy it in its fullest glory, you've got to eat it smothered in a flour-thickened "cream" gravy made from pan-drippings, maybe some bits of bacon, milk or just occasionally cream, and black pepper. And, by the way, one of the favorite times of day to eat chicken-fried steak this way is at breakfast.

**Chile verde**

The mild to only moderately hot long fresh green chilies of New Mexico form the basis for what is largely known as chili in this state—a sauce of the roasted and peeled peppers. To make a main course of it, chunks of pork are often simmered with the chilies. It's possible that this dish, not the red kind known as chili, is what legendary frontiersman Christopher "Kit" Carson (1809-1868) meant by his dying words at his home in Taos, New Mexico: "Wish I had time for just one more bowl of chili."

**Chili**

What most people regard as American chili hails from Texas but has spread nationwide: a meat stew generously flavored with moderate to spicy red chili peppers. The dish's full name is *chili con carne*, chili with meat. That meat can be beef, pork, lamb, game, poultry, or other more arcane proteins such as rattlesnake. Beans are optional.

**Chowder**

The name may come from the French *chaudière*, meaning "heater," a vessel in which large seafood soups were traditionally cooked. And the dish may indeed descend from such French specialties as *bouillabaisse*. But chowder has evolved into an all-American soup-stew, most often featuring seafood.

New England-style clam chowder is based on milk or cream along with seafood broth, and also includes cubed potatoes, onion, and bacon. Manhattan-style chowders, by contrast, are tomato-based. You'll also see the term applied to other robust, chunky soups such as corn chowder.

**Cioppino**

You'd be forgiven for thinking this is an Italian word, since this spicy tomato-based seafood stew was in fact developed by the Italian immigrant fishermen of San Francisco Bay. However, you'd be mistaken. The dish, in fact, evolved as a communal specialty, made after all the fishing boats had returned to harbor and sold off their catch. Any scraps of seafood left over would be "chipped into" the pot, and those words were given an Italian twist to name the resulting dish.

**Clambake**

This New England-style feast couldn't be more elemental. Dig a big pit in the sand. Line it with rocks and build a big wood fire in it to heat the rocks. When the fire dies down and the rocks are blazing hot, line the pit with seaweed and pile inside it layer upon layer of fresh clams in the shell, lobsters, corn, and potatoes. Cover the pit with a tarp and wait until everything bakes/steams to perfection. Then uncover the pit and enjoy the bounty of sea and land, with great lashings of melted butter and plenty of beer.

**Corn pone**

This very basic Southern cornbread preparation is made by combining cornmeal, a touch of wheat flour, salt, milk, and rendered bacon fat, then forming the dough into sticks and baking them. So fundamental a form of sustenance is corn pone that Mark Twain remarked, in his *Corn-Pone Opinions*, "You tell me whar a man gits his corn pone, en I'll tell you what his 'pinions is."

**Country captain**

A favorite of Georgia, this mild chicken curry with apples and raisins has quite a provenance. It was most likely brought to the state back in the 19th century by a British sea captain who had first encountered it in India. The dish gained special favor in the 1940s when it was served to President Franklin Roosevelt and General George Patton at Warm Springs, the health retreat where FDR found some relief from his polio.

**Crawfish**

"Pinch my tail and suck my head" may sound like a provocative invitation, and you will see some form of the exclamation stretched across well filled T-shirts in New Orleans. But all it really refers to is the right way to eat crawfish, the local term for freshwater crayfish, also sometimes called by the more casual "crawdads" or "crawdaddies" or the even more off-the-cuff "mudbugs." Whatever you call them, these little sweet-fleshed crustaceans, which look like finger-length lobsters, are generally boiled in a spicily seasoned pot of water, sometimes with accompaniments of baby potatoes and rounds of corn on the cob, then drained and dumped out onto newspaper-covered tables to be eaten by hand. Their tails are pinched and twisted to reveal the succulent meat inside, then the heads sucked to extract every last trace of delicious juice.

**Dirty rice**

This Louisiana rice dish only looks dirty if you find the flavor of finely minced "variety meats" such as chicken livers and gizzards less than tasteful, in which case you might apply the adjective to the flavor as well. Good seasonings, however, including garlic, hot red pepper, onion, and bell pepper, make the dish more palatable.

**Eggs Benedict**

Arguably America's most popular brunch item, this combination of poached eggs and griddled Canadian bacon on toasted English muffin halves, all topped with French Hollandaise sauce, was reputedly invented in 1894 by maître-d'hôtel Oscar Tschirky at the Waldorf-Astoria Hotel in New York City as a hangover palliative for Wall Street stockbroker Lemuel Benedict. I say "reputedly" because that's what Benedict told a reporter for *The New Yorker* magazine. But that same year, Charles Ranhofer, chef of Delmonico's in New York, published a recipe for eggs Benedict in a cookbook, which he reputedly created three decades earlier for Mrs. LeGrand Benedict. Since the dish is generally served in pairs—two eggs, two slices of Canadian bacon, two muffin halves—let the creators share the credit!

**Fajitas**

In Spanish, *fajita* means a small skirt or belt. The term is also applied to the similarly shaped beef skirt steak, a tough and inexpensive cut traditionally marinated, grilled, thinly sliced, and eaten in flour *tortillas* by northern Mexican ranchers. During the 1960s, Sonny Falcon, a butcher in Austin, Texas, created his own version of that preparation, selling it at weekend fairs. The dish was so popular that he came to be known as the "Fajita King." Soon, the dish caught on in restaurants all over the Southwest and beyond, with the thinly sliced beef usually combined with sliced onions and peppers and brought to the table sizzling on a hot cast-iron griddle. Today, the preparation style more than the cut of meat defines *fajitas,* which may also features chicken, shrimp, or just vegetables.

**Fried green tomatoes**

This Southern specialty—immortalized in a humorous and heartwarming novel by Fanny Flagg called *Fried Green Tomatoes at the Whistle Stop Café* and a subsequent movie that shortened the title to the first three words—may be found in homes and down-home cafes all over the region. Thick slices of firm, still-green tomato, which have a refreshingly tangy flavor, are coated with seasoned cornmeal, cracker crumbs, or bread crumbs and then pan-fried, often in bacon grease. Enjoy them as a side dish with breakfast, lunch, or dinner, or as an appetizer.

**Fry bread**

The Navajo people of the Southwest make this traditional bread by mixing a simple dough of wheat flour, baking powder, salt, and milk, forming it into flat rounds that they fry in hot oil until golden brown. Sometimes, chili peppers or onions might enhance the mixture. Fry bread is served alongside meals as a perfect tool for sopping up sauces. It may also be used as a wrapper for ground beef or other fillings to make what is known as a Navajo *taco*.

**Grits**

The name may come from *gyrt*, a Middle English term for bran, but grits are a true Southern phenomenon—coarsely ground particles of hulled white corn, or hominy. Cooked to a thick porridge, the process can take about three quarters of an hour with coarse stone-ground grits, or as little as five minutes with fine, precooked and redried "instant" grits. A popular side dish at breakfast and other meals, they're usually served with a big pat of butter melting in their center, which gives rise to the popular Southern expression of surprise and exasperation: "Well, don't that just butter your grits!"

**Gumbo**

The Congolese word for okra, *gombos*, gives the name to this Louisiana favorite, a generous stew of smoked meat or poultry; local seafood such as shrimp, oysters, crab, or crayfish; tomatoes, bell peppers, onions, garlic, and hot pepper sauce. One other key ingredient completes the profile: *filé*, a seasoning of powdered sassafras leaves, which together with the naturally mucilaginous okra gives the stew its luscious, almost gummy consistency. The dish's African roots have also brought forms of gumbo to the Caribbean islands. In fact, the defining quality of a good, thick gumbo has given rise to the Haitian proverb, "It takes more than one finger to eat gumbo."

## FUN ON THE BAYOU

*"Jambalaya, crawfish pie, filé gumbo,*
*Son of a gun we'll have big fun on the bayou."*

TRADITIONAL CAJUN SONG

**Hash**

This breakfast treat may get its name from the French *hacher*, "to chop." But hash is all-American, a mixture of diced potato and usually either corned beef or roast beef (a great way to use leftovers), flavored with onions and seasonings, then pan-fried in individual patties or a skillet-full at a time until hot and crusty. Some cooks will add a bit of cream to the mixture to help bind it and enhance the crust. "Red flannel" hash includes chopped beets, which contribute its characteristic color. Creative cooks might substitute seafood or turkey, chicken, or seafood for the meat; or do a vegetarian version. Most cooks will top or accompany the hash with eggs, usually poached or fried.

## **The first** Thanksgiving

Americans celebrate the national festival of Thanksgiving every year on the fourth Thursday of November, a date set in 1939 by President Franklin D. Roosevelt and approved by the U.S. Congress two years later. Previously, in 1863, President Abraham Lincoln had officially established the *final* Thursday of that month as Thanksgiving Day, culminating a campaign begun by Sarah Joseph Hale in 1827 to make it an official national holiday.

Thanksgiving feasts today, largely celebrated as family events at home but also served as special menus in large hotel dining rooms and some other restaurants, typically feature a whole roast turkey with bread-based stuffing or dressing and gravy, accompanied by cranberry sauce and seasonal vegetables. Pumpkin pie is traditionally served for dessert.

The first Thanksgiving, however, was actually celebrated in October of 1621 by the Pilgrims of the Plymouth settlement to mark their first full year and successful harvest in the New World. The Pilgrims invited the Indian chief Massasoit and about 90 of his men to join them in three days of feasting. The menu included wild "fowl," with turkey likely among them, as well as seafood, corn, beans, pumpkins and other hard-shelled winter squashes, and at least five deer that the Native guests contributed to the celebration.

**Hoecakes** The simplest of old-fashioned Southern breads got its name because, in the colonial era and the early days of the nation, slaves would bake individual patties of the humble mixture of cornmeal, water, salt, and butter on the forged-iron blade of a hoe held over an open fire.

**Hoppin' John** This rich-tasting, well seasoned mixture of the ivory-and-black dried beans known as black-eyed peas, white rice, sausage, garlic, onions, and hot pepper is a favorite dish of the deep South, probably evolved from recipes originally brought over by African Americans. Enjoyed year-round, it's a must-have dish on New Year's Day, promising prosperity year round. You'll find a number of explanations for the name, among which the two most popular are an expression of hospitality to share the dish, "Hop in, John!"; and a tradition of children hopping around the table for good luck before eating it.

**Huli huli**

In Hawaii's native language, the name means "turn turn," describing the cooking process for a spit-roasted or barbecued chicken. Nowadays, the term refers to a favorite way of grilling chicken with a baste made from soy sauce, sugar, ketchup, garlic, and ginger, similar in spirit to Japanese *teriyaki*.

**Indian candy**

Not really candy, but just as addictive, this term from the Pacific Northwest refers to thin strips of salmon that have been cold-smoked, that is, very slowly cured away from the heat of a smoky fire built from fragrant wood usually after having been marinated with honey or brown sugar. As chewy and intensely flavored as beef jerky, it makes a satisfying snack.

**Indian pudding**

No, Native Americans did not invent this soul-satisfying dessert, though they certainly can take credit for introducing the Pilgrims, who did develop it, to all the ingredients involved. A cooked mush of dried cornmeal (hence the name, from what the Pilgrims called "Indian corn") is enriched and sweetened with milk, cream, eggs, butter, molasses, sugar, cinnamon, and ginger to make a simmered or sometimes baked dessert you can spoon up like a breakfast cereal.

**Jambalaya**
From Louisiana comes this thick, soupy main-course rice dish, in which the grains are simmered with wine, broth, ham, sausage, chicken crab, shrimp, tomatoes, okra, hot chilies, sweet bell peppers, and garlic. Some more rustic—or refined, depending on how you look at it—versions even feature alligator meat, leading their creators to say, "you'd better eat it before it eats you."

**Jerky**
A term reputedly derived from the French *char cuit*, for "cooked meat," this refers to a popular treat of the American West: thin strips of beef or other meat, marinated with salt and spices and then smoked or air-dried to preserve it. Originally a great way for pioneers and cowboys to keep meat for a long time, jerky could be easily reconstituted by simmering or simply shredding it into cooking dishes. Today, it's more common as a snack sold largely in convenience stores.

**Key lime pie**
The small, fragrant, zesty, and sweet Key limes of southern Florida give distinctive character to this favorite pie, found in that area and just about everywhere else nowadays. The juice and zest flavor a custard filling (which turns out yellow, not lime-green) for a shell usually made of either crushed graham crackers or sometimes regular pie pastry. Whipped cream may be spooned atop the whole pie or individual servings; a light egg-white meringue appears less often.

**Laulau**
See **Luau: feasting Hawaiian-style**

**Loose meat sandwiches**
A favorite in the Midwestern state of Iowa, this is made by sautéing ground beef, breaking it up into fine particles, then adding beef broth and continuing to cook it until the liquid has

## **Luau:** feasting Hawaiian-style

The luau, Hawaii's traditional communal feast, owes its origins to the Islands' King Kamahameha II, who in 1819 abolished the longstanding practices of separating men and women during meals and of restricting certain foods to royalty only. To impress upon the people his sincere support of these measures, the good king held a feast to which men and women, commoners and royals alike were invited.

Today, as then, Hawaii's finest recipes were featured, including *luau,* a stew of chicken, pork, or fish, taro leaves, and coconut that gave the occasion its name. Also featured will be such dishes as *poke,* a dish of chopped raw salmon or other fish mixed with sesame oil, onions, seaweed, and soy sauce; *lomi lomi* salmon, a mixture of chopped salt-cured fish fillets, tomatoes, sweet onions, chilies, and maybe some splashes of lime juice and pineapple juice; *laulau,* a mixture of chopped salmon or other fish and pork steamed inside the leaves of the tropical *ti* plant; roasted sweet potatoes; assorted tropical fruits; and *poi,* a sour fermented puree made from the roasted and pounded starchy root of the taro plant. The star attraction, however, is *kalua* pig, a whole suckling pig roasted over smoking embers in a deep fire pit referred to as an *imu.*

The feast is traditionally enjoyed while sitting on grass mats on the ground, and is eaten with the hands. This gives rise to an interesting bit of trivia about the *poi,* which varies in thickness depending on how much liquid is added to the final puree; thus, very thick *poi* is referred to as "one-finger *poi,*" slightly thinner *poi* as "two finger," and the thinnest as "three-finger."

evaporated, leaving its extra savor in the beef. The loose meat is then generously spooned into a hamburger bun and dressed to taste with ketchup and mustard, plus chopped onion. A proper loose meat sandwich should come with a spoon to scoop up what falls out.

**Maryland chicken**

Take your basic Southern fried chicken—chicken pieces dusted with seasoned flour or coated with egg and bread crumbs, and shallow-fried in hot oil or fat until crisp and deep golden-brown on the outside and juicy within—and then smother it in a flour-thickened cream gravy made with the pan drippings. There you have it: chicken done in the traditional style of the Mid-Atlantic State of Maryland.

**Muffuletta**

The name for this popular Louisiana-style lunchtime sandwich comes either from a Sicilian word for a mushroom cap, describing the large round loaf of bread on which it is based, or a similar word for a mold, describing how solidly its ingredients are packed in. It's generously stuffed with such cold cuts as ham, salami, and *mortadella,* along with provolone cheese and a spicy, juicy salad of marinated chopped vegetables including green olives, pimientos, capers, celery, and garlic. Credit for its creation usually goes to Salvatore Lupa's Central Grocery in New Orleans, which started serving them late in the first decade of the 20th century.

**New England boiled dinner**

Undoubtedly owing its heritage to such European favorites as French *pot-au-feu* and Irish corned beef and cabbage, this one-pot meal consists of corned beef or ham poached with staple vegetables like onions, carrots, turnips, cabbage, potatoes, and sometimes beets. Often, a whole chicken will be added to the pot. The sliced meats and vegetables are served in shallow soup plates, moistened with their broth and accompanied by creamed horseradish and mustard.

**Oysters Rockefeller**

Created in 1899 at Antoine's restaurant in New Orleans, this dish of oysters on the half shell baked beneath a creamy money-green puree of watercress, green onions, and parsley—liberally laced with anise-scented Pernod aperitif and topped with buttery bread crumbs—was deemed so extravagant that it had to be named after the nation's richest man, capitalist John D. Rockefeller (1839-1937). Interestingly, most versions served today feature spinach as the primary green.

**Po'boy**

Named because it supplies a convenient and nourishing meal even for folks of limited means, the signature sandwich of New Orleans starts with a long loaf of French bread, split and slightly hollowed out. Inside goes a generous helping of fillings that can range from sliced cold cuts or roast meat and gravy to deep-fried seafood, of which the most popular option is freshly shucked plump oysters. You can enjoy a po'boy dressed or undressed—the sandwich, that is, which comes with such garnishes as mayonnaise, sliced tomatoes, and shredded lettuce, or plain.

**Prairie oysters**

In size, shape, and color, calves' testicles may indeed resemble oysters. But you won't find many true oyster lovers lining up to enjoy this specialty of the American West, also called Rocky Mountain oysters. In fact, once cleaned, peeled, floured or breaded, and fried, prairie oysters are surprisingly palatable, being tender, fairly mild in flavor, with a faint mineral edge. How do I know? Back in the mid-1990s, I was fortunate to be a guest for a few days in the Amarillo, Texas, home of the great cowboy poet Buck Ramsey, now sadly gone. One morning, before I was set to interview him for an article I was writing, we sat down to a lavish breakfast prepared by his wife, Betty, who'd made scrambled eggs, bacon, biscuits, potatoes, and prairie oysters. I helped myself to lots of everything but the last item. When I sat down to eat, Buck took one look at my plate, gave me a warm smile, and said, "No balls, no interview!" I ate some, found them edible, washed them down with strong black coffee, and got my story.

**Red beans and rice** Jazz great Louis Armstrong signed all his correspondence with the words "Red beans and ricely yours," a sure sign of the fondness with which this humble but immensely satisfying New Orleans dish is widely regarded. Kidney beans are slowly simmered with ham, *andouille* sausage, garlic, onions, hot peppers, and other spices to form a rich, satisfying stew that is ladled over steamed white rice to make a complete meal.

**Redeye gravy** This traditional Southern gravy for pan-fried ham gets its name not only from the pinkish tint contributed by the meat but, more importantly, from the fact that strong black coffee is customarily used to deglaze the pan, dissolving the solidified meat juices and literally brightening the bleary eyes of those who eat it.

**Rocky road** The name describes the lumpy appearance of this mixture of nuts (usually almonds) and marshmallows, usually mixed into chocolate ice cream to make one of the most popular traditional American flavors. Or it can be embedded in chocolate and cut into thick squares of the same name to become an old-fashioned candy store treat.

**Runza**

If you haven't spent any time in Nebraska, you've probably never heard of the *runza*, even though fast-food restaurants selling them are almost as widespread as top-brand burger stands. They're German-influenced meat pies shaped into half-moons, like turnovers, filled with a well seasoned mixture of ground beef, onions, and finely shredded cabbage.

**Scrapple**

Enjoy this Amish and Pennsylvania Dutch dish at breakfast time. The name pretty much sums it up: scraps of cooked pork, often in the form of smoked ham, are mixed with cornmeal to form a thick paste that is left to set and then sliced and fried in butter. Served with fried or scrambled eggs, it makes a meal fortifying enough to power you while you plow the back 40 acres!

**Shoofly pie**

The name of this old Amish and Pennsylvania Dutch dessert attests to its sweetness. Basically, it's a single pie crust baked with a filling combining molasses, sugar, sometimes other sweeteners such as maple or corn syrup, and eggs. As if that weren't sweet enough, some cooks insist on drizzling the top of the pie with chocolate!

**Sloppy Joe**

A Midwestern relative of the loose meat sandwich, from which it may have evolved, this favorite since the Great Depression consists of ground beef sautéed and mixed with minced onion, ketchup, and other seasonings to form a very thick sauce that is scooped into burger buns, picked up by hand, and eaten—leading inevitably to the adjectival part of its name.

**Son-of-a-gun-in-a-sack** This dessert of chuckwagon cooks on cattle drives in the Old West, still found in some places today that practice authentic ranch cooking, was made by combining a mixture of bread crumbs, flour, sugar, molasses, suet (beef fat), evaporated milk, baking soda, raisins and other dried fruit, nuts, and sweet spices in a clean cloth bag. With so many ingredients and such a messy mixture, the special treat wasn't the easiest thing to make on the open range; hence the name. Tied up in its wrapper, the resulting soft dough was boiled in a potful of water, resulting in a treat very similar to a traditional English steamed pudding.

**Sopaipillas** I've seen at least two explanations of this word describing deep-fried square little yeast donuts of New Mexico, traditionally served there alongside meals and eaten with honey. One claims that the word means "honey bread." But you'll run into lots of Southwesterners who'll claim it's an Hispanic way of saying "sofa pillows," an apt description for the way they puff up when fried. They are a treat when fresh from the fat, hot and crisp. Tear off pieces to scoop up spicy sauces or to stuff with bits of meat or beans; or drizzle them with honey as a sweet counterpoint to hot chilies.

**Spoonbread** The name of this Southern specialty pretty much says it all. Cornmeal is mixed with flour, milk, beaten eggs, and seasonings and then baked to make a soufflé-like bread so soft that it needs to be dished up with a spoon. It makes a wonderful breakfast dish, on its own or as a companion to griddle ham or pork chops.

**Submarine sandwich** A Brit may have invented the sandwich back in the 18th century, but trust the Yanks to supersize it. Americans love to make big sandwiches on long rolls or slender loaves of bread, stuffing them with all manner of cold cuts, cheeses, carved meats, meatballs, poultry, seafood, vegetables, and sauces, and enjoying them hot or cold. The most ubiquitous name for such sandwiches is the descriptive "submarine." But various parts of the country apply their own nicknames, including Louisiana's "po'boy" and "muffuletta," the "hoagie" of the Philadelphia and southern New Jersey region, Maine's "Italian sandwich," the "grinder" in parts of New England and northern California, and other appellations including "rocket," "zeppelin," "torpedo," and "hero."

**Succotash**

A favorite Southern side dish, this sautéed mixture of fresh sweet corn kernels and lima beans or other beans takes its name from *misickquatash*, a word meaning "ear of corn" in the language of the Narraganset Native Americans. Other vegetables may also be included for flavor and color, the most frequent of which are minced onion and strips of roasted red bell pepper, and it's not uncommon to include some chopped bacon or ham as well. Alas, the dish is probably best known today for the exclamation uttered by Sylvester the Cat whenever he's thwarted in the Warner Bros.' "Looney Tunes" cartoons: "Sufferin' succotash!"

**Waldorf salad**

Maître-d'hôtel Oscar Tschirky invented this popular salad at New York City's Waldorf-Astoria Hotel in 1896. Elegantly simple in concept, it combines chopped apples, seedless grapes, celery, and walnuts in a dressing of mayonnaise, cream, lemon juice, and sugar. Still popular, the salad today sometimes becomes the foundation for lunchtime main courses with the addition of chicken or turkey breast or shrimp.

# Canada

Influenced by France, cultural womb of Quebec, and by that superpower behemoth to the south, Canada's own cuisine is undeniably enriched by a variety of sources.

## LET'S DINE CANADIAN TONIGHT!

*"Is there such a thing as Canadian cuisine? The idea of ordering 'Canadian' may have some scratching their heads. But Canada has given the world its share of gastronomic delights…from peameal bacon to poutine to pemmican…"*

"A TASTE OF CANADA: OUR HOMEGROWN CUISINE,"
Canadian Broadcasting Company Archives

While Canada is a nation and a culture worthy of respect in its own right, you'll gain an understanding of the best cooking there if you flip to the sections on Britain, France, and the United States, as well as to the cuisines of the many different immigrant cultures that make Canada such a thriving country. That observation is not meant to diminish any eating experience you might have there, since Canada has restaurant chefs and home cooks alike to rival some of the world's best.

It also has outstanding ingredients that contribute to the distinction of Canadian cooking—which, it should be noted, is no more one unified cuisine than are those of the United States, France, China, or any other sizeable country. Canadian maple syrup, produced predominately in the east, is one of the world's most distinctively complex-tasting sweeteners, made by boiling down the sap of the sugar maple tree. Canada's waters, lakes, and rivers yield up a wealth of fresh fish and shellfish; its open ranges produce rich crops of wheat and outstanding beef; and the fertile farmlands of the west, especially in British Columbia, provide a cornucopia of fresh produce as good as any in the world. All of these help make the experience of dining in good Canadian restaurants an unalloyed pleasure, especially when contemporary chefs employ them in creative combinations that highlight their freshness and bounty.

There are also, of course, a range of dishes that have become distinctly Canadian specialties, reflecting the nation's cultural history and its wealth of home-grown ingredients. Here's a representative sampling.

**Peameal bacon** What other parts of the world refer to as "Canadian bacon" is called here peameal bacon, so-named because during the early 20th century the lean top loins of pork used to make it were rolled in crushed dried yellow peas to help it keep during the salt-curing process. Nowadays, cornmeal is the preferred coating during curing, but the old name sticks. Thickly cut into round slices, the bacon has a dense, meaty yet tender texture and rich flavor, and is best enjoyed quickly seared on a hot griddle—as it is for the American classic eggs Benedict.

**Pea soup** This traditional French-Canadian recipe, cooked by the *voyageurs* who first explored and settled here in the 17th century, is just the thing to fortify you during a long, cold winter. Dried split peas are cooked in a big pot with a chunk of salted pork, onions, garlic, carrots, celery, bay leaves, and other seasonings to form a rich concoction as thick as a porridge. Before serving, the pork meat is cut up into little cubes or shreds and stirred back into the soup.

**Pemmican** If the more familiar jerky—chewy strips of air-dried seasoned meat—might be considered a simple ingredient or snack, than pemmican amounts to a recipe or full meal. This specialty developed by Native North American peoples was adopted by early pioneers and settlers. It is made by pounding together jerky, dried berries, animal fat, and sometimes dried chilies to make a sustaining ration that could be eaten as is or reconstituted by simmering in water.

**Poutine** A beloved French-Canadian comfort food, *poutine* (pronounced "poo-tseen") is based on thick-cut French fries cooked in lard, then topped with a thick, dark chicken gravy seasoned with vinegar and black pepper and, lastly, fresh curds from Cheddar cheese.

**Soupe a l'ivrogne**

Hard to tell if this French-Canadian "drunkard's soup" gets its name because it's a great hangover cure or because it's so easy to make even someone under the influence could put it together. Cubes of salt pork and chopped onion are sautéed with bread cubes until the bread is nicely browned, then simmered with beef broth and herbs.

**Tarte au sucre**

Translating as "sugar tart" but more accurately referred to in Canada by the English "maple sugar pie," this simple dessert from Quebec is a mixture of maple sugar (the granulated form of maple syrup), brown sugar, and cream baked in a one-crust pie shell.

**Tourtière**

This thick, savory two-crust deep-dish pie or torte from Quebec features a mixture of ground pork, mashed potato, and onion, generously seasoned with salt, black pepper, cinnamon, cloves, and allspice. It most likely evolved from the French *terrine*. Enjoyed year-round, the pie is a must for family meals following Christmas Eve Midnight Mass, and in some families it is made with chopped leftovers from a pork roast served at a family dinner the Sunday before Christmas.

**Voyageur stew**

Handed down generation to generation from French Canada's early settlers, this is a robust stew made with game, beef, or pork, braised with chunks of salt pork; vegetables such as onions, carrots, and mushrooms; wine and broth; and generous amounts of herbs and spices.

# The Caribbean

Since the Age of Exploration began, the islands of the Caribbean have seen a dynamic gathering of many different cultures: Native, Spanish, Portuguese, British, French, Dutch, and Indian. Each has contributed its own ingredients, cooking styles, and preparations to the home-grown bounty of seafood and tropical produce, yielding a lively, widely varied cuisine unique to the region.

## WELL-AGED PLEASURES

*"Cheese, wine, and a friend must be old to be good."*

CUBAN PROVERB

Part of the delight of dining on Caribbean food is the transformation it produces in dishes that may, at first glance, sound or look familiar. See what sounds like a French *pot-au-feu* on the menu? Don't be surprised to find bananas and sweet potatoes joining the poached meat in the pot. Tempted by curry, thinking it will resemble something you might find in an Indian retaurant? Well, you'll recognize the blend of spices, to be sure, while also being delighted by the papaya, pumpkin, or taro root that might be bathed by the rum-laced sauce. Think the *bacalao* of Portugal or Spain will be the familiar warm, whipped mixture or fritters of salt cod? Think again, as you savor flakes of the reconstituted fish tossed with the fresh flavors of avocado, onion, tomatoes, and chilies.

One of the most popular forms of Caribbean food outside of the region today is the cooking of Cuba. This robust, earthy cuisine is especially beloved for its garlicky, citrusy, altogether juicy treatments of roast pork and roast chicken; its vibrant seafood dishes, including paella-like shrimp in yellow rice; its interpretation of *ropa vieja*; and its generous griddle-cooked sandwiches like the *medianoche*. Fried bananas or plantains, white rice, and rich-tasting black beans are inevitable and welcome accompaniments to any Cuban meal.

Of course, the islands of the Caribbean have, down through the centuries, evolved other dishes that are uniquely their own, including the following highlights.

**Ackee**

Various experts describe the pale yellow pulp of this popular Jamaican tree fruit as tasting like mild banana, scrambled eggs, or soapy mashed potatoes. When you think about it, all such attempts point to the fact that this popular raw or cooked breakfast food, also found canned in markets, is so bland that you can pretty much describe it any way you like. The red-skinned fruit should only be eaten when it has ripened on the tree to the point of splitting open; before that point, it is considered mildly toxic.

**Blaff**

This popular seafood dish features white fish fillets, poached in a wine-based broth seasoned with garlic, green onions, hot chilies, allspice, cloves, and fresh lime juice. The name supposedly comes from the sound made when the pieces of fish are dropped into the fragrant, simmering liquid.

**Calaloo**

Reflecting the African heritage of cooking in the Antilles and other Caribbean nations, this leafy vegetable of the same name is often cooked along with okra, which also came to the islands with slaves transported there. They're combined with chicken broth, coconut milk, chilies, garlic, onions, cloves, salt cod, salt pork, conch, bananas, and other ingredients until tender. Before serving, the soup is beaten by hand to break up the solids into a more homogeneous but still chunky mass.

**Conch**

First, don't make the mistake of giving this the widespread soft pronunciation of "consh." The proper way to say the word is a hard "konk," befitting the way this shellfish—popular not only in the Bahamas and Jamaica but also in Florida—has to be prepared before sautéing it as a main

## **Do the** jerk

Jamaica's most famous culinary dish, jerk gets its name from the same source as American jerky—the French *char cuit,* meaning cooked meat. But what a bland etymology for such an exciting preparation!

Chicken and pork are the meats most often jerked (yes, the word functions as noun, adjective, and verb alike). Preparation begins by seasoning and marinating meats with the holy trinity of jerk spices—hot chili peppers (in fact, Scotch bonnet chilies, close cousins to *habañeros,* the hottest of Mexico's chilies), allspice, and thyme, to which sugar is often added along with other seasonings such as garlic, ginger, and cinnamon, according to the individual cook's whims or family traditions. Pulverized and blended together, the jerk seasonings are smeared all over the food, which is then covered and refrigerated for several hours or overnight.

Finally, the jerk is slowly barbecued by indirect heat, close to but not directly over a hot fire, until its surface is deeply browned and its interior is cooked through and tender. Bread and cold beer, both of which counterbalance the heat, are standard accompaniments.

course, deep-frying it to make conch fritter appetizers, or simmering it in a chowder or stew. The tough meat is removed from its shell, peeled, and then beaten mightily with a mallet or a pestle, or even pulverized in a food processor. The resulting meat will have a tenderness to match its mild sweet flavor.

**Lechón**

Derived from the word *leche,* Spanish for "milk," this refers most often throughout the Caribbean, and in particular in Spanish-speaking countries like Puerto Rico and Cuba, to a whole suckling pig, marinated and roasted to serve at a special feast, such as Christmas.

**Medianoche**

This "midnight" sandwich, a specialty of Cuba, consists of layers of thinly sliced roast pork and ham, cheese, mayonnaise, mustard, and tart dill pickle chips inside a soft bread roll. The sandwich is pressed and grilled in butter between the electrically heated plates of a sandwich press machine or underneath a weight on a griddle or in a saucepan. The name may refer to the sandwich's restorative effects after a night out on the town.

## PRIMITIVE—BUT DELICIOUS

*" Food is the most primitive form of comfort."*

PUERTO RICAN PROVERB

**Moros y Cristianos**

"Moors and Christians" poetically but accurately describes this mixture of equal parts black beans and white rice, mixed together to serve as a side dish with Cuban meals. Eat a plate or bowlful of this nourishing dish to see in the New Year, so folks on the island believe, and you'll have a year filled with good fortune.

**Patties**

Resembling and evolved from the pasties of Great Britain, these half-moon-shaped meat pies, popular in Jamaica and other island nations, are made distinctively Caribbean by the addition of lively spices, such as hot chili peppers.

## **A side of** bananas

Virtually any main course you order in a Cuban restaurant will more likely than not arrive with a side of what looks and smells like fried bananas, and is actually sometimes referred to as such. In fact, however, these are not bananas but the related fruit known as plantains, or *plátano*, a larger, tougher-skinned, less sweet cousin of the familiar table fruit. Often, the fruit will be cooked when still slightly underripe, with a flavor that's starchy and barely sweet, tasting more like a tuber than a fruit. These are usually peeled, sliced, deep-fried, and then each sliced flattened to pancake thinness before frying a second time to make *tostones*. When ripe and sweet, tasting more like a banana but still noticeably starchier, the plantains are cut into longer diagonal slices and pan-fried with lime juice until golden brown and slightly caramelized, becoming the side dish known as *maduros fritos*.

**Ropa vieja**

In Cuba, and also in Mexico and other Spanish-speaking countries of the Americas, you'll see stewed shredded beef with tomatoes, onions, garlic, and peppers referred to by the offhand term "old clothes," a fanciful reference to the finished dish's resemblance to old rags. The succulent meat mixture is served with rice to soak up the juices, and may also be used as a filling for Mexican *tacos, burritos,* and other casual treats.

**Vaca frita**

You've got to love a dish that's as simply, bluntly named as this Cuban favorite: "fried cow." Actually, the meat is more likely to be the brisket or flank of a steer, slowly braised to tenderness with onions and citrus juice, then shredded and fried with garlic in olive oil.

# Mexico

The wonder of Mexican cooking, and the fact that it enthralls more and more fearless gourmets, lies not merely in the fact that it features such lively spicing, highlighted by the wide range of chili peppers that contribute such variety to the cuisine (see **A chilies glossary**).

## PHILOSOPHIES OF THE KITCHEN

*"As women, what wisdom may be ours if not the philosophies of the kitchen? Lupercio Leonardo put it well when he said, 'How well one may philosophize when preparing dinner.' And I often say, when making such trivial observations, 'Had Aristotle cooked, he would have written more.'"*

SOR JUANA INÉS DE LA CRUZ (1648-1695), MEXICAN NUN

An even greater part of its intrigue is how ancient the cuisine's roots are, dating back many centuries to the glory days of the Aztec nation, which developed traditions of cooking with particular ingredients that remain evident today: corn, dried and ground to a coarse or fine meal used in the *tortillas* and *tamales* that are such standbys of the Mexican table; chilies (see **A chilies glossary**), source of the cuisine's often subtly spicy excitement; and chocolate, used to make not only sweets and hot chocolate drinks enjoyed throughout the country but also to make the best-known version of Mexico's preeminent sauce, *mole*.

Mexican cooking's roots also trace far back to the Mayan civilization of the Yucatán Peninsula. This wild tropical paradise gives rise to many of the country's signature seafood dishes, most notably *huachinango a la Veracruzana*, as well as its most famous way of preparing pork, *pibil*, in a fire pit lined with banana leaves.

As exotic as such dishes may be, the final part of Mexican cooking's appeal is its utter familiarity. After all, anyone who enjoys eating tomatoes, bell peppers, or chocolate can thank this New World country for sending its native ingredients eastward to enliven the cuisines of Europe.

**Agua fresca**

The "fresh water" of Mexico is actually a thirst-quenching nonalcoholic drink combining fresh fruit juice, sugar, water, and ice. A wide range of flavors may be found in restaurants and snack stands all over the country, including lemon, lime, orange, pineapple, watermelon, cantaloupe, passionfruit, and the popular *agua fresca de jamaica*—a ruby-red drink made from a tangy-sweet infusion of hibiscus blossoms.

**Albondigas**

Mexico's meatballs are made from a finely ground mixture of pork and beef, combined with bread crumbs or rice, egg, onion, and such seasonings as oregano or cumin. They may be enjoyed fried and then cooked in a chili sauce or, more often, simply poached in a rich broth with vegetables to make the satisfying soup known as *sopa de albondigas*.

**Buñuelos**

These popular treats, similar to southwestern *sopaipillas*, are squares or circles of a simple sweet dough, deep-fried in hot lard until they puff up and turn golden brown, then dusted with cinnamon sugar. Enjoy them as a breakfast or midmorning treat with coffee or hot chocolate.

**Burrito**

Just like its namesake "little burro," this casual main dish based on a large flour *tortilla* can carry a heavy load: a filling that will usually include beans, cheese, and salsa, as well as a wide variety of different meats, poultry, or seafood; rice; guacamole; and shredded lettuce or other vegetables. The ingredients are arranged in a strip across the *tortilla*'s diameter; then opposite edges are folded over the ends of the filling to contain it, after which the *tortilla* is rolled up to enclose the filling completely. Most *burritos* are meant to be picked up and eaten by hand. Some restaurants, however, offer them in an appealing form known as *enchilada*-style, covered with chili sauce and melted cheese, requiring knife-and-fork delivery from plate to mouth. For a really indulgent *burrito*, go for a *chimichanga*, a specialty from the state of Sonora, in which the filled and rolled *burrito* is deep-fried to a crisp, then often covered with sauce and cheese.

**Carnitas**

Marinated chunks of tender pork are slowly baked until crispy on the outside and yet so tender that they're easily shredded, resulting in an intensely satisfying filling main dish served with corn *tortillas* or used as a filling for *burritos, tacos*, or other dishes.

**Chalupa**

This bite-size deep-fried "canoe" of cornmeal mush, or *masa*, is served as a snack or a light lunch item, filled with meat or poultry, cheese, and chili salsa.

**Chapulines**

In the state of Oaxaca in west-central Mexico, as well as in authentic Oaxacan-style Mexican restaurants elsewhere, you're likely to encounter a light little bar snack called *chapulines*. As addictive to eat as peanuts, these are in fact a species of tiny cricket, fried along with red chilies and garlic until crisp. Truth be told, if you can get over the fact that they still look like tiny bugs, they're delicious, tasting mostly of their two seasonings along with a vaguely nutty edge. You'll also find *chapulines* folded into *quesadillas* along with soft, mild cheese, and I've been in some restaurants in Oaxaca that won't even bother to tell you that they've done that, so common is the ingredient. If you're at all likely to be squeamish, open up that unassuming *quesadilla* before you take a bite!

**Chicharrones**

This lively name refers to squares or strips of pork skin and the fat and tissue beneath it, more delicately referred to in English as pork rinds. You'll find *chicharrones* most often deep-fried and salted, in which form they have a remarkably light and crunchy texture to go with their meaty flavor, becoming a delightful snack that is sold in bags in the supermarket. But they may also be simmered in a sauce of green or red chilies, to be served as an appetizer that guests wrap in hot-from-the-griddle *tortillas* or spoon into other edible containers such as *chalupas* or *gorditas*.

**Chilaquiles**

One of Mexico's most satisfying breakfast or midday treats, and a sort of *sopa seca,* actually derives from kitchen economy. Stale, day-old corn *tortillas* are cut into strips or triangles, lightly fried, mixed with red or green chili sauce—along with cheese and sometimes embellishments like leftover meat or chicken—and then baked in a casserole. There are two equally plausible explanations for the word's derivation. One argues that it comes from the native Nahuatl tongue's *chil-a-quilitl,* for chili broth with herbs; the other that it's Mexican slang for a torn up old hat. Whatever the case, enjoy *chilaquiles* on their own or with fried or scrambled eggs.

**Chorizo**

This close cousin of the Spanish sausage of the same name is made from ground pork, liberally laced with hot chili peppers and garlic. In Mexican kitchens, the sausage is often sautéed with onions and tomatoes as a filling for *tortillas.*

# **A chilies** glossary

**ANCHO** Dried form of the *poblano*, dark purple-red in color, sweet and mildly spicy.

**ARBOL** A skinny little dark red dried chili that packs a powerful punch of heat.

**CHIPOTLE** A smoke-dried ripe *jalapeño*, deep reddish brown in color, with a rich, smoky-hot taste. They're sold either dry, packed in plastic bags; or canned in a tomatey *adobo* sauce that is added to dishes along with the chilies.

**GUAJILLO** Mexico's most popular dried chili, purple-brown and moderately hot.

**HABAÑERO** A notoriously hot, fresh, orange-colored chili, moderate in size and shaped like a lantern.

**JALAPEÑO** The best-known hot fresh chili, ranging in color from deep bright green to red when ripe, only moderately hot.

**MULATO** A dark blackish-red moderately hot dried chili with an edge of flavor reminiscent of chocolate.

**PASILLA** Dark blackish-red chilies of moderate hotness, with a distinctively sharp taste.

**PEQUÍN** Small, very hot little dried chili about the size of a fingernail.

**POBLANO** Long, tapered, triangular-shaped, sometimes twisted-looking fresh chili, fairly mild.

**SERRANO** Small to moderate sized fresh green chili of moderate spiciness.

**Churros**

These ridged, deep-fried, golden-brown doughnut sticks made from a soft dough of flour, sugar, water, and egg, are enjoyed as a breakfast, dessert, or snack. Fresh from the hot fat or oil, *churros* are traditionally rolled in plain sugar or a mixture of sugar and cinnamon. They're at their absolute best eaten with a cup of rich, thick, cinnamon-spiced Mexican-style hot chocolate, into which dipping is optional.

**Cochinita pibil**

Yucatán-style roast suckling pig is traditionally cooked in a pit, the *pibil* of the title. But today the dish refers more to the style of seasoning—with chilies, orange juice, and the bright red spice called *achiote*, known in English as annatto seeds—and to the fragrant, herbaceous-tasting banana plant leaves in which the pig is wrapped for baking, ensuring ultra-moist, tender results.

**Enchiladas**

Literally "chilied," this refers to corn *tortillas* that are briefly fried to soften them, then dipped in chili sauce. They are rolled up around a filling that may range from cheese to chicken or turkey, beef or pork to seafood, combined with other creative embellishments. Topped with cheese and briefly heated to melt that cheese topping, they are served with such accompaniments as sour cream and guacamole. The process may sound involved, but it all happens in moments, making *enchiladas* (they seldom come singly) one of the most satisfying casual main-course treats of the

Mexican kitchen. The result is so satisfying that it's become common in the United States to describe a major victory as "the whole enchilada."

**Flautas**

Shaped like "flutes," these tightly rolled corn *tortillas* contain a filling of meat, poultry, or cheese, and are deep-fried until crisp to serve as an appetizer, snack, or casual lunch or dinner main dish.

**Frijoles refritos**

Despite what their name might seem to imply, "refried beans" are fried just once; the adjective actually means "well fried." First, dried pinto or red beans are simmered with garlic, onion, and chilies until tender. Then the cooked beans are mashed and fried in a skillet with lard to form a thick, rich paste. Served as a standard side dish at Mexican meals, usually garnished with cheese, they may also be used as a filling for *tortilla* or cornmeal-based specialties such as *burritos, chalupas, gorditas,* or *tostadas.*

## BE PREPARED!

*"A la hora de freír frijoles, manteca es lo que hace falta."*

*"At the moment of frying beans, lard is what you'll be lacking."*

MEXICAN SAYING

**Gorditas**

These "little fatties" are thick, small-diameter, freshly made corn *tortillas,* either topped with or folded around the usual fillings you might find in a *taco*: beans, meats, poultry, seafood, cheese, some salsa, a dab of guacamole, and maybe some shredded lettuce or cabbage.

**Guacamole**

Oh, those earthy ancient Aztecs! They applied their word for "testicle," *ahuacatl,* to the creamy vegetable-fruit we know as the avocado. Add the word *mole,* meaning "sauce" to a Mexicanized word for the main ingredient, and you get this avocado dip, made by pounding or mashing the ripe flesh of the avocado along with lime juice and salt in the dish's most basic form, to which such elaborations as chopped onion, fresh cilantro, or tomato may also be added. Guacamole is most often served as an appetizer along with crisp corn tortilla chips for dipping. A dollop of it may also be used as a garnish for other dishes.

**Horchata**

To call this "rice water," it's technical term, doesn't begin to touch upon the pleasures offered by this cousin to *aguas frescas.* White rice is left to soak for hours in cold, fresh water until the water turns rich and milky; then the rice is strained out and the resulting liquid is sweetened and flavored with cinnamon and nutmeg. Served over ice, it's one of the most soothing drinks imaginable to enjoy with well spiced Mexican food.

**Huevos rancheros**

These "ranch-style eggs" start with a crispy fried corn *tortilla,* topped with a smear of *frijoles refritos,* then a couple of fried eggs sunnyside-up, and such garnishes as sour cream, sliced avocado or guacamole, tomato salsa, and cheese. It makes for a fortifying breakfast, whether you have to go out and round up cattle or just shuffle papers at your desk.

**Huitlacoche**

Some pretentious gourmets who've discovered *huitlacoche* like to refer to this as "corn caviar," which I suppose is an improvement on what farmers used to call it in English: "corn smut." When conditions are right, the grayish-black fungus may be found growing directly on the kernels of a cob of sweet corn still on the stock, hidden away beneath its green leaves and silk. Mexican cooks have long savored the surprisingly delicate-tasting yet earthy fungus, sautéing it to use as a filling for *tacos* or *enchiladas*; and it has become a popular garnish for main courses in upscale restaurant kitchens.

**Manchamanteles**

The name, "tablecloths stainer," gives you fair warning to tuck your napkin into your collar when eating this pork stew, to which an assortment of dried red chilies contribute not only a warm, fiery taste but also a brick-red color that you'll have a hard time removing from any cloth.

**Menudo**

Mexican restaurants proudly announce on their menus, or with signs in their windows, that they offer *menudo* on Sunday. That's because this (literally) gutsy soup of tripe—usually beef stomach lining—and plump corn hominy is a time-honored meal with which to begin the day of rest, not least because it's believed to possess restorative powers for those suffering from hangovers. That's more likely due to the soup's liberal doses of hot red chili peppers and garlic than to any curative properties inherent in the tripe.

**Mole**

Pronounced "MOH-lay," and derived from the Aztec word *molli*, for a chili-based sauce, this refers to a wide range of thick, complex sauces that contain not only chilies but also such ingredients as garlic, onions, tomatoes, raisins or other fruit, almonds or other nuts, spices, corn *tortillas*, and even chocolate. The most famous form of *mole*, considered one of Mexico's national dishes, is *mole poblano de guajolote*, a turkey (*guajalote*) cooked in the style of the city of Puebla. The dish was reputedly invented when nuns at the Santa Rosa convent suddenly had to rustle up a dish worthy of two unexpected exalted visitors, an archbishop and a viceroy.

**Nogada, en**

See this after the word *chilies* on a Mexican menu and you know you're in for a treat. Many locals regard it as the national dish because its colors are those of the Mexican flag and it was reputedly created to celebrate the nation's independence. A *chile relleno* with a filling of beef *picadillo* is smothered in a snowy cinnamon-scented sauce of pureed almonds, walnuts, and cream, then garnished with pomegranate seeds and fresh cilantro leaves.

**Nopalitos**

The flat, oval, juicy, fleshy young pads of the nopal or prickly pear cactus are enjoyed as a vegetable in many Mexican kitchens. Although they can be found canned and ready to use, many cooks still prepare them the old-fashioned way, starting with whole pads from which they carefully pare away the sharp spines before cutting the cactus into thin little strips and sautéing them with garlic, onion, and chilies to serve as a side dish, a *taco* filling, or an add-in to *huevos revueltos*, scrambled eggs. They taste surprisingly mild, not far removed from zucchini.

**Pibil, en**

The Mayan word *pib*, for a deep fire pit, explains the original way in which this specialty from the Yucatán Peninsula was cooked many centuries ago. Pieces of pork (*cochinita* or *puerco*), chicken (*pollo*), or other meat or poultry are marinated overnight with citrus juices, garlic, herbs, spices, and subtly pungent ground annatto seeds (*achiote*), which turn the meat bright red. Wrapped snugly in banana leaves, which keep the food moist and also subtly scent it, they are slowly cooked in a deep pot (replacing that fire pit) until fork-tender. The love such preparations evoke was immortalized by filmmaker Robert Rodriguez in his 2003 movie *Once Upon a Time in Mexico*, when Agent Sands, played by Johnny Depp, says, "El, you really must try this because it's *puerco pibil*. It is a slow-roasted pork, nothing fancy, just happens to be my favorite, and I order it with a tequila and lime in every dive I go to in this country."

**Picadillo**

To make *picadillo*, cooks sauté ground beef or sometimes ground turkey with a tart, sweet, hot combination of lime or lemon juice, onion, garlic, hot and bell peppers, green olives, tomatoes, and seedless raisins. The resulting mixture, thicker than a meat sauce for pasta and wonderfully fragrant, may be served in all its simplicity with rice as an accompaniment or stuffed inside *tacos, empanadas, tamales*, or hollowed-out vegetables.

**Pipián**

From the word for "seeds," this refers to chicken, or sometimes other main ingredients, cooked in a sauce enriched, thickened, and flavored with ground pumpkin seeds and sesame seeds. You'll sometimes see such a sauce also referred to as a green *mole*.

**Posole**

This stew, also spelled *pozole,* is based on big kernels of hominy—corn that has been slaked, that is treated with lime to remove its husk before drying. The earthy seeds are simmered in meat broth with red chilies and usually pork to make a satisfying soup-stew that is typically served with shredded cabbage, chopped radishes, chili sauce, fresh limes, and other garnishes that allow each diner to customize a serving to taste.

**Quesadilla**

Its name derived from *queso,* meaning "cheese," and *tortilla,* a *quesadilla* is Mexico's answer to the grilled cheese sandwich or toasted cheese but in this case, the sliced bread is replaced by a *tortilla.* Depending on where you go in Mexico, the details beyond that may vary. Sometimes it's a flour *tortilla,* sometimes corn. Sometimes the cheese is mild and white, other times yellow and sharp. In some places the cheese may be layered between two *tortillas,* while in others a single *tortilla* is folded in half over the cheese. Cooking, too, varies, with the *quesadilla* either cooked on a griddle or in a skillet with a little bit of butter or oil, the logical method for the layered version; or a folded *quesadilla* may be deep-fried in hot lard or oil. Then come the many additions to the filling, from *rajas* to shredded or grilled chicken, beef, or pork, to squash blossoms or *huitlacoche,* to a dab of *mole* or a sprinkling of *chapulines.* Such elaborations transform a basic snack into a satisfying casual meal.

**Rajas**

Literally "strips," this refers to slender pieces of roasted fresh chilies, often sautéed with onions, garlic, and herbs, plus a touch of cream to bind and enrich the mixture. Popular as a garnish for *tacos* or other *tortilla*-based treats, *rajas* are also frequently used as an embellishment for *huevos revueltos* (scrambled eggs).

**Relleno**

Though the term basically means "stuffed," it usually applies to a *chile relleno,* a mild green chili such as a *poblano* that is roasted whole, peeled, and seeded, then stuffed with mild cheese or *picadillo,* dipped in an egg-based batter, and deep-fried. The finished product is usually served on a plate covered with a sauce of tomatoes, bell peppers, and onions, though it's not uncommon to find it more casually stuffed into a *burrito.*

**Salsa**

The Spanish word for "sauce" covers a wide category of grace notes and complements in Mexican cooking. The salsa most people know is made from fresh tomatoes, chopped and combined with chilies, onions, cilantro, and maybe some lime or lemon juice; you'll find it on the table of every Mexican restaurant, ready to dip into with *tostaditas* or spoon over your meal. Playing a similar role is red chili sauce, which can range from mild to spicy. *Pico de gallo,* literally "rooster's beak," is still another popular table salsa, the term usually referring to either a fresh tomato salsa or to a chopped mixture of onions, orange segments, hot chilies, and cilantro with a lively flavor that pecks at the palate. Guacamole, too, is technically such a salsa, though it stands apart as a dish in its own right. Nowadays, innovative cooks are also using a wide variety of other salsa ingredients, including tropical fruit such as pineapple, papayas, mangoes, and bananas, and fresh berries; and starchy staples such as sweet corn kernels and black beans. Warm red and green chili sauces and green *tomatillo* salsas, all the sort in which the corn *tortillas* for *enchiladas* are dipped before filling and rolling, also quality as salsas, of course.

**Sopa**

Soups in Mexico fall into two basic categories. *Sopas aguadas,* literally "water" or "liquid" soups, cover all the many types with which people outside of Mexico are familiar. *Sopas secas,* however, are something entirely different: "dry soups," served like a soup course in a bowl, and even made with broth or liquid that is soaked up by featured ingredients such as the thin angel hair pasta known as *fideo,* rice, or the *tortilla* strips that, once bathed and softened in chili sauce, become *chilaquiles.*

**Sope**

Resembling a thick, round corn *tortilla* with a raised rim and made from fresh cornmeal dough, a *sope* is used in similar fashion to a *chalupa,* filled with *frijoles refritos* and maybe meat, poultry, or seafood, perhaps garnished with *rajas,* and sprinkled with cheese before being consumed with gusto as a nourishing, satisfying snack.

**Taco**

The *taco* is Mexico's basic sandwich, a corn or flour *tortilla* folded around a filling of meat, poultry, seafood, vegetables, or beans. Soft *tacos* are eaten just that way, garnished perhaps with a squeeze of lime, some salsa, some shredded lettuce, and cheese; hard *tacos* are deep-fried either before being filled, or the *tortilla* and filling are fried together before the garnishes are added.

**Tamales**

To begin, please note that the singular version of this word is *tamal*, not "tamale" as so many non-Mexicans say. Of course, *tamales* are so delicious that you'll likely never use the singular when ordering them. Cornmeal *masa*, a soft dough made from ground slaked corn, is stuffed with cheese, chilies, meat, poultry, seafood, *huitlacoche*, or even sweet fillings like fresh pineapple or dried fruit. Then, it's wrapped inside a soaked dried cornhusk, paper, or in tropical regions a larger wrapper such as a banana leaf. Finally, it's steamed to form a dense, satisfying dumpling that may be eaten out of the wrapper or more formally on a plate with sauce.

**Tomatillos**

Fortunately the days are largely past when this distinctive Mexican vegetable was referred to in English as green tomatoes. Yes, when they're ready to be cooked, or already cooked into a sauce, they could be mistaken for small unripened tomatoes, and their refreshingly astringent flavor may be reminiscent of them. But *tomatillos* in fact come from a different species of plant; and in markets, one look at the brown parchmentlike husks that completely enclose the small, pale-green, shiny ovoid shapes tells you you're dealing with something different. Chopped up like tomatoes, they cook down to a good, thick sauce that goes well with meats, poultry, and seafood.

**Tortillas**

Mexico's bread mainstay, *tortillas* are washcloth-thin rounds of flour or cornmeal dough cooked on a griddle. Though now mass-manufactured, the best are still made by hand, and the sound of someone slap-slapping the dough back-and-forth between her hands is a pretty sure sign of good *tortillas* if you hear it in a restaurant. Although they're often served alongside a meal, like bread, *tortillas* are also transformed into a wide range of dishes, as the vehicles for *tacos, burritos, quesadillas, tostadas, enchiladas,* and other treats. Even stale ones find new life in the breakfast treat called *chilaquiles.*

**Tostada**

Meaning "toasted," this casual dish starts with a deep-fried *tortilla,* usually flat if it's a smaller corn *tortilla* and sometimes shaped into a basket or bowl form if a larger flour *tortilla.* The golden-brown, crisp result is then topped or filled with *frijoles refritos,* meat, poultry, or seafood, lettuce and other vegetables, shredded or grated cheese, salsa, and perhaps dollops of sour cream and guacamole to make a truly indulgent sort of main-course salad.

**Tres leches**

The "three milks" of this Mexican celebration cake are canned evaporated milk, canned sweetened condensed milk, and heavy cream. Part of the trio joins flour and lots of beaten eggs and sugar to form a spongelike cake; most of that milk mixture's remainder is then poured over the baked, cooled cake, which soaks it up like a sponge. Slathered in whipped cream, and sometimes layered with it as well, the cake is usually served atop a pool of the remaining chilled milk trio, into which a dollop of jam is placed, then garnished with fresh berries or other fruits and accompanied by still more whipped cream to serve.

## *Tortillas:* Mexico's daily bread

It's actually an understatement to refer to these "little cakes" as the daily bread of Mexico. Whether perfectly thin and round from factory manufacturer, or rustic and homemade by hand in small bakeries and home kitchens everywhere, these unleavened flatbreads made from cornmeal or wheat-flour doughs are served hot, fresh from the griddle on which they're quickly cooked, and as an accompaniment to every meal.

Just as bread becomes the vehicle for all manner of sandwiches, so are *tortillas* employed as platforms or wrappers for an even greater variety of hold-in-your-hand or knife-and-fork treats, including *burritos, tacos, enchiladas, tostadas,* and *quesadillas.* Corn *tortillas* are also cut into triangles and deep-fried to serve as *tostaditas,* crisp corn chips enjoyed with salsa or guacamole. And, when stale, they're likely to be transformed into the treat called *chilaquiles,* much as stale bread becomes croutons, French toast, or bread pudding.

**Veracruzana, a la**

Meaning "in the style of Veracruz," the port city on the Gulf of Mexico, this term refers most often to *huachinango,* red snapper, cooked whole or in filets with a lively sauce of olive oil, lime juice, tomatoes, garlic, onion, *jalapeño* chilies, green olives, capers, and oregano.

**Zacahuil**

An ancient specialty of Mexico's eastern coastal regions around Veracruz, this is a gigantic *tamal* wrapped and steamed in banana leaves, its cornmeal mixture studded with big pieces of food—ears of corn, hard-cooked eggs, chicken pieces, jumbo shrimp, and more. I was present once when my friend John Rivera Sedlar, a noted Southwestern chef and self-taught scholar on the foods of the Americas, prepared a *zacahuil* at least eight feet long and three feet in diameter, which took all day to cook and overwhelmed more than a hundred hungry people.

# Central and South America

Don't confuse the cooking of Central and South America with that of Mexico, as some people mistakenly do. The cuisines of these countries are gaining a profile in their own right, and merit exploration for their own sake, particularly in the intriguing ways their cooking combines Native and colonial influences.

**THE POWERS OF FOOD!**

*"Good broth will resurrect the dead."*

LATIN AMERICAN PROVERB

The cooking of Brazil, for example, features many dishes inspired by the West African slaves who came to this country in Portuguese colonial days. Their influence is particularly evident in such glorious preparations as *feijoada,* the Brazilian national dish, a highly seasoned one-dish meal consisting of an abundance of smoked and fresh meats cooked with black beans and served with *manioc* meal and spicy garnishes. The Brazilian ranching tradition, meanwhile, presents itself the all-you-can-eat wonders of the *churrascaria.*

Peru, on the other hand, marries Spanish cooking traditions with those of the ancient Incan empire, resulting in such enthralling specialties as *anticuchos, ceviche,* and the chili-laced stews that go by the name of the hot *ají* pepper. Argentine cooking, meanwhile, shows a delightfully sophisticated mixture of Italian, German, and English influences; but, like Brazil with its famed *churrascaria* (see **Churrascaria: Brazilian barbecue**), it achieves perhaps its greatest glory in the *parrillada* (see **Argentine grilling, gaucho-style**), reflecting that nation's own great ranching traditions.

**Ají**

The small-but-intense chili peppers of Peru also give their name to stews that they season, including such dishes as *ají de gallina,* a mixture of boiled potatoes and shredded boneless chicken meat in a spicy sauce made with ground walnuts and milk-soaked bread.

**Ajiaco**

Colombia's national dish, this main-course soup features chicken pieces, chunks of several different types of potato, and rounds of fresh corn on the cob, seasoned with onions, garlic, cumin, and thyme. In upscale versions as you might find them in the capital of Bogotá, the soup is enriched before serving with heavy cream, and garnished with capers and cilantro.

**Anticuchos**

A snack or hors d'oeuvre enjoyed throughout Peru, this consists of chili-marinated chunks of ox heart or beef heart speared onto a small skewer and grilled over an open fire. Though the main ingredient may make the dish sound decidedly downscale, and you will indeed find it offered up by street vendors, it's just as likely to appear passed on trays at elegant parties.

**Arepas**

This staple of Columbia and Venezuela is like a very thick, starchy corn tortilla, generally cooked on a griddle or over an open fire. Not very appetizing alone, it comes to life as an accompaniment to flavorful stews or soups, or when topped with melted cheese.

**Borracho**

The Spanish word for "drunken" usually refers to any Latin American dish in which a plump bird is slowly simmered or baked submerged in white wine and broth. You can count on garlic and onion being primary seasonings.

**Carbonada**

Like a French or Belgian *carbonnade,* this popular Argentine main course features beef stewed with onions. From that point on it differs, tipped off by the adjective most often appended to the dish's name: *criolla,* "creole," reflecting Latin America's blending of indigenous Indian, European, and African cultures. Added to the stew, you'll find hot chili peppers, garlic, white potatoes, sweet potatoes, maybe beans and corn, squashes, and perhaps some fresh apples and tart dried fruit. The grandest versions are actually oven-baked inside a large hollowed-out pumpkin.

**Ceviche**

You'll find versions of *ceviche,* sometimes also spelled *cebiche, sebiche,* or *seviche,* all over Latin America, including Mexico, and many different countries will claim it as their own even though it probably originated in Peru. What *ceviche* is definitely not is a "raw" seafood dish, as it is sometimes mistakenly called. Yes, it starts with raw, ultra-fresh seafood, such as firm-fleshed white fish, shrimp, scallops, pieces of squid, and sometimes mussels or other shellfish. And they're never exposed to heat. However, the acid in the lime, lemon, or orange juice with which they're tossed has the same physical effect on the seafood that heat would, turning it opaque and firm. Add chopped onion, minced fresh chilies, and herbs such as cilantro or chives and you wind up with the most refreshing seafood cocktail imaginable—but, again, nothing that should really turn away those who might be leery of uncooked fish.

## **Churrascarias:** Brazilian barbecue houses

**Like the Thanksgiving meal of the United States, the original *churrasco*, or barbecue, of Brazil was a feast held by its ranchers to give thanks for the bounty of the earth, a tradition begun more than a century ago.**

Holding pride of place on the table were the finest cuts of beef, pork, lamb, and poultry, all cooked over an open fire.

Eventually, restaurants specializing in *churrasco*, known as *churrascarias*, or barbecue houses, became popular places for Brazilians to celebrate. And, for very good reasons—particularly the aspect of all-you-can eat grilled proteins—they've begun to spread beyond Brazil's borders.

Typical *churrascarias* will feature some sort of cold and hot buffet tables at which guests can fill up plates with assorted salads and marinated vegetables, along with side dishes like black beans, steamed rice, mashed potatoes, fried bananas, and cooked vegetables. But the real feast comes in the never-ending parade of fire-grilled main courses, carried from table to table by servers who carve individual portions directly from the spit onto each individual plate. Many restaurants feature some sort of coaster or poker chip at each table, green on one side and red on the other, which guests use to signal whether they want servers to keep coming or hold off for a while.

For inquisitive eaters, it's fascinating to be able to taste and compare various cuts of meat side by side on the same plate. Some highlights to watch out for include:

**ALCATRA** Top sirloin

**COSTELA** Beef ribs

**COSTELA DE PORCO** Pork ribs

**FRALDINHA** Bottom sirloin

**LINGUICA** Pork sausages

**PICANHA** Center-cut sirloin, one of the signature choices of a *churrascaria*

**Chimichurri**

Argentina's most popular table condiment is a coarse puree of garlic, parsley (and sometimes oregano or even cilantro), hot chili peppers, corn oil or olive oil, and a splash of red wine vinegar. If that sounds like a salad dressing, go ahead and spoon it over your greens. But the sauce is primarily enjoyed as an embellishment for grilled meats or poultry, and anything else savory that might arrive at the table, where a sauceboat or bowl of *chimichurri* will be a central feature. And just try to resist dipping your bread in it!

**Cuy**

If you had one as a pet when you were a child, you might be better off not knowing that this favorite dish of Peru (pronounced "qwee"), is named for its main ingredient, a kind of guinea pig. The plump little rodents are typically fried and then stewed with onions, garlic, the hot little local chilies known as *ají*, and potatoes.

**Dulce de leche**

This "milk sweet" is one of the most popular ingredients of Argentina and other Latin American countries. Whole milk is slowly cooked until its natural sugars caramelize, turning it deep golden brown, and the mixture thickens to the consistency of a jam. You'll find jars of *dulce de leche* on the breakfast table, to be enjoyed as a spread on toast or other morning breads, and it's also used as a deliciously sweet flavoring or filling in pastries and desserts.

**Empanadas**

Literally "breaded," this refers to a hand-sized baked or fried Argentine pastry turnover filled with a mixture of chopped meat, olives, onions, nuts, and raisins, served for lunch, as a snack, or—when made in smaller bite-size portions—as an hors d'oeuvre. You'll also find good empanadas in other parts of Latin America, with fillings ranging from seafood to game, vegetables to fruits to cheese. Other fillings may be used as well. Some I've enjoyed especially include one filled with a thick, garlicky mixture of sautéed chopped mushrooms, and another dessert-style example stuffed with soft white cheese and a generous smear of sweet, tangy quince paste.

**Escabeche**

This "pickled" treatment for chicken, seafood, or meat is enjoyed all over Latin America, employing vinegar as the primary liquid in which the featured ingredient is cooked along with vegetables and spices—or sometimes pickling it with the vinegar right after it has been cooked. When done, the dish is left to cool and served chilled as a refreshing warm-weather main course.

**Feijoada**

Brazil's national dish is a feast based upon black beans (*feijão*) slowly simmered with assorted meats, chilies, garlic, and tomatoes. The meat, presented at table in slices on a platter, include fresh and dried beef, smoked beef tongue, bacon, fresh and cured sausages, and pig's ears, feet, and tails. A separate bowl or casserole contains the beans, and alongside are served an assortment of garnishes including boiled greens such as kale or collard greens; boiled rice; toasted *manioc* meal, *farinha de mandioca*, from the starchy cassava root, sprinkled on as a seasoning; fresh orange segments; and a hot, tangy sauce of chili and lime juice. Since the preparation of a *feijoada* at its grandest, a *feijoada completa,* is time-consuming, you're more likely to see it offered as a restaurant special on weekends, particularly Saturdays.

**Humitas**

Just as Americans in the Deep South love their grits, made from dried and ground corn hominy, many South Americans—particularly the people of Chile and Argentina—consider this sweet-corn preparation (which takes its name from the word for corn in Quechua, the ancient Incan language) the ultimate comfort-food staple. Fresh corn kernels, grated right off the cobs or pureed in a food processor, are simmered with butter, milk, eggs, maybe a little sugar, and grated cheese to make a thick porridge that is served primarily as a side dish. Garlic, onion, hot chilies, and other vegetables such as squash or bell pepper may also be added. Sometimes you might find *humitas* steamed inside corn husks or banana leaves, like Mexican *tamales.*

**Matambre**

This favorite Argentine appetizer does indeed "kill hunger" as its name suggests. To make it, a thin sheet of flank steak is rolled up snugly around a filling that includes spinach, carrots, onion, peppers, garlic, bacon, and hard-cooked eggs, then tied, poached, and cooled. Cut crosswise into slices that reveal its mosaic-like colorful pattern, it is typically served with *chimichurri.*

**Pachamanca**

In this traditional Peruvian form of grand entertaining, a large pit is dug in the earth, lined with rocks, and transformed with a log fire into an intense oven. Moist tropical leaves are piled inside to create a cooking platform for a whole kid or piglet, chickens, and *cuy,* along with casseroles of pigs' feet, whole ears of corn, *tamales,* and other treats. Then, the pit is sealed with more leaves and hot rocks, leaving the ingredients to cook slowly until the pit is opened hours later when the party officially begins.

**Papas**

Potatoes, native to Latin America, are enjoyed in many national dishes. Peru's *papas huancainhas* (in the style of the town of Huancayo) are chunks of the starchy tuber enrobed in a sauce of onions, chilies, and cheese, while its *papas arequipeñas* (in the style of the city of Arequipa) complement potatoes with chilies, cheese, and peanuts. Colombian *papas chorreadas,* literally "dirty potatoes," are boiled chunks tossed with butter-sautéed onions, chilies, and tomatoes, which are then enriched with cream and cheese.

**Porotos granados**

The name for this Chilean national dish literally refers to the shelled fresh cranberry beans upon which it is based. They're stewed with garlic, onions, tomatoes, squash, corn, and herbs to make a dish widely enjoyed as either a vegetarian main course or as an accompaniment to meat, poultry, or seafood. Before serving, each guest usually douses the *porotos* with great lashings of *pebre,* a very spicy abounding in hot chili peppers and garlic.

**Provoleta**

One of Argentina's most beguilingly basic appetizers consists of a thick slab of Italian-style provolone cheese, quickly seared on a blazing-hot oil-coated grill until it is crusty and brown on both sides, melting within. It arrives at the table still sizzling, usually buried in a mixture of chopped fresh tomatoes, onions, garlic, and parsley. All that's left for you to do is use a fork or knife to cut off a piece, smear it on a crust of bread, add some of the tomato mixture and maybe a drizzle of *chimichurri,* and enjoy it.

## **Argentine grilling,** gaucho-style

Just as Brazil has its *churrascarias* (see **Churrascaria: Brazilian barbecue houses**), Argentina boasts its *parrilladas,* or grill restaurants, featuring meats cooked on a grill (*parrilla*) over live wood fires in the style of that country's cowboys, the gauchos. Unlike Brazil's popular all-you-can-eat affairs, however, *parrilladas* are typically menu-service restaurants, offering a range of choices from which each guest selects a main course, to be eaten liberally doused with *chimichurri.* However, for larger parties—or very hungry eaters—there's always the option of ordering a *parrillada completa,* which as its name implies provides a fairly exhaustive selection of the restaurant's grilled protein choices.

Unless you go for that option, however, you'll likely be ordering individual steaks or other cuts of meat or poultry. So it helps to have some familiarity with the basic beef options:

**ALCATRA** Sirloin

**ANCHO** Rib-eye

**BIFE DE CHORIZO** Rump steak

**CHORIZO** Spicy beef sausage

**COSTILLA** T-bone

**ENTRAÑA OR FALDA** Skirt steak

**LOMO** Tenderloin

**MURACHAS** Short ribs

**MILANESA** Minute steak, usually breaded and pan-fried in the Italian style

**Quinoa**

Pronounced "keen-wah," this grain, a staple of the ancient Incan civilization of the Andes, still enjoys popularity in Peru, Chile, and other South American countries. Indeed, creative contemporary chefs make use of it in stylish restaurant dishes. Traditionally, the rice is ground to make a flour and cooked to make porridges or mixed with water to form a dough from which thin flatbreads resembling *tortillas* are formed. The grains may also be boiled or steamed whole like rice for use in *pilafs,* soups, casseroles, and other dishes both savory and sweet. The delicately flavored grain is also prized as a high-quality protein source.

**Salteñas**

The Bolivian term for *empanadas.*

**Sudado**

From the Spanish *sudar,* "to sweat," this term describes a popular Peruvian preparation of fresh fish steamed (that is, sweated) or simmered with tomatoes, potatoes, and onions as well as a strong seasoning including garlic, paprika, and lemon. The juicy fish is typically served with boiled potatoes or yucca root or with steamed rice.

**Tostones**

A popular treat in Venezuela and elsewhere around Latin America and the Caribbean, these start with slices of ripe plantain, a large relative of the banana. They're fried, then smashed flat and fried a second time, resulting in a crisp, toasty, fruity chip that tastes so good you won't be able to stop at just one.